Healthy Dining
in San Diego
Fifth Edition

Restaurant Nutrition Guide

Featuring Healthy Entrees from
76 Popular San Diego Restaurants

Including:

✓ **Calories**   ✓ **Cholesterol**
✓ **Fat**   ✓ **Sodium**

Diabetic Food Exchanges, Fruit & Vegetable Servings,
Protein & Carbohydrate Information

by

Accents On Health, Inc.

Authors and Contributors:
Anita Jones-Mueller, M.P.H.
Esther Hill, Ph.D.
Erica Bohm, M.S.
Susan Goldstein
Rebecca Dawson, R.D.
Amy Sturm
Mikah Felago

Healthy Dining in San Diego

Healthy Dining
in San Diego

Fifth Edition

Restaurant Nutrition Guide
by
Accents On Health, Inc.

Authors and Contributors:
Anita Jones-Mueller, M.P.H., Esther Hill, Ph.D., Erica Bohm, M.S.,
Susan Goldstein, Rebecca Dawson, R.D., Amy Sturm & Mikah Felago

Published by:

Healthy Dining Publications
Accents On Health, Inc.
8305 Vickers Street, Suite 106
San Diego, CA 92111

(858) 541-2049
(800) 953-DINE
www.healthy-dining.com

Cover concept by Patricia Mattison, graphics by Mark Bentley, logo by Ramon Hutson, staff photos by Michael Ross

Library of Congress Cataloging in Publication Data
Jones, Anita
Healthy Dining in San Diego
1, Nutrition.
2, Diet.
3, Restaurant Food
91-71724
ISBN 1-879754-04-5

Table of Contents

Preface by the San Diego County Medical Society

As we enter a new century, we are becoming more conscious of the importance of nutrition and exercise in our daily lives. As physicians, we are seeing Americans becoming more overweight and unfit, and we are keenly aware that dietary factors are important links to obesity, cancer, heart disease, diabetes, hypertension, and more.

At the same time, we are finding that people are eating out more than ever before, with an average 4 to 5 meals eaten out of the house per week. In some groups of people, over 60% of meals are eaten outside the home. With this frequency of dining out, menu choices contribute significantly to our overall food intake.

Restaurant food tastes good, but it is usually loaded with fat, salt and sugar. And it usually has very few fruits and vegetables, which are so important for their fiber, antioxidants, phytochemicals and other components essential to our health. While many restaurants feature some healthier choices on their menus, getting people to choose these items is another story. There are many factors that interfere with healthy eating. Social and cultural pressures often play critical roles in reinforcing bad eating habits.

Believe it or not, it is possible to dine out well and still be health-conscious. *Healthy Dining in San Diego* is truly a book on the cutting edge of health and nutrition. This fifth edition is being released in conjunction with a landmark campaign called **TrEAT Yourself Well**, a cooperative effort between the California Department of Health Services, the California Five a Day Campaign, the California Restaurant Association, and Healthy Dining. The San Diego County Medical Society is proud to support the efforts of these organizations in providing our community with nutritious, good-tasting alternatives when dining out.

We're certain that once you start flipping through the pages of *Healthy Dining in San Diego*, you'll be as excited as we are that we all can make positive changes in our lives with such easy and delicious choices.

Edward Singer, M.D., President,
San Diego County Medical Society

Jeffrey Krebs, M.D., FACP, Council Member
San Diego County Medical Society

A Message from Marilu Henner

Marilu at the March 1, 2000 media launch of
***Healthy Dining's* TrEAT Yourself Well** *campaign.*

With good health, you can do it all. And without health, what do you really have? Health is the single most important factor in your life. It's the basis from which every aspect of your life stems. You can have all the money in the world, you can have all the power in the world, but if you do not have your health, you have nothing. You have been dealt a certain hand in life, and you have been given all the opportunity to play that hand the best you can. Disease doesn't discriminate.

Everything you need to live a longer, happier, healthier life is literally at your fingertips. And, **what you eat makes all the difference**! Whole, natural, high-quality foods will get -- and keep -- you in top form. Lots of fresh fruits and vegetables, whole grains and lean proteins will bring you health and vitality and add years to your life.

Congratulations to the chefs and restaurants participating in the *Healthy Dining* program. They truly have your health <u>and</u> tastebuds in mind. Enjoy the delicious dishes featured in this book. And, best wishes for a very happy, healthy and balanced life!

Sincerely,

Marilu Henner

"With good health you can do it all." And "do it all," she does. Marilu Henner is a celebrated television and film actress, best known for her role as Elaine Nardo on *Taxi* and her role opposite Burt Reynolds in *Evening Shade*. She recently starred in the smash Broadway musical *Chicago*. Marilu is the author of two *New York Times* best-selling nutrition books: *Total Health Makeover* and *30-Day Total Health Makeover*. She has just released a new recipe book called *The Total Health Kitchen*. Marilu is the mother of two young boys and is also the author of a parenting book, *I Refuse to Raise a Brat*.

About **Healthy Dining** and Accents On Health

Healthy Dining's team of highly qualified nutrition and health professionals is committed to an ambitious and exciting vision: to foster an ever-expanding trend toward healthier menu selections in restaurants. The ***Healthy Dining*** project began in San Diego in 1990 and expanded to Orange County and Los Angeles. The team has worked with hundreds of restaurants throughout Southern California and has analyzed over 7,000 menu items for nutrition content. ***Healthy Dining*** is earning respect from all corners -- health professionals, the media, the restaurant industry, and tens of thousands of consumers, many of whom write and call, expressing appreciation for the impact that ***Healthy Dining*** continues to make in Southern California. In 1998, ***Healthy Dining*** won the Meritorious Service Award from the California Dietetic Association. In 1999, Accents On Health, Inc. was awarded a three-year research grant from the California Department of Health Services, resulting in the landmark study/campaign called **TrEAT Yourself Well**. The goals of the campaign are to 1) inspire California chefs to create dishes which emphasize fruits and vegetables, whole grains and lean proteins and 2) provide restaurant diners with healthier choices.

Anita Jones-Mueller, M.P.H. – Director

Anita earned her Master's Degree in Public Health from San Diego State University. Her background includes extensive work in the health and nutrition fields, both with individuals and with community group education and support sessions. Anita is one of the founders of the ***Healthy Dining*** program and the lead author of the book series. She has directed the ***Healthy Dining*** project from its inception into a growing community program. Anita oversees the nutrition analysis, directs public relations and promotion, and speaks frequently to health professionals and community groups. She is also the Campaign Director for the **TrEAT Yourself Well** campaign.

Esther Hill, Ph.D. – Editor/Publisher

Esther Hill, a physiologist with a Ph.D. in Biomathematics, worked for over 15 years in medical research at the University of California at San Diego. Her motivation for being involved in this project comes largely from dealing with her son's unstable diabetes. Dr. Hill's family has found traveling and restaurant dining difficult, and she understands why nutrition information is so important to those with dietary restrictions. Dr. Hill is one of the founders of the ***Healthy Dining*** program. She assists with editing and publishing and is now the Principal Investigator of the **TrEAT Yourself Well** research study.

Erica Bohm, M.S. – San Diego Regional Director

Erica Bohm earned her Master's Degree in Community Health Sciences from New York City's Hunter College. Her experience includes nutrition education, cholesterol reduction, weight control and smoking cessation. During her 20+ years in the health field, Erica has worked for the American Red Cross, the American Health Foundation, and other health organizations, research projects and businesses. Her roles in ***Healthy Dining*** include seminars, program promotion, and networking with the restaurants, health professionals, community organizations and the media. Erica also serves as Campaign Manager for the **TrEAT Yourself Well** campaign.

Susan Goldstein – Orange County Regional Director

Susan earned her Bachelor of Science degree with distinction in Human Development and Family Studies from Cornell University. She has a strong background and knowledge in nutrition, health promotion, human resources and fundraising with over 15 years professional and volunteer experience in small and large corporations. Susan works directly with restaurant owners, managers and chefs to create the *Healthy Dining* books and expand the program in the community. Through ongoing events and activities, Susan promotes *Healthy Dining* with health professionals, the media, corporate and retail sales, special seminars, marketing and community relations.

Rebecca Dawson, R.D. – Staff Dietitian

Rebecca earned her Bachelor of Science degree in Dietetics from Michigan State University and her Registered Dietitian credential after an internship at the Oakland County Health Division in Pontiac, MI. Her background includes over three years' experience working for the Women, Infants & Children Supplemental Food Program, where she taught group classes and conducted individual nutrition counseling. At *Healthy Dining*, Rebecca calculates the nutrient analyses of recipes using a nutrition software program, researches nutrition information on ingredients and communicates with chefs regarding recipes.

Amy Sturm – Publishing Coordinator

Amy recently received her Bachelor of Science degree in Foods and Nutrition from San Diego State University, where she served as president of the Student Nutrition Organization, was involved in many nutrition related volunteer projects, and graduated with distinction. Most recently, Amy was elected as the Outstanding California Dietetic Student of the Year. She is currently working toward her Registered Dietitian credential. Amy's roles at *Healthy Dining* include working with chefs of participating restaurants to verify and review recipes for nutrition analysis, and coordinating the typesetting, editing and publication of the *Healthy Dining* books.

Mikah Felago - Projects Coordinator

Mikah Felago recently earned her Bachelor of Science degree in Foods and Nutrition from San Diego State University, graduating cum laude. The newest member of the *Healthy Dining* team, Mikah brings a wide range of experiences from the field of health and nutrition and contributes additional enthusiasm and creative ideas. Mikah is involved with managing the *Healthy Dining* corporate office, telephone and Internet communications, promotion and marketing, and the coordination of projects and events involving the *Healthy Dining* series of books and the **TrEAT Yourself Well** study/campaign.

Healthy Dining,
Recipient of the 1998
Meritorious Service Award
of the California Dietetic Association

Healthy Dining Director Anita Jones-Mueller (center), dietitian Sherri Corey (right) and Publishing Coordinator Amy Sturm (left) accept the 1998 Meritorious Service Award from the California Dietetic Association at its annual meeting in May, 1998. This award was presented to **Healthy Dining** in recognition of exceptional service to and support of the profession of dietetics.

The **TrEAT Yourself Well**
Campaign and Research Study

If you're like most Americans, you probably find yourself eating out more and more. Good news! The California Department of Health Services has recognized the importance of restaurant nutrition to Californians' health and has funded a study to encourage the selection of healthier restaurant meals. San Diego has been chosen as the pilot city for the landmark study. The study/campaign is being implemented by *Healthy Dining* in partnership with the Department of Health Services, the California 5 a Day Campaign and the California Restaurant Association. The campaign includes the largest social marketing and advertising program conducted to date to promote healthy restaurant dining.

The campaign's goals are (1) to inspire California chefs to create great-tasting dishes emphasizing fruits and vegetables, grains, and lean proteins and (2) to provide restaurant diners with healthier choices. The campaign/study extends from March 1, 2000 to April 30, 2001.

The study restaurants include:

Publicity includes advertising, public relations, an in-restaurant awareness program, and a community relations program. Advertising includes full-page color print ads, TV spots and educational programming. Additional promotion is occurring through participating restaurants, local health organizations, hospitals, medical offices and other community organizations.

The research study involves collection of weekly sales data at each of the San Diego "intervention" restaurant locations and at their "comparison" locations outside the San Diego promotion area. Three times during the campaign, customers are being surveyed in the restaurants to measure attitudes towards the healthful menu dishes and the **TrEAT Yourself Well** campaign. The evaluation of the **TrEAT Yourself Well** project is being conducted by Juárez & Associates of Los Angeles.

Please visit www.healthy-dining.com or call (858) 541-2049 for additional information.

Distinguished *Healthy Dining* Advisory Board

The following individuals serve on **Healthy Dining's** Advisory Board. Each advisor completes a comprehensive review of one of our publications -- the San Diego, Orange County, or Los Angeles edition -- and provides feedback and suggestions. The **Healthy Dining** team is proud, honored, and fortunate to gain the input of such a distinguished group. We thank every Advisory Board member for his or her commitment to this important community health program.

Margot J. Aiken, MD, FRCPC, FACE, Scripps Clinic. Dr. Aiken is in full-time clinical practice at Scripps Clinic and involves herself in education programs and professional societies related to maternity, menopause and endocrinology. She is a member of numerous professional organizations including The Am. Assoc. of Clinical Endocrinology, The Am. Soc. of Reproductive Medicine and The North Am. and Int'l. Menopause Societies.

Robert Ashley, Director Hospitality Services/Executive Chef - UCSD Medical Center, Thorton Hospital. As a world traveler with 102 countries visited, Chef Robert's exposure to the cuisines of the world has driven him to develop authentic regional food creations that have won national and international acclaim. By using indigenous ingredients, Chef Robert improves the nutritional profile of his dishes. A television show evolved from "Chef Robert's Healthy and Exotic Cuisines of the World" brunches that are open to the public at Thorton Hospital. Chef also lectures, consults and conducts cooking classes with numerous government and private organizations in California.

Paula Benedict, MPH, RD, Nutritionist, San Bernadino County Dept. of Public Health & Nutrition Program. Paula is the Coordinator of the Better For You Restaurant Program, a healthy restaurant/menu labeling program for San Bernadino County restaurants. She is also a nutrition columnist for the *San Bernadino County Sun* newspaper and a Board Member of the National Council Against Health Fraud and the American Cancer Society, Loma Linda Unit.

Marilyn Biggica, Instructor of Foods & Nutrition, San Diego Comm. College. Marilyn teaches low-fat cooking at San Diego Community College and is active in the Community College District, where she serves on the Curriculum Council and Advisory Committee. Marilyn also advises restaurants about healthier alternatives on their menus. She teaches that healthy food can taste good, as reflected in her cookbook *"101 Ways to Eat for Health and Pleasure."*

Antonio Cagnolo, Owner/Operator, Antonello Ristorante. A native of northwestern Italy, Antonio has emerged as a dynamic force in the field of dining, having received honor after honor for his many contributions both in and out of culinary circles. He has earned national acclaim for the award-winning Italian cuisine served at Antonello Ristorante in Santa Ana. Antonio has been the recipient of the prestigious Golden Scepter Award several times and has been named "Restaurateur of the Year" by the Southern California Restaurant Writers.

Marie Connors, Special Services Manager, Weight Watchers of San Diego and the Inland Empire, Inc. Marie has been with Weight Watchers since 1984, lecturing on weight management and nutrition. She coordinates and supervises Weight Watchers' involvement in health fairs, sports expos, charitable events, Wellness at the Worksite as well as their annual participation in the Del Mar Fair.

David G. Daniels, MD, Private Practice. Dr. Daniels practices medicine in San Diego, where he has maintained a private office for 24 years. Dr. Daniels has been involved with *Healthy Dining* since its inception. His continued interest in nutrition, weight control and the *Healthy Dining* publications demonstrates his commitment to helping everyone make healthier choices.

Gayle A. DeBrosse, President, KOO KOO ROO Restaurants. Gayle has over 16 years experience in the food service industry, primarily in quality assurance, product development, and public relations. Presently, she oversees the strategic direction and operation of the KOO KOO ROO restaurant chain. Gayle received a B.S. degree in Nutritional Sciences and a Master's degree in Agribusiness form Arizona State University.

Danna Demetre, RN, Founder and Director, Lifestyle Dimensions. Danna has been actively involved in the health and fitness industry for over 20 years as a registered nurse, fitness professional, corporate marketing manager and professional trainer. Her company, Lifestyle Dimensions, offers a comprehensive program designed to equip and empower women to meet their long-term health and fitness goals.

Aya Dinning, RN, Director of Community Relations, Healthcare Partners Inst. for Applied Research & Education. As Director of Community Relations, Aya coordinates the Institute's fundraising and community education programs. Prior to her current position, Aya was Director of the Healthcare Partners Medical Group's highly successful clinical trials program for 10 years, where she managed the overall operation of the drug research program, working on new pharmaceutical medications.

Mary Donkersloot, RD, Nutrition Therapist, Personal Nutrition Management. Mary is a nutritionist with a private counseling practice in Beverly Hills. She is the author of *Fast Food Diet: Quick and Healthy Eating at Home and On The Go* and *The Everyday Gourmet Diabetes Cookbook.* Mary is a graduate of the Professional Chef Training Program at the Epicurean Cooking School in Los Angeles.

Karen C. Duester, MS, RD, Owner, Nutritionist, The Food Consulting Co. Karen provides nutrition analysis services and custom food labels to restaurants, cookbook authors, publishers and food manufacturers through her company The Food Consulting Co., which she founded in 1993. Karen was named "Recognized Young Dietitian of the Year" in 1987 and has been listed in *Two Thousand Notable American Women, Who's Who in Young Professionals, Who's Who in Emerging Leaders* and *Who's Who in American Women.*

Judith Ewing, Adult Education Instructor, San Diego Community College District. With a Bachelor's degree in Home Economics, Judith is involved in a variety of projects and programs related to health. For the past 21 years, she has been an Instructor at the San Diego Community College, where she teaches cooking classes. Judy is also a consultant in menu and recipe development for Creative Culinary Concepts.

Mary Felando, MS, RD, Cardiac Rehab Dietitian. With a Master's degree in Human Nutrition from Cornell University, Mary has worked in the nutrition field for 18 years. Currently employed as an Administrative Dietitian in the Los Angeles area, she is responsible for the development and implementation of the nutrition component of one of the largest cardiac rehabilitation programs in the country.

Tom Feltenstein, CEO, Feltenstein Partners; Chairman & Founder, Neighborhood Marketing Institute. Tom's energetic, dynamic style and proven marketing strategies have gained him celebrity status for 20+ years with restaurant and hospitality associations and corporations worldwide. His successful career stems from his association with powerhouse corporations such as McDonald's and Burger King, plus owning a chain of 14 restaurants. Tom's high-level executive training and hands-on, "in the trenches" experience provide him credibility as the most respected and highly sought after marketing consultant in the foodservice industry.

Sally Fenton, Executive Director, American Heart Association. Sally has over fifteen years of professional experience in the areas of management and fundraising, in which she combines creative and analytical abilities to reach targeted goals. Sally has also been very active in professional organizations and community activities including the American Cancer Society, Directors of Volunteers in Agencies (DOVIA), and the Women's Health Initiative, where she currently serves as the President of the Orange County Advisory Board.

Evelyne Fleury-Milfort, MSN, C-RNP, CDE, Diabetes Program Coordinator, USC Center for Diabetes & Metabolic Diseases. Evelyne is the past president of the Diabetes Teaching Nurses of Southern California. She is an active member of the American Diabetes Association, as well as a member of the American Assoc. of Diabetes Educators. In addition to her position at the USC Center for Diabetes, she is on the faculty for Eli Lilly Diabetes Interactive Network Program and is a guest lecturer for the USC Family Nurse Practitioner Program.

Gaetano Foiani, Owner and Food & Beverage Manager, Il Moro Restaurant. Gaetano has over 20 years experience in restaurant management, including 3 years as a professional instructor at the Hospitality Industry School in Italy. He currently owns and manages Il Moro, a popular restaurant in Los Angeles that serves fresh, wholesome and healthy Italian food.

Gail C. Frank, DrPH, MPH, RD, CHES, Professor of Nutrition, Cal. State University Long Beach. Gail has been active in the fields of nutrition and health for over 25 years. Along with directing many programs at Cal State Univ. Long Beach, Gail is an Adjunct Professor of Pediatrics at Univ. of Cal., Irvine, and Co-Principal Investigator for the Women's Health Initiative. She is active in many professional organizations, and has served as the Media Spokesperson for the American Dietetic Association for 14 years. Gail has had over 600 media interviews including the LA Times, CNN, NPR, US News & World Report and USA Today.

Annette Globits, R.D., Nutrition Educator and Counselor. Annette graduated from Cornell University, completed her internship at the University of Michigan Medical Center, and has worked as a dietitian at the UCLA Medical Center and the Los Alamitos Medical Center. She teaches classes on various subjects from weight reduction to nutrition during pregnancy, and has lectured extensively throughout the community. She now operates a private practice in nutrition and believes "What you eat can make a difference."

Robyn L. Goldberg, R.D., Private Practice. Robyn began her career at Cedars-Sinai Medical Center in Los Angeles as the inpatient dietitian in the Department of Cardiology. She currently has her own private practice in Beverly Hills, CA, where she specializes in medical conditions, disordered eating, preventative nutrition and athletes maximizing optimal nutrition. Robyn promotes opportunity to excel in personal health and fitness maintenance through a lecture series in association with several medical groups. She serves as a Nutrition Consultant for the Celiac Disease Foundation.

Micheline Erika Hansen, RD. Micheline is the Corporate Dietitian and Nutrition Specialist for Albertsons Supermarkets, making regular appearances on television and radio to give nutrition information to consumers. Micheline was formerly the coordinator of Nutrition Programs for Centinela Hospital's Fitness Institute, working with individuals associated with the Los Angeles Lakers, Dodgers and Kings, and the LAPD.

Michelle Heilpern, President, Heilpern & Associates. Michelle has over 15 years of professional experience in the health care field. Her company specializes in strategic planning, marketing, public affairs and fund-raising for health care and non-profit organizations. She is the winner of nearly a dozen national awards for communications excellence.

Connie Hippensteel, Manager, San Diego Tech Center/Fitness Center. With a Master's degree in Exercise Physiology, Connie manages one of the most unique and modern fitness centers in San Diego. The Tech Center leases office space to 30 different companies and provides them with a state-of-the-art gym where over 2500 employees have the opportunity to get fit.

Elizabeth James, MPH, RD, President, Elizabeth James & Associates, Inc. With an educational background in nutrition and dietetics, Elizabeth has over 20 years experience in food styling, design, journalism and nutrition consulting. She has contributed articles and presentations to publications such as *Bon Appetit*, *NFL Properties*, *Valley Magazine* and *The Los Angeles Times*. As a Food Stylist and Consultant, some of her clients include Del Monte Foods, Healthy Choice, General Foods, McDonald's and Proctor and Gamble.

Jeanne Jones, President, Jeanne Jones, Inc. Jeanne is a prolific author, having completed 30 popular cookbooks. Her most recent book is *Healthy Cooking for People Who Don't Have Time to Cook* (Rodale Press, January 1997). Her internationally syndicated column "Cook It Light" is eagerly anticipated by millions each week. She regularly speaks to medical and lay audiences and has appeared on radio and TV shows such as "Donahue" and "Good Morning America." Jeanne's consulting services have been sought by such varied clients as the Pritikin Longevity Center, Canyon Ranch Fitness Resorts, Windstar Cruises and The Golden Door.

Barbara Kar, MA, MPH, Cancer Control Program Manager, American Cancer Society, San Fernando Valley Unit. As Manager for the Cancer Control Program at the American Cancer Society, San Fernando Valley Unit, Barbara manages public and professional education programs for a population of two million, including youth programs in schools and adult programs in clinics and hospitals, clubs, industries and other community groups. She also serves as regional liaison to the L.A. Unified School District.

Cindy Stack Keer, RD, MPH, Senior Health Educator, Kaiser Permanente Medical Center. As an educator and trainer, Cindy works as a consultant in developing, coordinating, implementing, evaluating and teaching educational programs. She manages a variety of projects such as a Latino Diabetes Education Program, where she utilizes her fluency in Spanish. Cindy works closely with physicians, nurses, managers and other health professionals in facilitating multi-disciplinary groups to improve the continuity of care for Kaiser members.

Kay Kimball, RN, MSN, Coordinator of Cancer Wellness Programs, Palomar Medical Center. Kay has worked as a Registered Nurse in various medical and surgical units and has been the Coordinator of the Cancer Wellness Program since 1994. She earned her Master's Degree as a Certified Family Nurse Practitioner.

Shirley Klein, Personal Trainer. As a Certified Personal Trainer and Weight Management Consultant in Leucadia, California, Shirley is committed to helping others get in shape and live a healthy lifestyle. Current positions include San Diego Regional Training Instructor for Secure Horizons and Senior Fitness Instructor at the YMCA. She is associated with the Am. Council on Exercise and the International Dance & Exercise Association.

Jeffrey Krebs, MD, FACP. Dr. Krebs has been practicing Internal Medicine in San Diego County since 1989. He is an Assistant Clinical Professor of Medicine at the UCSD School of Medicine. Dr. Krebs is on the Council of the San Diego County Medical Society and is the Chair of the California Medical Association's Young Physician Section. As a former competitive athlete, Dr. Krebs has always had an interest in nutrition.

Rieva Lesonsky, Senior Vice President/Editorial Director, Entrepreneur Media, Inc. Rieva has over 18 years experience at Entrepreneur media, currently serving as VP/Editorial Director of *Entrepreneur and Business Start-Ups* magazines. Rieva served on the Small Business Administration's (SBA) National Advisory Council from 1994 - 2000. The SBA has also honored her as a Small Business Media Advocate and a Woman in Business Advocate. For five years, Business News Reporter has named her one of the Top 100 Most Influential Journalists.

Phyllis Ann Marshall, FCSI, Principal, FoodPower. Phyllis is a foodservice industry consultant specializing in concept development and strategic plans to increase sales and profits of full-service restaurants and foodcourts. She holds a B.A. degree from Cornell University and has extensive experience in the areas of market positioning, menu development, merchandising and four-walls marketing. Phyllis develops growth strategies with an eye to adding new profit centers and establishing brands. She assists shopping centers with the development of new foodcourts and the retrofitting of existing properties in order to create destination restaurant locations.

Barbara Kuntz Mallman, RD. Since 1977, Barbara has been guiding her clients, readers and audiences to a healthier lifestyle. She has been in private practice since 1985 and is currently a Registered Dietitian for Scripps Clinical Research Studies. Prior to 1985, Barbara was the head spa dietitian at La Costa Health Spa in Carlsbad, California and chief nutritionist at Cardio-Fitness Centers in New York City. Barbara has reached thousands of people through her lectures, interviews on *Hour Magazine* and Channel 10's "Staying Fit" program.

Cindy Maynard, MS, RD. Cindy is a health and medical writer with articles appearing in national publications. She has a private practice in San Diego and currently consults for Healthy Within, a day treatment program for women with eating disorders. She has appeared on Channel 10 News for the Staying Healthy series and has been interviewed for AM 1000 Talk Radio Show in San Diego.

Agnes McGlone, Senior Vice President, Youth Market Programs, American Heart Association. Agnes has been in the non-profit industry since 1989. Her work with the AHA began in the Inland Empire as a fundraiser. She then transferred to LA as Director of Special Events, fundraising for many large events. Agnes then became the Executive Director in Orange County where the office experienced a 30% increase in income in two years. Currently, she oversees all aspects of the AHA programs serving the youth of California, Nevada and Utah.

Patti Tveit Milligan, MS, RD, Registered Dietitian, Henry's Marketplace. As Corporate Dietitian at Henry's Marketplace, Patti is responsible for customer education and nutrition updates to staff. In her previous position as Director of Nutrition and Marketing for Daily's Fit & Fresh Restaurants, she assisted with the development of the restaurant and provided nutritional expertise to the foodservice operation. Patti is also the Sports Team Nutritionist at San Diego State University's Aztec Gymnastics Club and lectures throughout San Diego.

April Morgan, Director of Member Programs, The Sports Club Company. April has over 20 years experience in the fitness industry. She holds a Bachelor's degree in Commercial Recreation and an A.C.E. Certification. In her current position, she oversees all member programs such as private training, group exercise, sports and children's programs for The Sports Club company which operates upscale health and fitness clubs throughout the country under The Sports Club and Spectrum Club name.

Eileen Packer, RD, CAE, Chief Executive Officer, California Dietetic Association. Eileen has several years' experience in managing operations, fundraising and creating innovative programs for non-profit organizations. Prior to her current position as CEO of the California Dietetic Association, she was the Director of Food and Nutrition Services at AMI Tarzana Regional Medical Center for 11 years, where she managed a 50-employee Food Service Department in a 212 bed medical center.

Victoria Pepper, MS, RD, Marketing Coordinator, Kaiser Permanente Preventive Medicine. Victoria has worked for Kaiser Permanente for over 12 years as a Lifestyle Educator teaching weight management, stress management, cooking classes and theatre workshops. In 1989 she became the Marketing Coordinator for Kaiser Permanente's Positive Choice Wellness Center and Health Appraisal Clinic. Before joining Kaiser Permanente, Victoria worked as a Dietitian for Scripps Clinic and was in private practice.

Patricia Perrault-Mattison, Writer and Designer, Write to Design. Patricia's professional career includes more than 10 years of experience as a writer and editor and 8 years in graphic design. In fact, Patricia designed the covers of several editions of *Healthy Dining*. She has a Bachelor's degree in English from the University of Oregon and has been employed in the public relations field for the last 6 years.

Susan Plese, Public Information Specialist, San Diego County Sheriff's Department. Susan has extensive experience in marketing, communications, public relations, desktop publishing and special event management. She has a Bachelor's degree in Journalism.

Diane Powers, Owner, Bazaar del Mundo. Diane is the founder, owner and operator of Bazaar del Mundo, the landmark San Diego tourist destination that helps attract over 5 million visitors to Old Town State Historic Park each year. She received the "Entrepreneur of the Year" Award from the California Travel Industry Association and the "San Diego Woman of Achievement" Award from the League of Women Voters, along with numerous honors for her achievements in design, recycling/environment, marketing and management.

David Priver, MD, Past President, San Diego County Medical Society. Dr. Priver served as the president of the San Diego County Medical Society in 1996 and 1997. He has been in private practice as an OB/GYN since 1974 and is on the staff of several prestigious hospitals in San Diego, including Sharp Memorial Hospital and UCSD Medical Center. He is a member of the American Medical Association and the California Medical Association. His special interests include a healthy diet approach to good prenatal care and menopause.

Elyse Resch, MS, RD, FADA, Nutrition Therapist. Elyse has been in private practice in Beverly Hills for 17 years, specializing in eating disorders, intuitive eating and preventative nutrition. She is the co-author of "Intuitive Eating" and does regular speaking engagements. She is a certified child and adolescent obesity expert and was the treatment team nutritionist on the Eating Disorder Unit at Beverly Hills Medical Center. She participates in a variety of organizations and activities including the Sports, Cardiovascular and Wellness Nutrition Practice Group of the American Dietetic Association.

Paul Rosengard, Director of Educational Services, SPARK Physical Education at San Diego State University. Paul is the Exec. Dir. of SPARK Phys. Ed. at SDSU, the Dir. of the Physical Activity Intervention for Project M-SPAN (Middle School Physical Activity and Nutrition) at SDSU, instructs the Univ. of California at San Diego and Cal State Univ., San Marcos, and is the former Deputy Dir. of the Governor's Council on Physical Fitness and Sports. He is also employed as a consultant and trainer by a number of Federal and State grants that study physical activity, behavior change, and/or environmental change with many different populations and cultures.

Joan W. Rupp, MS, RD, Director, Project LEAN (Lowfat Eating for Americans Now) and Assistant Professor, University of California San Diego. Joan is an Assistant Professor in the Department of Family and Preventative Medicine at the University of California San Diego and a Lecturer in the Department of Exercise and Nutritional Sciences at San Diego State University. She is also the Director of the Southern Coast Region of Project LEAN, a state-wide nutrition education program involving restaurants, chefs, grocery stores, schools and the media promoting the healthy eating message.

John Ryan, General Manager, Walt's Wharf. John has been in the food industry business for over 20 years. He is a firm believer in healthy dining and its counterpart, physical fitness. His position at Walt's Wharf has been a perfect fit, with a menu emphasizing freshness and healthy choices. John, wife Dana and two sons have many fitness accomplishments that currently include swimming and triathlon competition.

Mary Ryzner, MS, RD, Clinical Dietitian, Palomar Medical Center. Since receiving her Master's Degree in Nutrition in 1988 from California State University, Northridge, Mary has worked as a Clinical Dietitian for various hospitals and care centers. Currently, she is responsible for patients' dietetic needs and is the Preceptor for 10 San Diego State University AP4 Program dietetic students. In addition, Mary organizes and teaches "The Heart of the Matter" community class.

Sheri Sachs, Executive Director, Conner's Cause for Children. Sheri attended the City University of New York, majoring in psychology, while her husband completed his residency in Internal Medicine. Sheri managed two medical practices before becoming active in philanthropic organizations. She served as a board member of the San Diego County Medical Society Alliance. Currently, Sheri is the Executive Director of Conner's Cause for Children and an active mother of two boys.

Debra Sarokin, Vice President of Research and Development, La Salsa Holding Company. Debra has many years of experience in the restaurant field. For over 9 years she has been associated with La Salsa, where she first started as the Vice President of Human Resources. Prior to 1990, she worked for California Pizza Kitchen as Director of Operations. Debra has also been affiliated with Cabo Cabo Cabo, RJ's and Gladstones.

Clarice M. Schickling, RD, CDE, Diabetes Wisdom, Inc. Clarice has been a Certified Diabetes Educator since 1986 and is a past President of Orange County Chapter of the American Association of Diabetes Educators. Trained at the Univ. of Minnesota, Clarice has since worked in California as a therapeutic, teaching, administrative and consulting dietitian, college teacher and administrator. She is a member of the American Dietetic Association, American Diabetes Association and the American Association of Diabetes Educators.

Jamie Steele, President & Fitness Director, Steele Bodies. Jamie has been in the health and fitness industry for over 20 years. His company, Steele Bodies, a personalized fitness, wellness and nutrition program, specializes in high-intensity training principles. Jamie has owned and operated 10 health and fitness facilities in California and Arizona and worked in upper level management and business development for a large California health and fitness chain.

Stacy Steinberg, MS, RD, Associate Executive Director, Cedars-Sinai Comprehensive Cancer Center. Stacy is the past President of the LA Dietetic Association and recipient of the Young Dietitian of the Year Award by the American Dietetic Association. She has served as the National Nutrition Services Coordinator for Salick Health Care and is now responsible for the associate management and direction of operations at the Cedars-Sinai Comprehensive Cancer Center.

Allyson Thurber, Executive Chef, Water Grill Restaurant. Allyson's innate talent, eye and taste for innovation, dedicated determination and commitment to quality have made her instrumental in establishing Water Grill as one of the best seafood restaurants in the country. She is a leader in perfecting the art of creating exquisite cuisine that couples good nutrition with exceptional taste. Allyson graduated Valedictorian from the famed Culinary Institute of America and was named the "#2 Seafood Chef" in the country for 1996.

Debra L. Tindle, RD, Clinical Dietitian, Garden Grove Hospital & Medical Center. Debra received her Bachelor's degree in Dietetics & Food Admin. from Cal. State Univ., Long Beach and has over 20 years experience as a health educator in areas of nutrition, internal medicine and weight management. She served as a reviewer for the *Journal of Nutrition Education* and the *National Weight Control Resources Directory*. Debra presently manages clinical nutrition, food service and community education at the Garden Grove Hospital & Medical Center.

Christopher Trela, Journalist, *OC Metro Magazine*/"Metro Menus." Christopher is the restaurant writer for Metro Menus and the theatre critic for the *OC Metro Magazine*. He also writes a Health & Fitness column for the *OC Metro Magazine*, and is a freelance writer and photographer for many local magazines, a public relations consultant, and the President and owner of Paradise West Creative Services.

Evelyn Tribole, MS, RD, Nutrition Editor, *Shape Magazine*. Evelyn is an award-winning registered dietitian with a counseling practice in Beverly Hills. She reaches over 3 million readers with her monthly column in *Shape Magazine*, "Recipe Makeovers." Evelyn has served as the "Good Morning America" Nutritionist and is author of several books including *Healthy Homestyle Cooking, Eating on the Run* and *Intuitive Eating.*

Patricia Van Donck, CVT, ADN, Clinical Research Associate, Advanced Tissue Sciences, Inc. Patricia spent 10 years in the Navy, specializing in cardiovascular medicine. She earned an Associate's degree in Nursing and is certified as a Clinical Research Associate.

Gene Warneke, Freelance Tour Director & Commercial Photographer. Gene has a special interest in food and dining. In his prior position as Executive Director of the American Institute of Wine and Food (San Diego Chapter), Gene administered and planned the organization's food and wine events. Gene now works as a freelance tour director for a destination management company and as a commercial photographer specializing in food.

Terry Zierenberg, RN, CDE, Program Coordinator, Diabetes Care Center at Encino-Tarzana Regional Medical Center. Terry has spent several years educating nurses, patients and the community about diabetes. Previously, she was a Diabetes Nurse for Northridge Hospital Medical Center and a Diabetes Nurse Clinician for the Diabetes Treatment Center at Encino-Tarzana R.M.C. Her affiliations include the American Association of Diabetes Educators, the American Diabetes Association and the Juvenile Diabetes Foundation.

Disclaimer:

The purpose of this book is to provide nutrition information for selected menu items from restaurants that have chosen to participate in the ***Healthy Dining*** program. Please note that the items listed in this book are not necessarily appropriate or healthful for all individuals. Some people need to be more careful about certain items such as salt or sugar, or have food allergies which put additional restrictions on their food choices. Each individual is responsible, in cooperation with his or her physician, dietitian or other health consultant, for making personal dietary decisions. We have not included all the restaurants that serve healthy food, nor are we recommending all entrees from restaurants that are included in this book.

It is also important to note that the numerical values for the nutrition information included in this book are approximations only, and that the categories "Good Choice" and "Excellent Choice" give a better overall indication of the nutrition content of the menu items.

The nutrition information provided is based on the United States Department of Agriculture (USDA) nutrition information database, the source most commonly used for estimating nutritional content of foods. Participating restaurants supplied their recipes for the computerized analysis. The analyses were completed using the Nutritionist IV Computer program. Research shows the Nutritionist IV program to be one of the most current and reliable nutrition analysis programs available. If values for recipe ingredients were not available from the USDA database, the manufacturer was contacted for the nutrition information. If the manufacturer did not have nutrition information, ingredients were closely matched to a similar product's nutrition information. Data were rounded as follows: for calories, cholesterol and sodium, to the nearest 5 (mg). For fat, protein and carbohydrates, to the nearest whole number, and for diabetic exchanges to the nearest ¼ exchange.

All information contained in this book has been carefully compiled and reviewed by qualified health professionals. Nutrition information is based on recipes supplied by the restaurants. Participating restaurants have agreed to prepare food according to the recipes submitted for a period of one year, or to clearly notify customers otherwise.

The authors are not responsible for maintaining quality control over the food that is prepared by the restaurants. The restaurants are ultimately responsible for the quality of the food they serve.

An Important Message from the *Healthy Dining* Team

Welcome to the ***Healthy Dining*** "family." This program has grown from San Diego to Orange County to Los Angeles. More than 1000 individuals have participated in this effort, including restaurant chefs and management, health professionals, and members of community organizations. You, the ***Healthy Dining*** reader and restaurant diner, play an essential role as well.

Why? Because restaurants are responsive to their customers. They need to hear from you that health-conscious menu items and nutrition information are important to you.

Here's how you can help ***Healthy Dining*** grow in your community:

1. Dine at the restaurants listed in the book, and tell the restaurant staff and owners that you appreciate and value their participation in ***Healthy Dining***. Also, request the ***Healthy Dining*** menus at participating restaurants and use the discount coupons.

2. Tell friends, family and business associates about ***Healthy Dining***.

3. Tell other restaurants about ***Healthy Dining*** and recommend that they participate next year.

4. Give ***Healthy Dining*** books as gifts for birthdays, holidays, etc.

5. Use ***Healthy Dining*** as a fund-raiser (call for information).

6. Use ***Healthy Dining*** restaurants for your catering and party needs.

7. Invite a ***Healthy Dining*** representative to give a presentation to your organization.

8. Please call us with your suggestions and feedback: (858) 541-2049.

Thanks! Together we can make Southern California a healthier place to live and dine.

Part I

Healthy Dining Tips

Realistic Guidelines and Practical Information

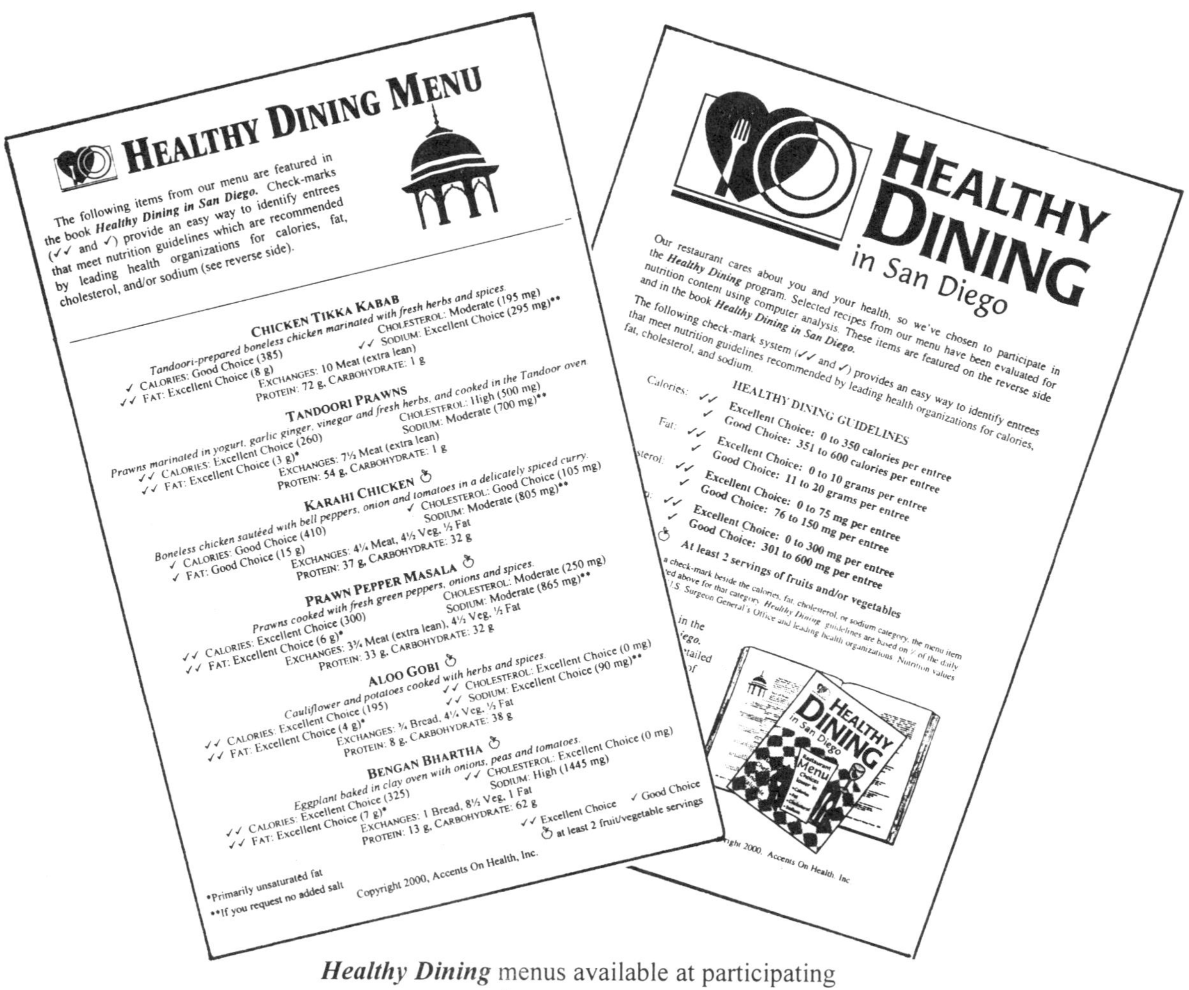

Healthy Dining menus available at participating
restaurants for customer convenience.

The *Healthy Dining* menus illustrated above are condensed versions of the menu pages in your book. We encourage all the restaurants to pass out their *Healthy Dining* menus along with their regular menus. Some restaurants, however, don't automatically provide them -- *you must request these special menus*. And please do! The more that restaurants hear customers asking for specific nutrition information and ordering "Special Requests," the more they will recognize how important healthy dining is to many people.

If nutrition information is important to you, if you want to have the choice to "order healthy," please request *Healthy Dining* menus in the restaurants and let them know that you appreciate the healthy menu choices.

How to Use This Book

This introduction summarizes how to interpret the nutrition information for the restaurant menu items. Part I of the book provides more in-depth information to help you become better informed about health and restaurant dining. Part II features nutrition profiles for specific entrees at 76 restaurants at over 300 locations in San Diego. Part III includes a Health Resource Guide, Part IV presents a wonderful selection of Chefs' Recipes, Part V contains a Survey, a Book Order Form, and over $200 in Coupons, and finally, Part VI lists three Restaurant Indexes for quick reference.

The Check Mark System - An easy way to find entrees to fit your goals

First, let's define "healthy entree." In this book, a healthy entree is one with high-quality, nutritious calories. In general, these are low in fat, cholesterol, calories and sodium. Because many entrees are not low in all areas, the check mark system will help you easily and quickly identify which entrees best fit your individual dietary goals.

Nutritional guidelines are difficult to set because each individual has different nutritional needs. For example, caloric needs vary according to age, gender, activity level, body weight and health goals (e.g., reducing body fat, lowering cholesterol, etc.). Nevertheless, the following are general guidelines to make the menu information easy to interpret. These guidelines are based on recommendations by the U.S. Surgeon General's Office and the American Heart Association. Details about how the values were developed are included in Chapters 3 through 6, but here's a quick summary of the check mark meanings:

ENTREE GUIDELINES

Calories	✓✓ Excellent Choice = 0 to 350 calories/entree ✓ Good Choice = 351 to 600 calories/entree
Fat	✓✓ Excellent Choice = 0 to 10 grams (g)/entree ✓ Good Choice = 11 to 20 grams (g)/entree
Cholesterol	✓✓ Excellent Choice = 0 to 75 milligrams (mg)/entree ✓ Good Choice = 76 to 150 milligrams (mg)/entree
Sodium	✓✓ Excellent Choice = 0 to 300 milligrams (mg)/entree ✓ Good Choice = 301 to 600 milligrams (mg)/entree

It's important to note...

Although some individuals prefer stricter criteria for their meal guidelines (especially people on very low-fat or low-sodium diets), the *Healthy Dining* guidelines represent fairly high standards for restaurant entrees and are realistic goals for most diners, as discussed in Chapters 3 through 6.

We occasionally include a menu item that is described as "moderate" in one of the nutrient categories. "Moderate" means that the item does not meet the guidelines, but it is less than twice the cut-off value for "Good Choice." Some items are listed as "high" in sodium (meaning above 1000 mg. sodium per entree) and are **not** recommended for those watching sodium intake.

The *Healthy Dining* guidelines are general guidelines developed for the general public. You, your physician and your dietitian are responsible for setting individual nutritional guidelines according to your particular health needs. **Please note also that the numerical values for the nutrition information are approximations only, based on recipes supplied by the restaurants**.

If you are health-conscious and looking for better ways to eat and enhance your overall health, this book will provide an easy way to choose entrees that don't have the hidden calories, fat, cholesterol and sodium you'd rather avoid.

If you want to lose weight, take special note of the calorie and fat categories and select items listed as Excellent Choice (✓✓) or Good Choice (✓) in these areas (see Chapters 3 and 4). For information on calculating percentage of calories from fat, see Chapter 3.

If you want to reduce your blood cholesterol level, choose from items that are listed as Excellent Choice (✓✓) or Good Choice (✓) for both cholesterol and fat (see Chapter 5).

To reduce dietary sodium, select those menu items that are shown as Excellent Choice (✓✓) or Good Choice (✓) in sodium, and request no added salt (see Chapter 6).

If you have diabetes, the "Exchanges" (i.e., Diabetic Exchanges used by the American Diabetes Association) are particularly useful, along with values for carbohydrate and protein. For more details, see Chapter 7.

If your physician or dietitian has given you daily limits in terms of sodium, cholesterol, etc., by all means note the numerical values as well as the check marks, and be sure they fit your restrictions. You may need to ask for additional modifications to your meal.

We've included brief entree descriptions, but they are not complete ingredient lists. Therefore, if you have food allergies or sensitivities, be sure to emphasize this to the restaurant personnel so they will understand how important it is to prepare your meal according to your specifications.

Comments about serving sizes, dressings and sauces, and side dishes

The nutrition information published in this book is based on the FULL SERVING (unless stated otherwise). Restaurant portions are frequently large, so you may not want to eat the full serving. If you eat only ⅔ of the entree, you're only consuming ⅔ of the calories, fat, cholesterol, sodium, etc.

In some cases the nutrition analysis includes dressings or sauces, and in other cases it does not. We generally recommend that you order sauces and dressings on the side and use them sparingly.

Dressings and sauces usually contain 5 to 10 grams of fat (45 to 90 calories) per tablespoon. Depending on your goals, you may choose to completely avoid them, or order them on the side and limit the amount you use. You will likely be served more than one tablespoon, so don't assume you can pour it all on your meal. You can measure out the amount you want using your teaspoon, keeping in mind that 3 teaspoons (tsp.) is equivalent to one tablespoon (Tbs.) or ½ ounce (oz).

The check mark system and guidelines listed on the previous page apply to main entrees only. We also feature some side dishes, appetizers, and desserts, and have set the guidelines for calories, fat, cholesterol and sodium equal to ⅓ of the Entree Guidelines. Other items such as breads are not generally shown because the nutrition values are fairly standard.

GUIDELINES for SIDE DISHES, APPETIZERS & DESSERTS†

Calories   ✓✓ Excellent Choice = 0 to 117 calories/serving
✓ Good Choice = 118 to 200 calories/serving

Fat   ✓✓ Excellent Choice = 0 to 3 grams (g)/serving
✓ Good Choice = 4 to 7 grams (g)/serving

Cholesterol   ✓✓ Excellent Choice = 0 to 25 milligrams (mg)/serving
✓ Good Choice = 26 to 50 milligrams (mg)/serving

Sodium   ✓✓ Excellent Choice = 0 to 100 milligrams (mg)/serving
✓ Good Choice = 101 to 200 milligrams (mg)/serving

KEY to FOOTNOTES

† Side dish guidelines are ⅓ of Entree Guidelines
* Primarily unsaturated fat (see Chapter 4)
** If you request no added salt (see Chapter 6)
🍎 at least 2 fruit/vegetable servings (see Chapter 8)

PRICE RANGE SYMBOL

At the end of each restaurant's introductory paragraph, a price range symbol appears:

$ Average entree under $10
$$ Average entree $10 - $20
$$$ Average entree over $20

How are restaurants selected to be included in Healthy Dining?

Our goal is to include a wide variety of restaurants. We do not specifically look for restaurants that specialize in serving "health food," but for a selection of popular restaurants that have a sincere interest in providing healthy foods and nutrition information. If you want organic and natural foods, we include restaurants that cater to these preferences as well. Vegetarian dishes are available at many of the restaurants. A good clue for vegetarian dishes is to look for items with no cholesterol (no animal products) or very low values, which may indicate small quantities of cheese or dairy products. You may, of course, double check with the restaurant personnel before ordering.

Restaurants participating in this book have a genuine interest in offering healthy choices. They pay a fee for the nutrition analysis, and they have signed an agreement with Accents On Health to prepare the selected entrees in accordance with the recipes they submitted or clearly notify customers otherwise. We highly respect the restaurants included in this book for their interest and commitment to serving healthy entrees. We purposely include many different types of cuisine with a wide range of prices and believe this will have the greatest impact in encouraging all restaurants to offer healthy, delicious choices.

How are entrees selected?

When a restaurant participates in the *Healthy Dining* Program, our staff of qualified health professionals works with the chef to select recipes low in fat, cholesterol, calories and sodium.

Our first choice is to find items already on the menu, without making any modifications. This would be the easiest for you and for the restaurant. However, in some cases the recipe analysis doesn't meet the *Healthy Dining* guidelines. So we work with the chef to develop a "Special Request" version that is lower in calories, fat, cholesterol and/or sodium than the original dish (see Chapter 2). The analyses listed in this book for the "Special Request" items correspond to the lower calorie, fat, etc. content that you will be served <u>if and only if you make the "Special Request."</u> Otherwise you will be served a meal with considerably higher fat and higher calorie values.

We need your help!

The restaurants in this book devote time, money and effort to participate in *Healthy Dining*. In many cases the restaurants have modified recipes to meet your needs. Now they need to hear that this nutrition information is important to you and that you appreciate their participation in *Healthy Dining*.

We encourage all the restaurants to pass out *Healthy Dining* menus along with their regular menus. The *Healthy Dining* menus are condensed versions of the book pages. Some restaurants, however, do not automatically provide them -- *you must request the Healthy Dining menus*. And please do! The more that restaurants hear customers asking for specific nutrition information and ordering "Special Requests," the more they will recognize how important healthy dining is to many people.

So, if this information is important to you, if you want to have the choice to "order healthy," **PLEASE tell the *Healthy Dining* restaurants**! Please tell other restaurants that you'd like them to participate. This will enable us to include more restaurants and an even greater variety of healthy choices in the next edition of *Healthy Dining in San Diego*.

> Please ask for the *Healthy Dining* menus
> at participating restaurants.

We welcome your ideas

This program is growing, and we welcome your ideas on how to enhance it. Please write to us with your comments. We update this publication periodically and will continue to add more restaurants, more healthy entrees, and more nutrition information.

CHAPTER 1

Health, Lifestyle, Diet, Misconceptions & ... Dining Out

In 1988, the Surgeon General made a startling announcement to the American public:

> "If you don't smoke, what you eat may be
> the biggest factor influencing your health."

We've come a long way...

Diet has always strongly influenced health and disease. Until the early decades of this century, our country suffered from problems of *undernutrition*. Rickets, pellagra, scurvy, beriberi and goiter plagued our nation. Fortunately, in the United States, advances in medicine, fortification of foods, and successful cures virtually eliminated the vicious diseases caused by a lack of essential nutrients.

Currently, we've reached a whole new perspective on health and disease. A large body of medical research shows that lifestyle greatly influences health status. It is well recognized that daily health habits -- what we eat and drink, whether or not we smoke, how much exercise we get and how effectively we manage stress -- contribute to *how well and how long* we live.

The 1988 Surgeon General's Report on Nutrition and Health outlines the substantial impact of dietary practices on health. Today, the four leading causes of death by disease (heart disease, cancer, stroke, and diabetes), which together account for over ⅔ of all deaths in the U.S., are directly related to diet. The main conclusion of the 1988 report is:

> "*Overconsumption* of certain dietary components is now a major concern for Americans. While many food factors are involved, chief among them is the disproportionate consumption of foods high in fats, often at the expense of foods high in complex carbohydrates and fiber that may be more conducive to health."

> -- 1988 Surgeon General's Report on Nutrition and Health --

Clearly, a priority for Americans is to reduce intake of total fat, and especially saturated fat, because of the relationship between excess dietary fat and the development of many leading chronic disease conditions.

Dietary guidelines for Americans

Based on extensive scientific evidence, the following recommendations were developed by the Surgeon General's Office and the American Heart Association:

1.   Reduce overall consumption of fat, especially saturated fat. The American Heart Association recommends that <u>no more than 30%</u> of total calories come from fat (the average American diet contains approximately 35% fat). Saturated fat should comprise no more than 10% of the daily diet. Choose foods low in fat such as vegetables, fruits, whole grain foods, fish, lean meats and non-fat dairy products. Use food preparation methods that add little or no fat.

2. Reduce cholesterol consumption to less than 300 mg. per day, as recommended by the American Heart Association. The average American consumes about 400 - 600 mg. daily.

3. Reduce intake of sodium by choosing foods relatively low in sodium and limiting the amount of salt in food preparation and at the table. The American Heart Association recommends less than 3,000 mg. per day. The average American consumes about 4,000 - 6,000 mg. daily.

4. Achieve and maintain a desirable body weight. To do so, choose a balanced diet in which energy (caloric) intake is consistent with energy expenditure. To reduce caloric intake, limit consumption of foods relatively high in calories, fat, and sugar, and minimize alcohol consumption. Increase energy expenditure through regular exercise.

5. Eat a variety of foods. Increase consumption of complex carbohydrates and fiber, such as whole grain foods, cereals, vegetables, fruits, dried beans, peas, and lentils.

6. Limit sugar in your diet, and if you drink alcoholic beverages, do so in moderation.

Americans are catching on!

We're watching what we eat. Learning more about what we eat. Making healthier choices. We're beginning to cherish our health for its influence on all other aspects of our lives. For top performance, we're eating more high-quality fuel -- fruits, vegetables and whole grains -- and less beef, butter, whole milk and other foods high in saturated fat.

Since the mid-1970s, consumption of saturated fats has decreased significantly. In addition, U.S. death rates from heart disease have fallen dramatically, close to 25 percent in the last decade. Leading health organizations attribute some of this decline to better medical care but give most of the credit to healthier diets and lifestyles.

Food manufacturers are catching on, but...

Marketing efforts toward our increasingly health-conscious society have intensified in the past several years. Close to 30% of food advertising includes some type of health message. Although this spiraling emphasis on healthy eating from food makers is encouraging, it can be very misleading. For example, lunchmeats frequently flaunt a "96% FAT FREE" label, yet this means that only 4% of the meat's <u>weight</u> is fat, not 4% of the calories (a high percentage of the weight is water, thus decreasing the percentage weight from fat). Cookies, crackers and chips leap out from shelves with bright "NO CHOLESTEROL" or "FAT FREE" labels, yet the nutritional value seems to be of little concern (at least to the manufacturer).

Reading between the lines

Until recently, deciphering food labels was a difficult task. Nutrition information on labels was often misleading, confusing and incomplete. Terms such as "low-fat," "light," "natural," and "healthy" had virtually no standardized meaning and could be added to any package, regardless of contents.

In 1994, the Food and Drug Administration (FDA) implemented guidelines requiring almost all food packages to display a universal nutrition information label. The revised labels help you more easily identify important nutrition information. The FDA has also developed strict guidelines for several nutritional claims commonly used by food manufacturers. For example, any food package stating the product is "low-fat" must have 3 grams of fat or less per serving. A "low-calorie" food must contain 40 calories or less per serving. A food package promoting the product as "light" (e.g., light mayonnaise) must contain 50% less fat or one-third fewer calories than the food with which it is being compared (e.g., regular mayonnaise). If the original product contains more than 50% calories from fat, the fat must be reduced by at least 50% in the "light" product.

The guidelines set by the FDA for food packages are different from the *Healthy Dining* guidelines because the *Healthy Dining* guidelines represent a full meal, whereas the FDA guidelines are designed for a single product or serving.

A crusader for healthier fast foods

In April 1990, Phil Sokolof and his non-profit organization, The National Heart Savers Association, attacked American fast food restaurants with full-page ads in large newspapers accusing them of "poisoning" Americans with foods high in saturated fat. A Gallup poll showed that almost 40% of those who saw the ads immediately decreased their visits to fast food restaurants. Just three weeks later, McDonald's responded by removing beef tallow from their French fries. Other fast food chains quickly followed. Sokolof points out that his major goal was to stop fast food from being a *"fast track to a heart attack."*

With Sokolof paving the way, consumers began demanding to know -- just what are we getting in fast food meals? In response, most fast food restaurants now provide nutrition information for menu items. At last, the fast American favorites have exposed their "fat facts."

Some fat facts

A McDonald's Big Mac has 560 calories, 31 grams of fat and 1070 milligrams of sodium. Even the Filet-O-Fish has 450 calories, 25 grams of fat and 870 milligrams of sodium. Add fries and a shake, and you're drowning in fat and sodium.

Three pieces of Original Recipe Kentucky Fried Chicken contain a whopping 790 calories, 51 grams of fat and 2285 milligrams of sodium. Add coleslaw, mashed potatoes with gravy and a biscuit, and you get a total of 1270 calories, 76 grams of fat and 3565 milligrams of sodium. That's over a full day's recommended allowance for both fat and sodium in just one meal, and 54% of the total calories come from fat!

Salads are usually considered a safe choice. However, many salads have close to 1000 calories, over 50 grams of fat, and over 1000 milligrams of sodium. Sometimes salads are higher in calories and fat than many other items on the menu.

Better alternatives

In response to their new "fat visibility," many fast food restaurants added items that look much better on the nutritional charts. Jack in the Box now serves a Chicken Fajita Pita with under 300 calories and 9 grams of fat. Their Chicken Teriyaki Bowl, with lots of rice, is filling and very low in fat (but watch the sodium). They also provide a low calorie Italian salad dressing.

In place of traditional fast food, many people are finding healthier meals at the growing number of convenient "quick-service" restaurants. For example:

Subway offers sandwiches and salads with fresh, high quality ingredients. They bake bread fresh throughout the day and use only garden fresh veggies. Each sandwich and salad is made to your exact specifications. Light mayonnaise, low-fat potato crisps and fat-free pretzels are available.

La Salsa specializes in fresh and healthy Mexican food prepared without lard. Many of their items meet recommended nutritional guidelines. La Salsa's unique salsa bar provides flavorful toppings with little or no fat.

Koo Koo Roo California Kitchen features a diverse menu, including their Original Skinless Flamebroiled Chicken Breast with only 160 calories and 4 gram of fat, chicken and turkey sandwiches, and a variety of side dishes such as Confetti Rice and Vegetable Soup which can add extra variety and nutrition to your meal.

Consumer power

As a result of health-conscious consumers speaking out, we now have the choice to "order healthy" at fast food restaurants. "The public does not realize the dramatic power it wields," Sokolof emphasizes. "The consumer's wish is big business' command."

But what about dining out in restaurants?

What's healthy and what's not?

If dining out were only for special occasions, the rich and creamy dishes could be wonderful treats. An occasional splurge might not be so bad. But because restaurant dining for business, pleasure and convenience has become so common, it is important to find healthier choices.

That's what *Healthy Dining in San Diego* is all about. It's the first book of its kind. Never before has so much information been available for restaurant menu items. Each restaurant has its own unique recipes, prepared in its own special way. So nutrition information must be compiled restaurant by restaurant, recipe by recipe. And that's a lot of work.

There are books that give general information for dining out. They list common entrees to avoid and those that are probably best to order. However, as restaurants become more specialized and creative, "common" entrees are not so common, and so general guidelines are not always accurate or useful.

As you read on about what we've discovered in our research, you'll find that often you can't tell what you're getting by the menu description. It may portray a healthy item, but many times there are hidden ingredients, and the method of preparation is not specified. Without complete nutrition information, you don't know what you're getting, and that can be dangerous! *Healthy Dining* makes the process of ordering healthy food much easier.

Goals of *Healthy Dining in San Diego:*

1. **To guide you in choosing low-fat, healthy entrees served at popular San Diego restaurants.**

2. **To provide you with easy-to-read nutrition profiles for selected entrees.**

3. **To give you useful, practical guidelines and advice for healthier restaurant dining.**

4. **To encourage restaurants to prepare and serve a wide variety of healthy choices.**

CHAPTER 2

Is Restaurant Food Fattening and Unhealthy?

<u>*It can be if you're not careful! But it doesn't have to be.*</u>

Many restaurants smother meals with excess fat, sodium, cholesterol and calories. Butter, oil, cream, cheese and salt are frequently added to achieve the taste and texture that the average American expects. To make matters worse, many restaurant diners have the habit of adding "extras" such as salad dressing, sour cream, and butter (which push up the calorie and fat count even more). Let's take a shocking look at a favorite restaurant dinner:

Chicken Breast
Topped with a Creamy Parmesan Sauce
Served with Dinner Salad, Baked Potato and Sautéed Vegetables

	Calories	Fat (g)	Cholest. (mg)	Sodium (mg)
Dinner Salad	32	0	0	53
Blue Cheese Dressing (4 Tbs.)	308	32	36	668
Chicken Breast with Sauce	1312	91	481	1517
Baked Potato	220	0	0	16
Butter (2 Tbs.)	200	23	61	232
Sour Cream (2 Tbs.)	62	6	13	15
Sautéed Vegetables	117	11	0	207
Meal Total	2251	163	591	2708

Now let's evaluate these numbers relative to daily recommendations:

Calories: Close to a FULL day's recommended calories <u>in one meal</u>.
Fat: <u>Almost three times</u> the recommended fat intake for a FULL Day.
Cholesterol: <u>Almost twice</u> the recommended cholesterol intake for a FULL Day.
Sodium: <u>Almost the entire</u> recommended sodium intake for a FULL Day.

Other fat-filled favorites: Calories   Fat   Cholest.   Sodium
    (g)   (mg)   (mg)

	Calories	Fat (g)	Cholest. (mg)	Sodium (mg)
Italian manicotti with garlic bread	1393	79	411	2330
Beef & cheese enchiladas, rice & refried beans	1510	88	210	3516
Chicken fried steak with fries	1119	77	205	1895
Ultimate cheeseburger with fries & shake	1625	96	165	1708
Chicken sandwich with onion rings & shake	1282	68	82	2290
Seafood platter - fried - with tarter sauce	1195	70	97	1780
Salmon - smothered in a cream sauce	1024	76	283	1017
Fried chicken - with potato salad & cole slaw	1124	71	239	2552
Stir fry chicken with rice & egg rolls	1213	62	99	2907
Lasagna with garlic bread & salad	1538	77	194	2805
Omelet with hashbrowns	850	53	892	852
Pizza - sausage & mushroom	1290	48	84	1656
Chimichanga with sour cream & cheese	922	68	205	2125
Salad bar - with potato & tuna salad, dressing, and muffins with butter	1715	89	310	2954

Does dining out have to be so destructive to our health?

Some say, "Order grilled fish, salads or vegetarian dishes. By avoiding red meat, fried foods and creamy sauces, you can dine out and stay on your diet."

Be careful! We've analyzed hundreds of apparently "healthy" entrees and found that many were diet disasters. Frequently, "healthy" dishes are laced with unhealthy, hidden ingredients. The menu descriptions portray healthy items, but when we looked into the preparation methods, we found the items contained too much of certain unhealthy ingredients.

Surprising nutrition information about apparently "healthy" meals:

Grilled Swordfish - *Marinated in herbs and olive oil.*

884	Calories	
71	Fat (g)	Over a full day's recommended fat intake.
115	Cholesterol (mg)	Too much olive oil used in the preparation!
846	Sodium (mg)	

Vegetarian Pasta Primavera - *Fresh vegetables and garlic sautéed in a vegetable broth. Served over fettucini noodles and tossed with Parmesan cheese.*

816	Calories	The menu description didn't mention that the pasta was
45	Fat (g)	heavily tossed with oil, and the vegetables were sautéed
139	Cholesterol (mg)	in both broth *and butter*. This brings the fat total to 75%
892	Sodium (mg)	of a FULL day's recommended fat intake.

The "Healthy" Sandwich - *Avocado, tomato & cheese on whole wheat bread.*

746	Calories	
50	Fat (g)	This is a healthy sandwich?
66	Cholesterol (mg)	Avocado, cheese, and mayonnaise add
958	Sodium (mg)	up to too much fat and sodium.

Cobb Salad - *Crispy greens topped with chicken, avocado, bacon, tomato, hard-boiled egg and blue cheese crumbles. Served with a generous portion of your favorite dressing.*

1296	Calories	
102	Fat (g)	Very unhealthy. Much too high in fat,
647	Cholesterol (mg)	cholesterol, sodium and calories.
2553	Sodium (mg)	

Shrimp Stirfry - *Shrimp and assorted vegetables with chow mein noodles.*

866	Calories	Too much fat, calories, cholesterol and sodium.
64	Fat (g)	1 oz. oil to sauté (27 g fat), butter/cream
392	Cholesterol (mg)	sauce (25 g fat), and the chow mein noodles
668	Sodium (mg)	(9 g fat) quickly add up.

Tostada - *Mexican beans, guacamole, lettuce, tomato and cheese.*

1416	Calories	
77	Fat (g)	The cheese alone contributes 519 calories,
288	Cholesterol (mg)	43 grams of fat, 137 mg cholesterol and
2010	Sodium (mg)	802 mg sodium.

We also found other items labeled "Light" or "Light-Fare" that included potato skins (deep fried), vegetables with cheese sauce, a hamburger patty and cottage cheese (too much saturated fat), cheese quesadillas (there's that saturated fat in the cheese again) and deep fried fish tacos.

Accents On Health has even analyzed entrees with a ♥ next to them, and we discovered that many were too high in fat. Here are a few examples:

??? Heart Healthy Entrees ???

♥ Eggplant Salad	34 grams fat - 86% of calories from fat
♥ Pasta with Tomatoes & Garlic	42 grams fat - 50% of calories from fat
♥ Greens Topped with Grilled Ahi	26 grams fat - 73% of calories from fat
♥ Grilled Halibut	64 grams fat - 75% of calories from fat

How can these items be designated as "healthy" or "light" when if fact they aren't? A bit of history is in order. As we noted in Chapter 1 when discussing packaged foods, <u>health sells</u>; and so food manufacturers were quick to tout the health benefits of their products. Restaurants soon followed, with menus and banners promoting the healthfulness of certain dishes.

As demonstrated above, however, many dishes described as "healthy" actually are not. A restaurant may designate a meal as healthy simply because it is vegetarian or contains no butter, but in most cases, dishes with health claims have never been analyzed for nutrition content. And until recently, there were no standards for what really constituted a healthy or low-fat restaurant meal.

New restaurant regulations

In an attempt to protect consumers from vague, incorrect, or misleading information, the Food and Drug Administration (FDA) recently implemented regulations for those restaurants that make health and nutrition claims about their food. The regulations require that dishes with descriptions such as "low fat" or "low calorie" meet specified criteria; and that restaurants provide nutrition information to substantiate any health claims made. As awareness and implementation of the new regulations get underway, we hope to see increasing numbers of restaurants providing healthier choices along with nutrition information for these meals.

Unfortunately, however, the large majority of restaurants choose <u>not</u> to provide healthful menu items with credible nutrition information. This leaves diners, in most cases, at a loss for determining the nutritional content of restaurant meals.

The restaurants featured in this book lead the nation in providing meals with an eye on nutrition <u>and</u> taste, substantiated by credible nutrition data. Instead of smothering foods with excessive amounts of unhealthy ingredients, these talented chefs creatively use herbs, spices, small amounts of unsaturated oils and healthy preparation methods. They have your health <u>and</u> your tastebuds in mind.

Some scrumptious and healthy examples:

SandCrab Café (Escondido)
SEAFOOD GUMBO

✓✓ CALORIES: Excellent Choice (255)   ✓✓ CHOLESTEROL: Excellent Choice (70 mg)
✓✓ FAT: Excellent Choice (6 g)   ✓✓ SODIUM: Excellent Choice (255 mg)

Healthy Gourmet (Conveniently located Pick-Up throughout San Diego County)
HONEY THYME PORK

Roasted pork loin glazed with honey and seasoned with garlic, dijon, and thyme.

✓✓ CALORIES: Excellent Choice (325)   ✓✓ CHOLESTEROL: Excellent Choice (55 mg)
✓✓ FAT: Excellent Choice (5 g)   ✓✓ SODIUM: Excellent Choice (220 mg)

Leucadia Pizzeria and Italian Restaurant (Encinitas, La Jolla and Rancho Santa Fe)
PASTA WITH MARINARA SAUCE

Homemade marinara sauce served over your choice of hot pasta.

✓✓ CALORIES: Excellent Choice (335)   ✓✓ CHOLESTEROL: Excellent Choice (0 mg)
✓✓ FAT: Excellent Choice (6 g)   ✓✓ SODIUM: Excellent Choice (220 mg)

Whole Foods Market (La Jolla, Hillcrest)
IT'S ALIVE (8 OZ. SERVING)

Tons of sprouts and cubes of tofu mingle with a spicy Szechwan sauce to create this very exceptional salad

✓✓ CALORIES: Excellent Choice (120)   ✓✓ CHOLESTEROL: Excellent Choice (0 mg)
✓✓ FAT: Excellent Choice (6 g)   ✓ SODIUM: Good Choice (315 mg)

Some scrumptious and healthy examples (continued):

La Costa Resort and Spa (Carlsbad)
BEEF TENDERLOIN STUFFED WITH ARTICHOKE & PIMENTOS
*Tender beef tenderloin stuffed with artichoke hearts and pimentos covered
with a wild mushroom sauce, and served with seasonal vegetables.*

✓✓ CALORIES: Excellent Choice (270)   ✓✓ CHOLESTEROL: Excellent Choice (65 mg)
✓✓ FAT: Excellent Choice (8 g)   ✓✓ SODIUM: Excellent Choice (240 mg)

Star of India (La Jolla, Del Mar and Downtown San Diego)
ALOO GOBI
Cauliflower and potatoes cooked with herbs and spices.

✓✓ CALORIES: Excellent Choice (195)   ✓✓ CHOLESTEROL: Excellent Choice (0 mg)
✓✓ FAT: Excellent Choice (4 g)   ✓✓ SODIUM: Excellent Choice (90 mg)

Prego Ristorante (Mission Valley)
PESCE SPADA ALL'AMALFITANA
Marinated thinly sliced Pacific swordfish with baby French green beans, carrots, celery, daikon sprouts and capers.

✓✓ CALORIES: Excellent Choice (275)   ✓✓ CHOLESTEROL: Excellent Choice (55 mg)
✓✓ FAT: Excellent Choice (10 g)   ✓ SODIUM: Good Choice (505 mg)

Trellises Garden Grille (at the Town & Country Hotel in Mission Valley)
SWORDFISH CAPONATA
Grilled swordfish served over caponata.

✓ CALORIES: Good Choice (525)   ✓ CHOLESTEROL: Good Choice (115 mg)
✓ FAT: Good Choice (14 g)   ✓✓ SODIUM: Excellent Choice (300 mg)

Chin's Szechwan Cuisine (9 San Diego Locations)
SZECHWAN BRAISED STRING BEANS
*A famous Szechwan dish! A fresh selection of string beans, dry braised with
imported Chinese preserved cabbage in a Chef's spicy garlic sauce and stir-fried
with or without ground pork. Analysis does not include ground pork.*

✓✓ CALORIES: Excellent Choice (200)   ✓✓ CHOLESTEROL: Excellent Choice (0 mg)
✓✓ FAT: Excellent Choice (10 g)   ✓✓ SODIUM: Excellent Choice (265 mg)

Andiamo! Italian Restaurant (Tierrasanta)
CAPPELINI CON VEGETALI ARROSTITI
Angel hair pasta, fresh basil, garlic and olive oil tossed with assorted charbroiled vegetables.

✓ CALORIES: Good Choice (425)   ✓✓ CHOLESTEROL: Excellent Choice (0 mg)
✓✓ FAT: Excellent Choice (9 g)   ✓✓ SODIUM: Excellent Choice (300 mg)

French Market Grille (Rancho Bernardo)
VEGETABLE RAVIOLI WITH RATATOUILLE PROVENCALE
Vegetable raviolis with ratatouille provencale.

✓ CALORIES: Good Choice (395)   ✓✓ CHOLESTEROL: Excellent Choice (60 mg)
✓✓ FAT: Excellent Choice (10 g)   ✓✓ SODIUM: Excellent Choice (255 mg)

The menu items on the previous pages and in the following chapters are just a taste of the wonderful entrees served at the restaurants participating in *Healthy Dining in San Diego.* We invite you to visit the restaurants featured in this book. You'll discover a whole new world of menu items that are marvelously delicious and so good for you!

"Special Requests"

In some cases, after we analyzed the restaurant recipes, we found dishes that contained too many calories and/or too much fat, cholesterol or sodium. So we recommended that the chef modify the dishes to meet the *Healthy Dining* guidelines. We note these dishes as "Special Requests." "Special Requests" may be prepared with less oil or butter, salad dressing or sauce served on the side, less cheese, etc. When you order, <u>you must ask for the "Special Request"</u> for it to correspond to the published nutrition information. See the examples below to find out how many calories and grams of fat you save by ordering some of these "Special Requests."

Examples of "Special Requests:"

Café Japengo (La Jolla)
PAN ROASTED SALMON – SPECIAL REQUEST
Salmon filet with mushroom duxell, Thai green curry sauce and served with stir-fried spinach and soba noodles. <u>Request no butter and for spinach to be prepared without oil.</u>
This "**Special Request**" saves 450 calories and 50 grams of fat.

Bernard'O Restaurant (Rancho Bernardo)
ANGEL HAIR PASTA WITH TOMATOES, BASIL & GARLIC – SPECIAL REQUEST
Angel hair pasta with white wine tomato concasse. <u>Request less oil (1 Tbs)</u> <u>and no butter</u>.
This "**Special Request**" saves 230 calories and 25 grams of fat.

Acapulco (9 San Diego locations)
HALIBUT FILET WITH TOMATILLO SAUCE – HEALTHY DINING PREPARATION
Filet of halibut grilled with distinctly delicious tomatillo sauce. Served with vegetables and rice.
This "**Special Request**" saves 605 calories and 34 grams of fat.

Rock Bottom Restaurant & Brewery (Downtown San Diego, La Jolla)
TAOS CHICKEN SALAD – SPECIAL REQUEST
Spice-rubbed, grilled and chilled chicken breast, with crisp greens, roasted corn, green chilies, fire-roasted tomatoes and black beans. <u>Request less dressing (2 oz)</u>. Analysis does not include corn chips or croutons.
This "**Special Request**" saves 118 calories and 12 grams of fat.

Remember: Any dish marked "**Special Request**" means you must specifically order the "Special Request" for it to correspond to the published nutrition information.

CHAPTER 3

Do Your Calories Have a Purpose?

Calories have a bad reputation in our society. We're counting calories and cutting calories, as though we've forgotten that calories are what keep us alive. Food and water fuel our bodies to do the miraculous tasks we perform each day. Instead of focusing on just cutting calories, we need to look at the _quality_ of the calories we consume.

Just what are you getting from your calories?

Calories add up from the amounts of protein, carbohydrate and fat in foods. Each type of calorie has a very different function in the body. The following chapters explain the functions in more detail, but briefly:

Protein calories help the body to build and restore.

Carbohydrate calories are the body's main energy source.

Fat calories turn to fat -- _easily_.

In general, protein and carbohydrate calories supply our bodies with nutrients necessary to function optimally. We need a very small amount of fat each day, but because fat is very easy to get, most Americans suffer from an excess of dietary fat, not a deficiency.

We should strive to eat foods with high-quality, nutritious calories. Recommendations vary according to individual needs, but generally 50% to 65% of total daily calories should come from carbohydrates, 10% to 20% from protein, and 15% to 30% from fat. Because most Americans get enough protein and too much fat, the best way to determine the quality of your calories is to determine the percentage of calories from fat, and keep it under 30%.

Percentage of calories from fat

The 30% fat recommendation is the suggested average for the whole day. Some foods will add little, if any, fat to your diet, while other foods may supply a big chunk of the fat for the day. Of course, it's best to avoid (or use sparingly) foods which have a high percentage of fat (e.g., butter, margarine, oils, sour cream, cheese, cream cheese, etc.).

A fattening example:

Salmon - *Smothered in a cream sauce*
    Total Calories: 1024
    Protein: 77 grams
    Carbohydrate: 8 grams
    Fat: 76 grams

How to calculate the percentage of calories from fat:

Each gram of fat has nine calories. Using this information, you can calculate the percentage of calories from fat as shown in the following example. For the **Salmon with Cream Sauce**:

1. Multiply the number of grams of fat by 9 (number of calories per gram of fat):
   76 grams x 9 cals/gram = 684 calories from fat

2. Divide by total calories to get the fraction of calories from fat:
   684 calories ÷ 1024 calories = 0.67

3. Multiply by 100 to get the percentage:
   0.67 x 100 = 67%

67% of calories in this dish come from fat!

Carbohydrate and protein percentages can be calculated in a similar way, except that the number of grams of each is multiplied by 4 rather than 9, because carbohydrates and proteins provide 4 calories per gram. The division step is the same. For this example, these calculations show that 3% of calories come from carbohydrate and 30% from protein. Cholesterol and sodium do not contribute to calories.

The small percentage of carbohydrate is common for meat, poultry, and fish entrees, but a nutritious entree should contain less fat. In this example, most of the fat comes from the cream and butter used in the sauce; however, it's not necessary to add excess fat to get a delicious tasting entree.

Let's look at a healthier salmon dish:

Grilled Salmon (French Gourmet)
Grilled 7 oz. filet of fresh salmon, served with papaya
salsa, steamed seasonal vegetables and herbed rice.

Analysis for salmon alone:
    Total Calories: 275
    Protein: 40 grams
    Carbohydrates: 0 grams
    Fat: 13 grams

To calculate the percentage of calories from fat:

   1. Multiply grams of fat by 9 calories per gram:
      13 grams x 9 cals/gram = 117 calories from fat

   2. Divide by total calories and multiply by 100 to get a percentage:
      117 calories ÷ 275 calories x 100 = 43%

43% of calories from this dish come from fat --- much less than the example above, but still above the recommended guideline of 30% of calories from fat.

Remember, the guideline of 30% or fewer calories from fat applies to the overall diet --- an entire day or week, not just one entree. Restaurants differ greatly in the ways meals and side dishes are presented. If you order a lean meat or fish entree, it consists mainly of protein and fat, and the percentage of fat will generally appear to be high. By themselves, many lean meats and fish contain 30% to 50% fat. Even soybeans contain about 40% of their calories from fat. But generally these high-protein entrees are not eaten by themselves. If you choose quality carbohydrate side dishes such as vegetables, grains, breads, and fruits, the percentage of fat for the overall meal will be significantly less. Entrees that are made up largely of carbohydrates (such as pasta or rice dishes) will generally have a lower percentage of calories from fat.

As an example of how the side dishes change the overall percentage fat, let's include the side dishes that are served with this entree:

	Calories	Fat (g)
Salmon	275	13
Papaya Salsa	80	4½
Steamed Seasonal Vegetables	30	½
Herbed Rice	270	3
Totals	655	21

To calculate percentage of calories from fat:

   21 grams of fat x 9 cals/gram = 189 calories from fat
   189 calories from fat ÷ 655 total calories x 100 = 29%

Only 29% of total calories from this meal come from fat, which is within the recommended guidelines and significantly less than the percentage of fat calculated for the salmon alone.

This example demonstrates how a meal can be a good choice even when the protein-rich part of the meal by itself (the salmon in this case) exceeds 30% of calories from fat. Also, remember that a meal like this one will probably be the largest of your day, and your choices for the remainder of the day can also bring the overall percentage of fat down.

Grams of fat vs. percentage of calories from fat

We list grams of fat for each of the dishes on the menu pages rather than percentage of calories from fat. The previous example illustrates how calculating the percentage of calories from fat for a single menu item does not adequately reflect values for the entire meal or the entire day. Chapter 4 discusses in more detail how to choose guidelines for fat intake that are appropriate for you.

How the check mark guidelines for calories are set

The *Healthy Dining* guidelines assume an average intake of 2,000 calories per day. Next, we assume that the restaurant meal accounts for the largest of the day's meals, or at least ⅓ of the daily total calories. So 600 calories for the main entree would fit into the calorie budget. Thus, an upper limit of 600 calories is labeled as a "Good Choice" for calories. The "Excellent Choice" value of 350 calories represents a proportionately lower level, corresponding to about 1200 calories per day:

    ✓✓   Excellent Choice = 0 to 350 calories/entree
     ✓   Good Choice = 351 to 600 calories/entree

> Glance through the restaurant pages and use the quick, easy check mark system to see the wide variety of entrees which contain high-quality, nutritious calories and are "Excellent Choice" (✓✓) or "Good Choice" (✓) for calories.

CHAPTER 4

Fat - How Much and What Type?

Fat -- it clogs our arteries and builds up around the stomach, thighs and buttocks. Too much body fat, almost always caused by <u>too much fat in our diet, too many calories</u> and/or <u>too little exercise</u> in our day, increases the risks of high blood pressure, elevated blood fats (triglycerides and cholesterol), heart disease, stroke, diabetes, cancer and other health problems.

How much is too much?

The guidelines recommended by the American Heart Association and the Surgeon General's Office (see Chapter 1) suggest that fat should contribute no more than 30% of total calories. Chapter 3 shows examples of calculating percentage of calories from fat. This section deals with counting grams of fat. If we assume a daily intake of 2000 calories, then no more than 600 calories per day (30%) should come from fat. Since each gram of fat contributes 9 calories, then about 66 grams of fat (600 ÷ 9) is the suggested upper limit of fat intake per day. If you're not careful, it's very easy to exceed that with just one meal!

How the check mark guidelines for fat are set

What is a reasonable limit per meal or per entree? If we divide the day's allotment (66 grams) into three equal meals, then a <u>reasonable limit per meal is 22 grams of fat</u>. Main entrees usually contribute the largest amount of fat to the meal (unless you load your side dishes with too much fat, as discussed below), so we set guidelines of:

✓✓ Excellent Choice = 0 to 10 grams of fat/entree
✓ Good Choice = 11 to 20 grams of fat/entree

If you're very active and take in more calories, then a higher limit would be appropriate. If you're on a <u>weight loss diet</u> or <u>very low fat diet</u>, then the "<u>Excellent Choice</u>" <u>guideline of up to 10 grams</u> of fat per entree is probably more appropriate.

Notice that these recommended guidelines represent an average intake for an average meal. Don't be overly concerned about the cutoff between our designations of "Good Choice" and "Excellent Choice." Unless you're on a very restricted diet, the difference between an entree with 11 grams of fat (which would receive one check mark) and one with 9 grams of fat (two check marks) is probably not worth worrying about. An occasional meal with somewhat more fat (but don't overdo it!) can be fairly easily compensated for by reducing fat intake during other meals.

Portion sizes

Be aware of portion sizes. Restaurant portions tend to be very large. The entrees listed in this book often represent 6 to 10 ounces of a <u>very</u> filling, protein-rich meal. In some cases, for a large serving, we may note that the nutrition information is based on only a part (e.g., ½ or ⅔) of a full serving. This means that only the recommended portion of the meal corresponds to the nutrition information. So, because it is a large serving, eat ½ or ⅔ and save the rest for the next day – or share with a friend.

Types of fat

Together with protein, fats form the structures in our bodies, including muscles, nerves, membranes and blood vessels. However, we need very little fat to perform these functions, and only *unsaturated* sources of fat aid in these processes. "Saturated" and "unsaturated" refer to the chemical structure of the fat molecules.

<u>Unsaturated Fats - Monounsaturated, Polyunsaturated</u>. These are the *"good"* types of fat. A <u>low total fat intake</u>, with the majority of fat from unsaturated sources, appears to lower blood cholesterol levels. The best sources for these "good" fats are natural grains, seeds and nuts, and fish. Many oils are primarily unsaturated, such as olive, canola, peanut, corn, safflower, sesame, cottonseed and soybean. Once again, these fats are "good" only in very small amounts! Look for menu items with the * alongside the fat content for dishes that contain primarily unsaturated fat.

<u>Omega-3 Fats</u>. Some types of fish contain unique polyunsaturated fats called Omega-3 fatty acids. These fatty acids seem to make blood platelets less likely to clot, thus decreasing risk of artery blockage and heart attack. Fish with high amounts of Omega-3 include salmon, albacore tuna, mackerel, herring and rainbow trout.

<u>Saturated Fats</u>. Saturated fats are the *very unhealthy* fats that raise blood cholesterol levels. Excess saturated fat is related to an increased risk of cardiovascular disease. Foods that contain saturated fats are usually hard at room temperature. Saturated fat is found mostly in animal products (beef, chicken, butter, ice cream, and cheese), processed and fast foods and some vegetable oils (palm oil, coconut oil, and partially hydrogenated oils).

<u>Hydrogenated Oils and Trans-Fatty Acids</u>. The vegetable oils found in most margarines and in packaged and processed foods (such as cookies, pastries, crackers, chips, etc.) are "hydrogenated." During the hydrogenation process, hydrogen is added to liquid oil, thereby changing its chemical structure. The result is a harder, more saturated fat product, which many people find appealing for spreads and in cooking. Manufacturers use the hydrogenation process because it increases product stability and shelf life, saving them money. Unfortunately, consumption of hydrogenated products contributes to elevated blood cholesterol levels and an increase in heart disease risk.

In addition to making the fat more saturated, hydrogenation also produces unnatural compounds called trans-fatty acids that have a more rigid molecular structure than natural fats do. Many scientists now believe that these trans-fatty acids are harmful because they block the important functions of the "good" types of fat. It is probably wise to opt for unprocessed foods rather than foods that contain "hydrogenated" or "partially hydrogenated" oils.

A summary of fat

When assessing the fat content of food, it is important to look at:
1. The <u>number of grams</u> of fat
2. The <u>percentage of calories</u> from fat
3. The <u>type</u> of fat - minimize or avoid saturated and hydrogenated fats

<u>One Last Word on Fat:</u> Although unsaturated fats do not raise blood cholesterol levels, too much fat -- saturated <u>or</u> unsaturated -- may make you fat, and excess body fat is a risk factor for many chronic diseases.

On the restaurant menu pages, the asterisk (*) next to the grams of fat indicates that the fat is primarily unsaturated (the "good" type). Look for it!

Some delicious examples of "Excellent" and "Good" choices for fat:
Notice that many contain primarily unsaturated fat (designated with the *).

Kabul West (Sorrento Valley)
FISH KABOB
Grilled fish served with fresh garden salad, basmati and homemade bread.
✓✓ FAT: Excellent Choice (3 g)*

Nicolosi's (Mission Gorge)
SPAGHETTI WITH MARINARA SAUCE
✓✓ FAT: Excellent Choice (2 g)*

The Greek Palace (Kearny Mesa)
VEGETARIAN DOLMADES
Grape leaves rolled with rice and tomato, and then topped with tomato sauce. Analysis is for 5 stuffed leaves.
✓✓ FAT: Excellent Choice (8 g)*

The Old Spaghetti Factory (Downtown San Diego, San Marcos)
SPINACH & CHEESE RAVIOLI
Tender pillows of pasta stuffed with spinach and three kinds of cheese, topped with our savory tomato sauce.
✓ FAT: Good Choice (13 g)

Bully's (Mission Valley, La Jolla, Del Mar)
FRESH FISH OF THE DAY WITH MANGO CHUTNEY
Request charbroiled, broiled or prepared with white wine and lemon.
✓✓ FAT: Excellent Choice (6 g)*

Some delicious examples of "Excellent" and "Good" choices for fat (continued):

Spices Thai Café (Del Mar, Rancho Bernardo)
LARB KAI
Minced chicken spiced with lime juice, chili, rice powder and fresh mint.
✓ FAT: Good Choice (17 g)*

Jack in the Box
CHICKEN TERIYAKI BOWL
Strips of teriyaki-marinated chicken breast, broccoli florets, carrots and
teriyaki sauce, all served on a bed of steamed white rice.
✓✓ FAT: Excellent Choice (4 g)

Trattoria Acqua (La Jolla)
ORECCHIETTE CON GAMBERETTI E ASPA
Orecchiette pasta with spicy shrimp, Italian cured ham,
broccoli, white beans, white wine and lemon zest.
✓✓ FAT: Excellent Choice (9 g)

Ki's (Cardiff)
KIED RICE
Brown rice, fresh vegetables and tofu.
✓ FAT: Good Choice (14 g)*

Sammy's Woodfired Pizza (7 San Diego locations)
HEALTHY DINING GRILLED SHRIMP WRAP
Bean sprouts, julienne vegetables, Asian greens and Thai dressing.
✓ FAT: Good Choice (19 g)*

Pacific Coast Grill (Solana Beach)
LOBSTER TACOS
with roasted corn salsa, black beans and tortillas. Analysis includes 4 corn tortillas.
✓✓ FAT: Excellent Choice (4 g)*

Now - how well are YOU doing?

Now that San Diego restaurants are watching how much fat they're adding to your diet, just *how well are you watching?* Here are some easy ways to add too much fat to your diet - quickly!

High-fat culprits:

	Calories	Fat (g)	Cholest.(mg)	Sodium (mg)
Salad Dressings: (3 Tbs.)				
Blue Cheese	231	24	27	501
Thousand Island	176	17	15	327
French	201	19	6	642
Italian	206	21	0	348
Oil & Vinegar	215	24	0	0
Ranch	162	17	12	291

High-fat culprits (continued):

Toppings: (2 Tbs.)

Butter	200	23	61	232
Margarine	202	23	0	264
Sour Cream	67	6	13	15
Cream Cheese	100	10	31	85
Tarter Sauce	150	16	18	196
Mayonnaise	198	22	16	157
Cheese (1 oz. cheddar)	114	9	30	176

Desserts:

Cheesecake	386	24	82	284
Apple Pie	323	14	28	207
Chocolate Cake	407	17	5	300
Ice Cream (1 cup)	349	24	88	108

Instead try:

- Fat-free or low-fat salad dressings
- Salsa, low-fat cottage cheese, or plain yogurt as salad dressing or topping for potatoes
- Only very small amounts of regular or high-fat salad dressings
- Frozen yogurt, sorbet, sherbet or fruit for dessert

CHAPTER 5

Cholesterol - A Hot Topic

Cholesterol continues to be a hot topic enmeshed in controversy. Medical research is progressing on this subject, and we hope to clear up some misconceptions concerning cholesterol.

Where does cholesterol come from?

Most of the cholesterol in your blood is manufactured by your liver. The body produces about 1,000 milligrams (mg) of cholesterol each day. In addition, the average American consumes 400 to 600 mg daily from food. Cholesterol from our food is found only in animal products. The cholesterol we derive from our diets is essentially the same as the cholesterol our bodies manufacture. Our bodies use cholesterol to form hormones and cell membranes.

However, the average high-fat/high-cholesterol diet tends to add too much cholesterol to the bloodstream. The excess cholesterol and other substances accumulate in the walls of the blood vessels. Over time the arteries become narrowed, and eventually the flow of blood is cut off, leading to a heart attack or stroke.

How should blood cholesterol be measured?

For an accurate and complete cholesterol measure, a tube of blood should be drawn from the arm by a qualified health professional. You should not eat or drink anything (except water) for 12 hours before the blood draw. The laboratory which analyzes the blood sample should follow the reference methods set by the U. S. Centers for Disease Control. The fingertip method found in shopping malls and health fairs may not provide results that are as accurate.

What determines blood cholesterol levels?

1. **Genetics**. Some individuals, no matter how prudent their diet or how regularly they exercise, can't achieve a low cholesterol level without the help of a physician and cholesterol-lowering medications.

2. **Lipoproteins**. Cholesterol is carried through the blood in protein packages called lipoproteins. The amounts and types of lipoproteins are an important indicator of your heart disease risk.

LDLs (low-density lipoproteins) are commonly termed "bad" cholesterol. LDLs increase heart disease risk because they keep cholesterol in blood circulation and carry it to the arteries to be deposited. Excess body fat and a diet high in saturated fat tend to increase LDL levels.

HDLs (high-density lipoproteins) are the "good" cholesterol that protect against heart disease. They actually carry cholesterol AWAY from the arteries to the liver to be excreted from the body. Individuals with high HDL levels have a lower risk of heart disease. Regular exercise, maintaining appropriate body weight, and not smoking help to increase HDL levels.

3. **Diet**. Foods high in saturated fat <u>increase</u> cholesterol levels. These include butter, whole milk products, palm and coconut oils, cheese, beef, pork, and eggs. In addition, many packaged and processed foods are high in saturated fat or (partially) hydrogenated oils, which also have a cholesterol-raising effect.

A diet *low in total fat*, with fat intake primarily from unsaturated fat sources, <u>reduces</u> cholesterol levels. Unsaturated fats include olive, corn, safflower, sesame, canola, soybean, and sunflower oils. *High fiber foods*, especially oat bran, apples, carrots, oranges, and legumes (beans, peas and lentils) <u>decrease</u> cholesterol levels by inhibiting the absorption of cholesterol into the bloodstream. *Fish and fish oils*, which contain omega-3 fatty acids, also <u>decrease</u> cholesterol levels.

4. **Smoking, stress and some medications** also raise cholesterol levels.

Important facts on dietary cholesterol and fat

<u>Too much of any fat</u> (even unsaturated oils!) can increase body fat, and excess body fat may increase blood cholesterol levels. Oils, margarine, and butter all have approximately the same number of calories and fat grams per ounce, and so all have the same potential to make you fat. Therefore it's important to limit your total intake of all types of fat.

Even though oils, margarine, and butter have about the same calorie and fat counts, there is a big difference in the chemical make-up of these fats. Butter is high in saturated fat, and <u>saturated fats increase blood cholesterol</u> levels. Saturated fats stimulate the production of LDLs ("bad cholesterol"), resulting in increased blood cholesterol levels. Therefore, if you avoid only dietary cholesterol in the food you eat, without reducing the amount of saturated fat, you may not decrease your blood cholesterol level at all.

Avoid <u>hydrogenated fats</u> too, because they are also saturated. Margarine, although cholesterol-free, is partially hydrogenated and contains <u>trans-fatty acids</u>, which have been shown to have a cholesterol-raising effect.

Vegetable oils are generally <u>unsaturated fats</u>. Liquid oils (such as olive, corn, canola, etc.) in small amounts may help to decrease cholesterol levels. Remember though, that all oils are 100% fat, so use only small amounts.

The <u>amount of cholesterol</u> found in foods is not as important as the <u>amount of saturated fat</u>. But you should minimize intake of very concentrated sources of cholesterol such as egg yolks and liver. Shellfish is very low in saturated fat, but moderately high in cholesterol. Most medical experts agree that shellfish, in small quantities, is a healthy choice.

Cholesterol is found only in animal products. Don't be misled, though --- just because foods don't contain cholesterol doesn't mean they are also low in fat! In fact, many "no-cholesterol" foods are loaded with fat. Be sure to check the number of fat grams on nutrition labels.

How the check mark guidelines for cholesterol are set

The Surgeon General's Office and the American Heart Association recommend that cholesterol consumption be limited to 300 mg per day. If the day's total were evenly divided in thirds, this would suggest a limit of 100 mg per meal. We set our guidelines for cholesterol as follows:

    ✓✓   Excellent Choice = 0 to 75 mg cholesterol/entree
    ✓   Good Choice = 76 to 150 mg cholesterol/entree

If every meal in your day were at the "Good Choice" limit of 150 mg, you would exceed the recommended amount. But since a restaurant meal usually contains a larger portion of meat or other cholesterol-containing foods than side dishes or other meals of the day, we assumed that this cholesterol intake can easily be compensated for by choosing foods with little or no cholesterol for the remaining selections.

If you are watching your blood cholesterol level, select items which are:

1.   "Excellent Choice" or "Good Choice" for fat
2.   Primarily unsaturated (designated with the *)
3.   "Excellent Choice" or "Good Choice" for cholesterol

Some flavorful examples of "Excellent" and "Good" choices for cholesterol:

Casa de Pico (Old Town San Diego)
CHICKEN AND BLACK BEAN TOSTADA
Seasoned, shredded chicken, black beans, shredded lettuce, tomato and olives, spiced with salsa ranchera & sprinkled with parmesan cheese. Analysis does not include tostada shell.
✓✓ FAT: Excellent Choice (7 g)   ✓✓ CHOLESTEROL: Excellent Choice (25 mg)

St. Germain's Café (Encinitas)
FAMOUS VEGETARIAN BURGER
Made from lentils, walnuts, onions and delicious spices. Topped with lettuce, tomato and onion. Served with fresh fruit and cafe potatoes. Analysis does not include potatoes or cheese.
✓ FAT: Good Choice (14 g)*   ✓✓ CHOLESTEROL: Excellent Choice (40 mg)

Subway (over 100 San Diego County locations)
SUBWAY CLUB®
✓✓ FAT: Excellent Choice (5 g)   ✓✓ CHOLESTEROL: Excellent Choice (25 mg)

Examples of "Good" and "Excellent" choices for cholesterol (continued):

Roppongi Restaurant, Bar & Café (La Jolla)
POLYNESIAN DUNGENESS CRAB STACK
Mango, pea shoots, cucumber, tomato, avocado and peanuts served with spicy ginger lime dressing.
✓✓ FAT: Excellent Choice (10 g)*   ✓✓ CHOLESTEROL: Excellent Choice (45 mg)

Round Table Pizza (18 San Diego County locations)
SALUTÉ CHICKEN & GARLIC™ PIZZA (2 SLICES)#
Creamy garlic sauce, three cheeses, roasted chicken, mushrooms, Roma tomatoes, red and green onions & lots of chopped garlic. Topped with Italian herb seasoning, shredded Parmesan cheese & roasted red peppers.
Analysis for 2 slices large pizza.
✓ FAT: Good Choice (11 g)   ✓✓ CHOLESTEROL: Excellent Choice (40 mg)

Kabul West (Sorrento Valley)
VEGETARIAN COMBO
Served with fresh garden salad, basmati rice and homemade bread.
✓✓ FAT: Excellent Choice (7 g)*   ✓✓ CHOLESTEROL: Excellent Choice (0 mg)

Jimbo's (Del Mar & Escondido)
LILY ABOVE THE POND
Basmati rice, tofu, broccoli, burdock root, carrots, snow peas, mung beans & bamboo shoots, stir fried.
✓✓ FAT: Excellent Choice (6 g)*   ✓✓ CHOLESTEROL: Excellent Choice (0 mg)

French Gourmet (Pacific Beach)
RATATOUILLE
with steamed seasonal vegetables and your choice of herbed
rice or couscous. Analysis is for rice; couscous similar.
✓✓ FAT: Excellent Choice (9 g)*   ✓✓ CHOLESTEROL: Excellent Choice (0 mg)

Su Casa (La Jolla)
CARNE ASADA TACOS
Three "Street Style" soft tacos filled with green tomatillo salsa, cilantro, onions & spices.
✓✓ FAT: Excellent Choice (9 g)   ✓✓ CHOLESTEROL: Excellent Choice (75 mg)

Sushi On the Rock (La Jolla)
BARRIO ROLL
Tuna, cilantro and serrano chili reverse roll, served with salsa.
✓✓ FAT: Excellent Choice (4 g)*   ✓✓ CHOLESTEROL: Excellent Choice (65 mg)

The Fish Merchant (Mission Gorge)
SALMON MARINATED IN RED GINGER SOY VINAIGRETTE
Charbroiled fresh salmon marinated in a red ginger vinaigrette sauce.
✓ FAT: Good Choice (15 g)*   ✓ CHOLESTEROL: Good Choice (110 mg)

Koo Koo Roo (Del Mar, La Jolla, Mission Valley)
HEALTHY DINING COMBO #2:
ORIGINAL CHICKEN BREAST & WING, CORN & YAM
✓✓ FAT: Excellent Choice (8 g)   ✓✓ CHOLESTEROL: Excellent Choice (25 mg)

                    *Primarily unsaturated fat

CHAPTER 6

Sodium - To Salt or Not to Salt?

That is the question. Sodium is an essential nutrient. It helps to maintain blood volume, regulate the balance of water in the cells, and transmit nerve impulses. The kidneys control sodium balance by increasing or decreasing sodium in the urine.

In general, Americans consume more sodium than the body needs. Many foods contain sodium naturally, and it is commonly added to foods during preparation or processing. Sodium is also found in drinking water, prescription drugs and over-the-counter medications.

One teaspoon of salt contains about 2,000 milligrams of sodium, approximately ⅔ of the American Heart Association's recommended daily amount. Other condiments contain significant amounts of sodium, such as seasoning salts (1620 - 1850 mg per teaspoon), monosodium glutamate (MSG, 492 mg per teaspoon), soy sauce (343 mg per teaspoon), and meat tenderizer (1750 mg per teaspoon). Packaged and processed foods also tend to be very high in sodium.

In the United States, about one in four adults has elevated blood pressure. Sodium intake is only one of the factors known to affect blood pressure, and not everyone is equally susceptible. The sensitivity to sodium seems to be very individualized. At present, there is not a good method to predict who is salt-sensitive or who will develop high blood pressure. Low-sodium diets may help some people avoid high blood pressure. Low-sodium diets may help some people with high blood pressure to control their blood pressure. And in some individuals, a low-sodium diet will not affect blood pressure at all.

Since most Americans consume more sodium than needed, consider reducing your sodium intake. Use less table salt, read labels carefully, and eat sparingly those foods which have large amounts of sodium. Remember that a substantial amount of the sodium you eat may be "hidden" - either occurring naturally in foods or as part of a preservative or flavoring agent that has been added.

To avoid too much sodium:

- Learn to enjoy the flavors of unsalted foods.
- Cook without salt or with only small amounts of added salt.
- Flavor foods with herbs, spices, and lemon juice.
- Add little or no salt to food at the table.
- Limit your intake of salty foods such as potato chips, pretzels, salted nuts and popcorn, condiments (soy sauce, steak sauce, garlic salt), pickled foods, cured meats, cheeses, and canned foods.
- Read food labels carefully to determine the amounts of sodium.
- Use lower sodium products, when available, to replace those with higher sodium content.

To avoid too much sodium when dining out:

1. Order entrees listed as "Excellent Choice" or "Good Choice" for sodium levels, <u>and</u>
2. Request no added salt whenever possible.

The analyses shown in this book reflect the sodium content that occurs naturally in food, as well as salt that is included in a prepared sauce or recipe where the sodium cannot be reduced for an individual portion. In addition, many chefs cook with salt "to taste" that was not included in the recipes they provided for analysis. Therefore it's important to <u>specify very clearly</u> that you want "no added salt."

The double asterisk (**) next to the sodium values reminds you to specify "no added salt" to get the values as published.

Note: Many items included in this book are listed as "moderate" (meaning 600 to 1000 mg sodium per entree) or "high" in sodium (meaning above 1000 mg sodium per entree) and are <u>not</u> recommended for those watching sodium intake.

How the check mark guidelines for sodium are set

Of the 3000 mg of sodium recommended per day, we consider a value of 1000 mg per meal (⅓ of 3000) to be a reasonable level. We assume 600 mg can reasonably come from the main entree as a "Good Choice" value, and the remainder from side dishes. An "Excellent Choice" level is ½ of the "Good" value, or 300 mg:

    ✓✓ Excellent Choice = 0 to 300 mg sodium/entree
      ✓ Good Choice = 301 to 600 mg sodium/entree

Examples of "Excellent" and "Good" choices for sodium:

Rainwater's (Downtown)
SALMON IN PARCHMENT
Roasted in paper with julienne vegetables and fresh herbs
in a white wine sauce, and served with basmati rice.
✓   SODIUM: Good Choice (305 mg)**

Casa de Bandini (Old Town San Diego)
ARROZ CON POLLO A LA MEXICANA
Choice morsels of chicken breast specially cooked with bell peppers, tomatoes & onions.
Served with black beans, Mexican rice & tortillas (accompaniments not included in analysis).
✓✓   SODIUM: Excellent Choice (100 mg)**

Examples of "Good" and "Excellent" choices for sodium (continued):

The Fish Market (Del Mar, Downtown San Diego)
GRILLED SWORDFISH WITH CILANTRO PESTO
Grilled swordfish served with cilantro pesto sauce.
✓✓   SODIUM: Excellent Choice (255 mg)**

Lino's Italian Restaurant (Old Town San Diego)
LINGUINI PRIMAVERA
Spinach pasta and fresh vegetables prepared with olive oil, basil, garlic and chicken broth.
Parmesan cheese not included in analysis.
✓✓   SODIUM: Excellent Choice (100 mg)**

Bandar (Downtown San Diego)
SHISH KABOB (½ SERVING)
Juicy marinated chunks of filet mignon, skewered and charbroiled to perfection with charbroiled vegetables.
Served with basmati rice (not included in analysis). Analysis is for ½ of a full serving.
✓✓   SODIUM: Excellent Choice (185 mg)**

KC's Tandoor (Mission Valley, Sorrento Valley)
BAINGAN BHARTHA
Roasted eggplant cooked with tomatoes and onions, and
served with dal (lentils), rice and naan (bread, ½ piece).
✓   SODIUM: Good Choice (410 mg)**

El Indio (Downtown San Diego, India Street)
BURRITO INDIO
A whole wheat tortilla filled with specialty seasoned
zucchini, corn, onion, beans and jack cheese.
✓   SODIUM: Good Choice (585 mg)

Montanas American Grill (Hillcrest)
FUSILLI PASTA WITH BABY SPINACH AND SUNDRIED TOMATOES
Pasta with baby spinach, sun-dried tomatoes tossed with lemon olive oil dressing.
✓✓   SODIUM: Excellent Choice (90 mg)**

Ranchos Cocina (Ocean Beach)
RANCHOS SIETE MARES
Hot, fresh seafood soup served with two corn tortillas.
✓   SODIUM: Good Choice (500 mg)**

CHAPTER 7

Protein, Carbohydrates & Diabetic Exchanges

Protein: the building blocks

Protein is very important for a healthy body. Protein provides materials for growth, helps to maintain and repair tissues, manufactures the lipoproteins to carry fat, and assists in the maintenance of proper fluid levels.

Generally it's easy to get protein in your diet, and most Americans consume 2 - 3 times more than necessary. Excess protein does not create muscle, as many hope, but is stored as fat. Excess protein puts a strain on the liver and kidneys. In addition, some protein sources are also high in fat, cholesterol and calories, such as: beef, whole milk products, eggs, poultry with skin, cheese and nuts.

The best sources of protein are low-fat foods, including fish, poultry without skin, skim or low-fat milk products and tofu. Whole grains, vegetables and especially legumes (dried beans, peas and lentils) also contain some protein. Unless you are a very strict vegetarian, you probably get adequate protein with a balanced diet. If you are a strict vegetarian, a dietitian can analyze your present diet to make sure you're getting adequate amounts of protein.

Carbohydrates: energy

Total carbohydrates are made up of simple sugars, complex carbohydrates, and fiber.

<u>Simple carbohydrates.</u> Sources of simple carbohydrates include table sugar, candies and other sweets, sodas and bakery goods. These foods contain little or no vitamins and minerals. They provide empty calories, i.e., calories that supply no nutrients and should therefore be minimized.

Fruits and some vegetables contain sugar naturally, and they also provide other nutrients, so they are valuable to a healthy diet. The sugar in simple carbohydrates is in a form that is absorbed quickly by the body, as opposed to the slower-digesting complex carbohydrates.

<u>Complex carbohydrates.</u> These carbohydrates contain many essential nutrients and are the body's most effective source of energy. They are very low in fat and should be the primary source of calories. It is recommended that 50% to 65% of total daily calories come from nutrient-dense carbohydrates. Foods high in complex carbohydrates include:

- breads and cereals
- dried beans, peas, and lentils
- rice and other grain products
- vegetables
- pasta

Dietary Fiber. The typical American diet is much too low in fiber. The American Cancer Society recommends 20 - 30 grams of fiber daily. The average American consumes only 7 - 8 grams of fiber daily. Dietary fiber is a term used to describe parts of plant foods that are generally not digestible by humans. By increasing your intake of foods containing complex carbohydrates, you will add dietary fiber to your diet.

There are two main types of fiber: soluble and insoluble. Soluble fiber may help lower blood cholesterol and control blood sugar and is found in oats, beans, carrots, apples and oranges. Insoluble fiber helps to move food through the body quickly and protect against colorectal cancer. Insoluble fiber is found in wheat bran and whole grains. Because both types of fiber have different functions for improving health, a variety of foods with fiber should be included in your diet. Fruits and vegetables are a significant source of nutrients and fiber. Thus, a diet rich in whole grains, breads, cereals, fruits and vegetables will provide optimal amounts of nutrients, fiber and energy.

Diabetic food exchanges

A well-balanced and carefully controlled diet is essential for those with diabetes. Recently carbohydrate counting is becoming more common as a way of choosing foods and serving sizes. The grams of carbohydrate are listed on most menu items in this *Healthy Dining* book. However "Diabetic Exchanges" was the system traditionally recommended by the American Diabetes Association and it is still used extensively. Foods are grouped into the various exchange lists according to their similarities in calories, carbohydrate, protein and fat content, which influence how they are utilized by the body. Although carbohydrates have the largest influence on blood sugar levels, protein and fat also contribute calories and influence the rates of digestion, so they are important to the overall plan.

Even for those without diabetes, exchanges can give useful information about portion size and the overall balance between protein and simple and complex carbohydrates, as explained below.

One meat exchange is equivalent to approximately 7 grams of protein and 3 grams of fat. One bread (starch) exchange contains approximately 15 grams of carbohydrate and 3 grams of protein. Starchy vegetables (potatoes, corn, beans, etc.) are counted as bread (starch) exchanges rather than vegetable exchanges. Vegetable exchanges have less starch (5 grams of carbohydrate and 2 grams of protein) and lots of fiber. A fruit exchange contains approximately 15 grams of more easily digested (simple) carbohydrate. A milk exchange contains 12 grams of carbohydrate, 8 grams of protein, and only a trace of fat, assuming skim milk is used. A fat exchange represents 5 grams of fat.

Some diabetic exchange lists use separate categories for lean, medium-fat, and high-fat meats. The computerized system used for the *Healthy Dining* analysis uses the lean meat category, which assumes approximately 7 grams of protein and 3 grams of fat per meat exchange. In most entrees included in the book, the meat is very lean and the total fat from the meat is lower than the 3 grams of fat per meat exchange normally assumed. In these cases we have designated the meat exchanges as "(extra lean)," which indicates that the meat exchange contains less fat than the assumed standard of 3 grams of fat per meat exchange. Any added fat from additional ingredients (e.g., butter or oil used in preparation, sauces, spreads, etc.) is counted as separate fat exchanges. This means that the fat exchanges reflect additional fat added to the meat.

In many entrees shown in this book, extra fat (often unsaturated) is added, but with the very lean meat, the total grams of fat still come out very low. So you don't necessarily need to shy away from a selection that shows fat exchanges. Looking at the grams of fat probably gives better information about the overall fat content.

The food exchange system used by some <u>weight loss programs</u> is similar to the diabetic food exchange system. A dietitian can help you interpret these numbers to meet your own dietary needs.

CHAPTER 8

Fruits & Vegetables – Nutrition Heavyweights

Science is finding that the saying "An apple a day keeps the doctor away" may be closer to the truth than most of us realize. And your mother was right — you should eat your vegetables! An abundance of research is in progress, and it is becoming increasingly clear that natural, whole foods such as fruits and vegetables contain more valuable substances than previously imagined, and certainly a more diverse range than available in nutrition supplements.

Fruits and vegetables deserve a special chapter in this book because of their importance in a healthy diet, and because their contributions overlap those of the other chapters so much. In addition to providing carbohydrates and high quality calories, they are packed full of other essentials — vitamins, minerals, fiber, antioxidants, and the more-recently discovered classes of compounds called phytochemicals (discussed in more detail below). Although numerical values are generally not available for these other substances, they are important and deserve special consideration as you make your food selections.

The World Health Organization, the National Cancer Institute, the American Cancer Society and other organizations emphasize a clear relationship between the amounts of fruits and vegetables consumed and several diseases, especially cancer and cardiovascular diseases. These organizations encourage Americans to eat at least 5 servings of fruits and vegetables each day. Eating "5 a day" is important to ensure that your body gets a variety of health-promoting nutrients. Research has shown that people who eat at least 5 servings of fruits and vegetables a day have only half the cancer risk of those who eat only one or two servings a day.

Fruits and vegetables are nutritional powerhouses which:

- are excellent sources of vitamins and minerals
- contain fiber (most Americans don't eat enough fiber)
- are virtually fat-free (exceptions: coconut, olives and avocado) and cholesterol-free
- are particularly helpful in weight management, due to their high-fiber and low-fat content
- contain antioxidants and phytochemicals (discussed below)

Vitamins and minerals

Vitamins and minerals are essential for many bodily functions. They play a prominent role in maintaining the health of the brain, heart, bones, teeth and nerves, in making and repairing red blood cells, in regulating the body's balance of fluids, and in other vital functions. The absence of any one vitamin or mineral may result in a unique deficiency that can only be corrected by supplying that specific nutrient. In some cases, people who have a certain disease or condition may need to adjust their intake of a particular vitamin or mineral. However, consuming mega (large) doses of certain fat-soluble vitamins (particularly vitamins A and D) can be toxic. It's best to get most of your vitamins and minerals from natural, healthy foods.

It is important to consume a wide variety of fruits and vegetables in order to benefit fully from the antioxidants, vitamins and minerals they contain. For example, the following tables show fruits and vegetables that contain significant amounts of Vitamins A and C (the other major vitamins B, D and E come primarily from other food sources such as grains, seeds, nuts, dairy or meat):

<u>Fruits and Vegetables High in Vitamin A</u>:

Apricots (fresh or dried)	Broccoli	Carrots	Chinese cabbage
Cantaloupe & melons	Collards & other greens	Green onions	Mangoes
Papayas	Peaches & Nectarines	Persimmons	Spinach
Tomatoes	Sweet potatoes	Winter squash & pumpkins	

<u>Fruits and Vegetables High in Vitamin C</u>:

Bell peppers	Broccoli	Brussels sprouts	Cantaloupe & melons
Cauliflower	Grapefruit	Guavas	Kiwifruit
Lemons & other citrus	Mangoes	Oranges	Papayas
Raspberries	Strawberries		

Notice that there is little overlap among the fruits and vegetables that are high in vitamins A and C. Some fruits and vegetables that don't appear on either list may be high in other important nutrients. For example, bananas are high in potassium. Some fruits and vegetables, especially leafy green vegetables, citrus, berries, melons, and beans are high in folate (from "foliage"), a B vitamin important in preventing heart disease, some types of anemia, and neural tube birth defects. There is no one food that "has it all." So be careful not to depend on a limited selection of fruits and vegetables to supply your nutrients. A glass of orange juice at breakfast and carrots at dinner, for example, move you toward your "5 a day" goal, but a wider variety of fruits and vegetables throughout the day is optimal.

Antioxidants

Antioxidants are disease-fighting compounds found in many foods. They neutralize free radicals, compounds that damage cells and lead to cardiovascular disease, cancer, cataracts, premature aging, and impaired immunity. Antioxidants include some vitamins (A, C, and E), beta carotene, some minerals (for example, selenium, copper, zinc, and manganese) and some of the phytochemicals discussed below. Fruits and vegetables are excellent sources of many of these antioxidants.

Phytochemicals

Phytochemicals are substances found in plant foods that are now recognized as powerful disease-fighting compounds. They have been shown to protect against cancer, cardiovascular disease, diabetes, and other medical conditions. "Phyto" means plant, and chemicals — well not all chemicals are bad for you. Our bodies are made of chemicals, and some kinds are essential for our health. Fruits and vegetables contain thousands, perhaps tens or hundreds of thousands of different phytochemical compounds.

Scientists have grouped phytochemicals into at least 14 different classes, but still little is known about their functions and their interactions. Many appear to stimulate or block the effects of enzymes in the body, some of which can fight diseases such as cancer or cardiovascular disease. Some phytochemicals have received a great deal of media attention, such as resveratrol, a substance found in grapes that appears to lower blood cholesterol. The resveratrol in grapes may explain the initial studies showing a beneficial effect of wine in reducing the risk of cardiovascular disease. Soybeans contain genistein, which nutritionists now link to lowering hormone-related cancer risk and stimulating the immune system. Other examples include the vegetables from the cabbage family (cabbage, brussels sprouts and broccoli), which contain phytochemicals that interact with estrogens and prostaglandins in fighting cancer.

A phytochemical-rich diet includes lots of fruits, vegetables, legumes (beans, peas and lentils), herbs and spices, whole grains, soy products, and also tea and nuts. With literally thousands of different phytochemicals already identified, this area of nutrition continues to be a rich field for scientific study. The table below lists beneficial effects of some of the fruits and vegetables studied so far.

Food:	**Beneficial effects:**
Berries, melons, cucumbers, squash & pumpkins	Aids immune system and helps lower blood cholesterol
Broccoli & cabbage family and leafy green vegetables	Lowers risk of hormone-related cancers, boosts ability to fight cancer and protects DNA in cells
Carrots, apricots, other orange & deep yellow fruits & vegetables	Helps protect against cancer, plaque in arteries, blood clotting and loss of eyesight
Citrus (orange, grapefruit, lemon, lime)	Helps body resist carcinogens, avoid blindness, and prevents blood clotting
Grapes (red)	Prevents blood clotting, protects DNA in cells and helps body resist carcinogens
Onions, garlic, leeks & chives	Controls cancer cells, blocks carcinogens, eliminates toxins & lowers blood cholesterol
Soybeans and soy foods	Helps block hormone-related cancers, slow tumor growth, and stimulate the immune system
Tomatoes & eggplant	Shields against carcinogens, reduces cancer and heart attack risk

The most effective approach is to eat as wide a variety of foods as possible to gain benefits from many sources. Studies have demonstrated that not all the foods listed above have the same cancer or blood cholesterol-fighting substances, and the phytochemicals may appear in different concentrations or be absorbed differently. Even different varieties of foods within the same category (such as various varieties of apples or lettuce) may have widely varying concentrations and kinds of phytochemicals. Unfortunately, there is no "magic" pill or supplement which can supply as much as whole foods can, or we would have long ago found an easier way to combat diet-related diseases such as cancer, heart disease, diabetes, and obesity.

What is considered one serving?

<u>Fruits</u>
1 medium whole fruit (apple, banana)
½ cup of canned or fresh fruit
6 oz. (or ¾ cup) 100% fruit juice
¼ cup of dried fruit

<u>Vegetables</u>
½ cup of raw or cooked vegetables
1 cup raw, leafy vegetables
6 oz. (or ¾ cup) vegetable juice

How can I get more fruits and vegetables in my diet?

For a snack or on the go, select nectarines, plums, berries, apple wedges, baby carrots, broccoli spears, or cherry tomatoes. Also, dried fruit is a healthy option over candy. You can easily pack it in a bag and take it with you on the road or eat it at your office.

At home, top your hot or cold cereal with fresh fruit, and drink a glass of 100% juice for breakfast. Smoothies made with fresh or frozen fruits and juices make a great breakfast or lunch choice. Fruit and vegetable juices are also delicious, sweet alternatives to soft drinks. At dinner, include a salad or raw vegetables with low-fat/non-fat dressing to reduce fat and calories. Steamed vegetables are always a good side dish, but you can also add vegetables to your favorite entrees, like tacos, lasagna, casseroles, and pasta dishes. Add pureed vegetables to sauces to fortify them and help get your "5 a day." Try more vegetarian meals, like tofu, rice or pasta with vegetables, or Oriental stir-fries. For dessert, bake apples, peaches, pears, or bananas, or make fruit cobblers.

Experiment with new recipes that emphasize fruits and vegetables, such as those starting on page 133 of this **Healthy Dining** book. Many cookbooks specialize in fruits, vegetables and other natural foods so you can try great-tasting dishes that will help you toward your 5 a Day goal. The California 5 a Day — for Better Health! Campaign offers a recipe booklet "Discover the Secret" which has 37 wonderful recipes incorporating fruits and vegetables. You can obtain a free copy of this recipe booklet and other information by contacting 1-888-EAT-FIVE or www.ca5aday.com.

When dining out, order meals that include vegetables or fruits as a major component. For example, stir-fried chicken with vegetables, like Moo Goo Gai Pan from **Fortune Cookie**, will provide better nutritional balance than a dish with chicken alone. **Roundtable's** Gourmet Veggie Pizza, which includes artichoke hearts, zucchini, spinach, mushrooms and tomatoes, is a better choice than plain cheese pizza. For a quick meal and a great contribution to your "5 a day," try a blended fruit smoothie at **Jamba Juice**. You can also request substitutions for side dishes. For example, if French fries normally come as part of a meal, request steamed vegetables or seasonal fresh fruit instead. Most restaurants are happy to make substitutions if you ask.

In choosing a restaurant meal from this book, you can determine if the meal contributes significantly to your "5 a day" goal. Look for the ☼ symbol next to the entrée's name. The ☼ indicates the dish provides at least 2 servings of fruits or vegetables (one serving for side dishes).

Examples of Restaurant Meals with two or more servings of fruits or vegetables

Daily's Restaurant (La Jolla)
DAILY'S SPICY GRILLED CHICKEN PIZZA ☼
*Grilled chicken & red onions, peppers, spicy tomato marinade with skim milk
mozzarella cheese on our whole wheat pizza crust.*

✓ CALORIES: Good Choice (465)   ✓✓ CHOLESTEROL: Excellent Choice (60 mg)
✓✓ FAT: Excellent Choice (9 g)   ✓ SODIUM: Good Choice (445 mg)
EXCHANGES: 2½ Meat, 3 Bread, 2 Veg, ½ Milk
PROTEIN: 38 g, CARBOHYDRATE: 53 g

Pizza Nova (Hillcrest, Point Loma, Solana Beach)
BROCCOLI WITH PENNE ☼
Broccoli, fresh herbs, garlic, sun-dried tomatoes, extra virgin olive oil and parmesan cheese.

✓ CALORIES: Good Choice (485)   ✓✓ CHOLESTEROL: Excellent Choice (10 mg)
✓ FAT: Good Choice (19 g)*   ✓ SODIUM: Good Choice (330 mg)**
EXCHANGES: ¾ Meat, 3½ Bread, 2 Veg, 3 Fat
PROTEIN: 18 g, CARBOHYDRATE: 62 g

Examples of Restaurant Meals with fruits or vegetables (continued):

Royal Thai Cuisine (San Diego, La Jolla)
ROYAL YACHT (½ SERVING) ♨
A combination of seafood carefully prepared with cabbage, celery and silver noodles,
blended with spices and served in a royal yacht. Analysis is for ½ of a full serving.
- ✓ CALORIES: Good Choice (495)   ✓ CHOLESTEROL: Good Choice (140 mg)
- ✓ FAT: Good Choice (15 g)*   SODIUM: High (1400 mg)

EXCHANGES: 1½ Meat (extra lean), 3¾ Bread, 2 Veg, 2¾ Fat
PROTEIN: 17 g, CARBOHYDRATE: 75 g

Tio Leo's (Del Mar, Mission Gorge, Mira Mesa, Morena/Napa)
GRILLED EGGPLANT TACOS ♨
Two delicious marinated eggplant tacos grilled to perfection and served
with cabbage, pico de gallo and feta cheese in a corn tortilla.
- ✓ CALORIES: Good Choice (395)   ✓✓ CHOLESTEROL: Excellent Choice (25 mg)
- ✓ FAT: Good Choice (14 g)   ✓ SODIUM: Good Choice (540 mg)**

EXCHANGES: ½ Meat, 3¼ Bread, 2½ Veg, 2¼ Fat
PROTEIN: 12 g, CARBOHYDRATE: 61 g

Tutto Mare (La Jolla)
SAGGIO DI RIVIERA ♨
Mixed organic baby greens, grilled calamari, mixed citrus sections and lemon vinaigrette.
- ✓✓ CALORIES: Excellent Choice (285)   CHOLESTEROL: Moderate (265 mg)
- ✓ FAT: Good Choice (15 g)*   ✓✓ SODIUM: Excellent Choice (55 mg)**

EXCHANGES: 2½ Meat (extra lean), ¼ Veg, ¾ Fruit, 2¾ Fat
PROTEIN: 20 g, CARBOHYDRATE: 18 g

Café India (Sports Arena)
TOFU JALFARAZI ♨
Tofu sautéed with onion, bell pepper and vegetables.
- ✓ CALORIES: Good Choice (370)   ✓✓ CHOLESTEROL: Excellent Choice (0 mg)
- FAT: Moderate (25 g)*   ✓✓ SODIUM: Excellent Choice (265 mg)**

EXCHANGES: 2¾ Meat, 2¼ Veg, 3¼ Fat
PROTEIN: 23 g, CARBOHYDRATE: 19 g

Mucho Gusto (Del Mar, Kearny Mesa)
PESCADOR FISH BURRITO ♨
Charbroiled red snapper with melted jack cheese, salsa fresca, fresh shredded
cabbage and cilantro, wrapped in a warm Sonora flour tortilla.
- ✓ CALORIES: Good Choice (525)   ✓✓ CHOLESTEROL: Excellent Choice (60 mg)
- ✓ FAT: Good Choice (14 g)   SODIUM: High (1270 mg)

EXCHANGES: 4 Meat (extra lean), 3½ Bread, 1¾ Veg, 2 Fat
PROTEIN: 39 g, CARBOHYDRATE: 60 g

Chili's Grill & Bar (Seven locations in San Diego County)
GUILTLESS PASTA PRIMAVERA ♨
Fresh steamed veggies on penne pasta with Tomato Basil marinara sauce and Parmesan cheese.
- CALORIES: Moderate (680)   ✓ CHOLESTEROL: Good Choice (125 mg)
- ✓ FAT: Good Choice (15 g)   SODIUM: Moderate (760 mg)

PROTEIN: 34 g, CARBOHYDRATE: 102 g

---

* Primarily unsaturated fat

** If you request no added salt

CHAPTER 9

Additional Tips for Healthy Dining

Here are some additional dining tips, adapted from "Eating Better When Eating Out," from the USDA Human Nutrition Information Service:

Appetizers: Enjoy raw vegetables dipped in salsa or low-calorie dressing, fruit or steamed seafood. Limit rich sauces, dips and batter-fried foods.

Soups: Choose broth or tomato-based soups rather than creamed soups. Lentil, bean and split pea soups are high in fiber. Most soups are high in sodium.

Breads: Bread supplies complex carbohydrates, vitamins, and minerals. Whole grain breads provide fiber. Watch out for breads with added fat or sugar such as croissants, biscuits, cornbread, muffins (e.g., bran, corn, blueberry) and sweet rolls. Use toppings (butter, cream cheese and margarine) very sparingly.

Vegetables and Salads: Plain vegetables are high in fiber and nutrients and very low in calories, fat and sodium. However, butter, margarine and sauces increase calories, fat, cholesterol and sodium considerably. Look for vegetables seasoned with lemon, herbs or spices rather than fat and salt. Remember -- salad dressings and toppings can add a lot of calories, fat and sodium.

Watch out for prepared salads that contain mayonnaise, salad dressing or oil, such as macaroni salad, potato salad, creamy coleslaw, tuna and chicken salad, and marinated vegetables. Some pasta salads are made with large amounts of oily dressing.

Main Entrees: Ask how meals are prepared and what ingredients are used. Is the fish or chicken broiled with butter or other fat? Is it served with a sauce? How large is the portion? Are vegetables fresh or canned, buttered or creamed?

Fish or poultry that is broiled, grilled, baked, steamed or poached is a good choice. However, entrees are often basted with large amounts of fat. Ask to have your entree prepared without added fat, and that chicken be prepared without skin (or remove the skin before eating). Request that lemon juice, wine or only a small amount of fat be used and that no salt be added.

Watch out for menu selections termed "light fare" or "light." "Light" may or may not mean lower in fat and calories. We have found restaurants in which "On the Light Side" means anything from smaller portions to lower prices!

Choose dishes flavored with herbs and spices rather than rich sauces, gravies, or dressings. If that's not an option, ask for gravies, sour cream, sauces, and other toppings to be served on the side and use sparingly. Limit your use of soy sauce, steak sauce, catsup, mustard, pickles and other condiments to help control sodium.

Portions are often very large. Ask for a take-home bag and eat the remaining portion the next day. Or share an entree with a friend and get an extra appetizer.

Many stir-fried entrees are prepared with very little oil, while some are prepared with too much. Request that yours be prepared with very little.

Pizza can be a low-fat, nutritious choice if you order yours with half the cheese and only vegetable toppings.

Sandwiches can be an excellent choice if you choose lean deli meats such as turkey or ham (but watch portion size!) instead of higher fat cold cuts, such as bologna or salami. Choose whole grain breads and go easy on or avoid oil, butter, avocado, and mayonnaise.

Desserts: Fruits are great! Sherbet, sorbet and frozen yogurt are much lower in fat than ice cream. If temptation gets to you, share the dessert with a dinner partner.

Words that signal _high fat_ include:

buttered or buttery	creamed or creamy	rich
scalloped	fried	breaded
fritters	tempura	croquettes
crispy	with gravy	in cheese sauce
Hollandaise	au gratin	à la king
Béarnaise	Alfredo	Newburg

Words that signal _high sodium_ include:

smoked	barbecued	pickled
broth	soy sauce	teriyaki
Creole sauce	marinated	cocktail sauce
tomato base	Parmesan	mustard sauce

Appendix:
Analysis Methods and Accuracy

How is the nutrition analysis done?

Using recipes supplied by the restaurant, a computerized nutritional analysis is performed with the Nutritionist IV computer program. Research shows the Nutritionist IV Program to be one of the most current and reliable nutrition analysis programs available. It uses the US Department of Agriculture (USDA) database. We regularly update our program with new data values published by the USDA. When values for recipe ingredients are not available from the USDA database, we contact the manufacturer for nutritional information. If the manufacturer does not have nutritional information, we match ingredients as closely as possible to another product, which does have nutritional information.

The numbers coming from the USDA database and the computer analysis imply a high degree of accuracy. In reality, the USDA found that nutritional values of foods can vary between similar food samples by as much as 20%, and the numbers coming from their measurements represent their average data. As recommended by the FDA, we rounded the data as follows: for calories, cholesterol and sodium, to the nearest 5 (mg). For fat, protein and carbohydrates, to the nearest whole number, and for diabetic exchanges to the nearest ¼ exchange. Therefore it is important to note that the numerical values for the selected menu items published in this book are <u>approximations only</u>.

Notes about accuracy

The most accurate method to obtain nutritional information is a chemical analysis performed in a professional laboratory. That is, in fact, how the USDA obtained the information for their database. It is very expensive (over $1,000 per item) and time-consuming, and therefore not feasible for this project. Every effort was made to ensure accurate information from the computerized analysis and the USDA database.

Two main obstacles were encountered with the computerized analysis. First, how much marinade do meats actually absorb? Second, how much oil is absorbed in flash-frying (a method commonly used in Chinese foods)? After numerous conversations with experts throughout the U.S., we found that there has been very little research in these areas. As recommended by nutritionists at the USDA and the Human Nutrition Information Service, we calculate that one gram per one ounce of marinade is absorbed, and that one teaspoon per six ounces of meat is absorbed with flash-frying.

Part II
Healthy Dining Menus

Arranged alphabetically
Also see indexes at back, arranged by cuisine, location, and alphabetically.

Summary of check mark system:

ENTREE GUIDELINES†

Calories	✓✓ Excellent Choice = 0 to 350 calories/entree	✓ Good Choice = 351 to 600 calories/entree
Fat	✓✓ Excellent Choice = 0 to 10 grams (g)/entree	✓ Good Choice = 11 to 20 grams (g)/entree
Cholesterol	✓✓ Excellent Choice = 0 to 75 milligrams (mg)/entree	✓ Good Choice = 76 to 150 milligrams (mg)/entree
Sodium	✓✓ Excellent Choice = 0 to 300 milligrams (mg)/entree	✓ Good Choice = 301 to 600 milligrams (mg)/entree

Footnotes
  *   Primarily unsaturated fat
 **   If you request no added salt
  †   Side dish guidelines are ⅓ of entree guidelines
  🍎   at least 2 fruit/vegetable servings

Price Range Symbols
$ Average entree under $10
$$ Average entree $10 - $20
$$$ Average entree over $20

Special Request - modification of the usual restaurant recipe or preparation method. You must ask for the "Special Request" for it to correspond to the published nutrition information.

Voted #1 Mexican Restaurant for two years in a row by the Readers of La Opinion Newspaper. Acapulco Restaurant offers a festive atmosphere to enjoy deliciously prepared Mexican dishes. Acapulco's executive chef has worked with time tested recipes to refine their food for the more health conscious guest. Please stop in and enjoy a delicious, health-consciously prepared meal at Acapulco Mexican Restaurant. $

Acapulco

Escondido: 1541 E. Valley Pky. (760) 741-9922   Old Town: 2467 Juan St. (619) 260-8124
Hemet: 2599 S. San Jacinto St. (909) 929-3340   Rancho Bernardo: 16785 Bernardo Ctr. Dr. (858) 487-6701
Mira Mesa: 8998 Miramar Rd. (858) 578-6390   San Diego: 4060 Clairemont Mesa Blvd. (858) 483-9222
San Marcos: 1020-50 W. San Marcos Blvd. (760) 471-2150
For additional locations outside the San Diego area, call (800) 735-3501

CEVICHE TOSTADA – HEALTHY DINING PREPARATION ☼
Delicately seasoned halibut filet, shrimp, tomatoes, onions, cilantro and peppers. Served with black bean salsa and sweet yams. Analysis does not include tortilla shell.
✓ CALORIES: Good Choice (360) ✓ CHOLESTEROL: Good Choice (135 mg)
✓✓ FAT: Excellent Choice (9 g)* SODIUM: High (1200 mg)
EXCHANGES: 2¾ Meat, 1¾ Bread, 1½ Veg, ¼ Fruit, 1¼ Fat
PROTEIN: 30 g, CARBOHYDRATE: 41 g

HALIBUT FILET WITH TOMATILLO SAUCE – HEALTHY DINING PREPARATION ☼
Filet of halibut grilled with distinctly delicious tomatillo sauce. Served with vegetables and rice.
✓ CALORIES: Good Choice (540) ✓ CHOLESTEROL: Good Choice (80 mg)
✓ FAT: Good Choice (17 g)* SODIUM: High (1330 mg)
EXCHANGES: 4½ Meat (extra lean), 2 Bread, 1¾ Veg, 2 Fat
PROTEIN: 55 g, CARBOHYDRATE: 42 g

VEGGIE FAJITAS – HEALTHY DINING PREPARATION ☼
✓ CALORIES: Good Choice (590) ✓✓ CHOLESTEROL: Excellent Choice (0 mg)
✓ FAT: Good Choice (13 g)* SODIUM: Moderate (730 mg)**
EXCHANGES: ½ Meat (extra lean), 3¾ Bread, 6¾ Veg, ¼ Fruit, 2¼ Fat
PROTEIN: 20 g, CARBOHYDRATE: 105 g

ENCHILADAS RANCHERAS – HEALTHY DINING PREPARATION ☼
Two corn tortillas filled with chicken & topped with salsa ranchera. Served with charro beans & fresh vegetables.
✓ CALORIES: Good Choice (515) ✓ CHOLESTEROL: Good Choice (85 mg)
✓ FAT: Good Choice (11 g) ✓ SODIUM: Good Choice (535 mg)**
EXCHANGES: 5 Meat (extra lean), 3¼ Bread, 1¾ Veg, 1¼ Fat
PROTEIN: 43 g, CARBOHYDRATE: 58 g

TACOS AL CARBON – HEALTHY DINING PREPARATION ☼
Two soft corn or flour tortillas filled with grilled chicken, with charro beans, fresh vegetables & pico de gallo.
✓ CALORIES: Good Choice (585) ✓ CHOLESTEROL: Good Choice (110 mg)
✓ FAT: Good Choice (11 g) SODIUM: Moderate (990 mg)**
EXCHANGES: 6 Meat (extra lean), 3½ Bread, 1¾ Veg, 1¼ Fat
PROTEIN: 55 g, CARBOHYDRATE: 66 g

GARDEN TOSTADA – HEALTHY DINING PREPARATION ☼
Charro beans, fresh vegetables, lettuce, tomatoes and tropical fruit relish. Tostada shell not included in analysis.
✓✓ CALORIES: Excellent Choice (310) ✓✓ CHOLESTEROL: Excellent Choice (0 mg)
✓✓ FAT: Excellent Choice (8 g)* ✓ SODIUM: Good Choice (440 mg)**
EXCHANGES: ½ Meat (extra lean), 1¾ Bread, 3¾ Veg, ¼ Fruit, 1¼ Fat
PROTEIN: 13 g, CARBOHYDRATE: 52 g

☼ at least 2 fruit/vegetable servings

   ✓ Good Choice   ✓✓ Excellent Choice

Andiamo!
Italian Restaurant

Conveniently located on Santo Road just off Highway 52 in Tierrasanta, Andiamo offers an eclectic Italian menu. Chef-Owner Javier Ugarte provides a wonderful selection of pastas, salads, entrees, homemade desserts and wood-fired pizzas in his seasonal menus. Andiamo also has three separate ambiance settings to cater private events from 10 to 80 guests as well as a large patio dining area. $-$$

Andiamo! Italian Restaurant
5950 Santo Road, San Diego, CA 92124 (858) 277-3501

CAPPELINI CON VEGETALI ARROSTITI
Angel hair pasta, fresh basil, garlic and olive oil tossed with assorted charbroiled vegetables.
- ✓ CALORIES: Good Choice (425)
- ✓✓ CHOLESTEROL: Excellent Choice (0 mg)
- ✓✓ FAT: Excellent Choice (9 g)*
- ✓✓ SODIUM: Excellent Choice (300 mg)**

EXCHANGES: 4¼ Bread, 1½ Veg, 1¼ Fat
PROTEIN: 13 g, CARBOHYDRATE: 75 g

PENNE ARRABIATTA
Penne pasta tossed with capers and homemade pomodoro sauce.
- ✓ CALORIES: Good Choice (430)
- ✓✓ CHOLESTEROL: Excellent Choice (0 mg)
- ✓✓ FAT: Excellent Choice (7 g)*
- SODIUM: High (1100 mg)

EXCHANGES: 4¼ Bread, 1¾ Veg, 1 Fat
PROTEIN: 13 g, CARBOHYDRATE: 75 g

VEGETALI PIZZA (½ PIZZA)
Roasted eggplant, zucchini, portobello mushroom and goat cheese pizza. Analysis is for ½ of a pizza.
- ✓ CALORIES: Good Choice (500)
- ✓✓ CHOLESTEROL: Excellent Choice (35 mg)
- ✓ FAT: Good Choice (16 g)*
- SODIUM: High (1105 mg)

EXCHANGES: 1 Meat, 4¼ Bread, 1 Veg, 2¾ Fat
PROTEIN: 17 g, CARBOHYDRATE: 70 g

POLLO AL LIMONE E ROSMARINO
Chicken sautéed with garlic, fresh rosemary, lemon juice and white wine, served with roasted potatoes and mixed vegetables.
- ✓ CALORIES: Good Choice (590)
- CHOLESTEROL: Moderate (170 mg)
- ✓ FAT: Good Choice (18 g)
- ✓✓ SODIUM: Excellent Choice (170 mg)**

EXCHANGES: 9 Meat (extra lean), 1 Bread, 1 Veg, 2½ Fat
PROTEIN: 66 g, CARBOHYDRATE: 28 g

RIGATONI PRIMAVERA
Assorted vegetables tossed with rigatoni and pomodoro sauce.
- ✓ CALORIES: Good Choice (600)
- ✓✓ CHOLESTEROL: Excellent Choice (10 mg)
- FAT: Moderate (22 g)*
- ✓ SODIUM: Good Choice (545 mg)**

EXCHANGES: 1 Meat (extra lean), 4¼ Bread, 2¼ Veg, 3½ Fat
PROTEIN: 21 g, CARBOHYDRATE: 78 g

CAPELLINI CON GAMBERETTI
Angel hair pasta with sautéed shrimp, garlic, basil, broccoli and fresh tomato sauce.
- CALORIES: Moderate (630)
- CHOLESTEROL: Moderate (275 mg)
- ✓ FAT: Good Choice (17 g)*
- ✓ SODIUM: Good Choice (340 mg)**

EXCHANGES: 4¼ Meat (extra lean), 4¼ Bread, 1½ Veg, 2¾ Fat
PROTEIN: 44 g, CARBOHYDRATE: 76 g

MARGHERITA PIZZA (½ PIZZA)
Mozzarella cheese, pomodoro sauce and fresh basil pizza. Analysis is for ½ of a pizza.
- ✓ CALORIES: Good Choice (550)
- ✓✓ CHOLESTEROL: Excellent Choice (50 mg)
- ✓ FAT: Good Choice (20 g)*
- SODIUM: High (1170 mg)

EXCHANGES: ¾ Meat, 6 Bread, ½ Veg, 1¼ Fat
PROTEIN: 22 g, CARBOHYDRATE: 68 g

* Primarily unsaturated fat
** If you request no added salt

Welcome to Anthony's. Established in 1946, Anthony's Fish Grotto continues to provide the finest seafood dining our city has to offer. We are confident you will enjoy every aspect of your meal, from our vast selection of healthy, fresh seafood to the service provided by our friendly team members. $

Anthony's Casual Seafood Restaurants:

San Diego Bay: Harbor Dr. at Ash St.   (619) 232-5103
Chula Vista: Hwy. 5 at "E" St.   (619) 425-4200
La Mesa: Highway 8 at Severin Dr.   (619) 463-0368
Rancho Bernardo: Bernardo Center Dr. to Avena Pl.   (858) 451-2070

COMBINATION SEAFOOD LOUIE ✿
Crab and Gulf shrimp nested atop chopped romaine and iceberg lettuce, surrounded with cucumber, carrots, beets, sliced avocado and tomato wedges. Garnished with chopped parsley. Dressing is served on side, not included in analysis.
✓✓ CALORIES: Excellent Choice (240)　　　CHOLESTEROL: Moderate (165 mg)
✓ FAT: Good Choice (11 g)*　　　✓ SODIUM: Good Choice (440 mg)**
EXCHANGES: 3 Meat (extra lean), 1¼ Veg, 1¾ Fat
PROTEIN: 25 g, CARBOHYDRATE: 12 g

HALIBUT WITH ORANGE MINT BASIL BUTTER
Mild and tender mesquite charbroiled halibut with orange mint basil butter sauce. Served with citrus rice pilaf (not included, see analysis below) and dinner salad (not included in analysis).
✓✓ CALORIES: Excellent Choice (245)　　　✓✓ CHOLESTEROL: Excellent Choice (70 mg)
✓✓ FAT: Excellent Choice (8 g)　　　✓✓ SODIUM: Excellent Choice (135 mg)**
EXCHANGES: 5¼ Meat (extra lean), ¼ Fruit, ¾ Fat
PROTEIN: 38 g, CARBOHYDRATE: 3 g

FRESH SEABASS WITH POMODORO SAUCE
Charbroiled seabass brushed with olive oil and garlic and topped with a flavorful pomodoro sauce. Served with citrus rice pilaf (not included, see analysis below) and dinner salad (not included in analysis).
✓✓ CALORIES: Excellent Choice (245)　　　✓✓ CHOLESTEROL: Excellent Choice (75 mg)
✓✓ FAT: Excellent Choice (8 g)*　　　✓✓ SODIUM: Excellent Choice (130 mg)**
EXCHANGES: 4¾ Meat (extra lean), 1¼ Veg, 1 Fat
PROTEIN: 35 g, CARBOHYDRATE: 7 g

GRILLED SHRIMP WITH HONEY MUSTARD GLAZE
on a bed of rice and topped with chives. Served with dinner salad (not included in analysis).
✓✓ CALORIES: Excellent Choice (300)　　　CHOLESTEROL: Moderate (250 mg)
✓✓ FAT: Excellent Choice (3 g)*　　　SODIUM: Moderate (645 mg)**
EXCHANGES: 3¾ Meat (extra lean), 1½ Bread
PROTEIN: 30 g, CARBOHYDRATE: 36 g

GRILLED FISH TACO
charbroiled with Mexican seasonings, wrapped in a flour tortilla, with cheese, guacamole, salsa and creamy taco sauce.
✓✓ CALORIES: Excellent Choice (320)　　　✓✓ CHOLESTEROL: Excellent Choice (40 mg)
✓ FAT: Good Choice (16 g)　　　SODIUM: Moderate (720 mg)**
EXCHANGES: 2 Meat, 1¼ Bread, ½ Veg, 2¼ Fat
PROTEIN: 21 g, CARBOHYDRATE: 29 g

CITRUS RICE PILAF - CAL: 190, FAT: 1 g, CHOL: 0 mg, SOD: 620 mg; EXCH: 2¾ Bread; PROT: 6 g, CARB: 41 g

Low-calorie Ranch dressing is available for salads.

✿ at least 2 fruit/vegetable servings
✓ Good Choice　✓✓ Excellent Choice

Come to Bandar and experience what San Diego restaurant critic Eleanor Widmer has described as the "finest Persian gourmet restaurant in the city." Since our opening in 1996, we have received numerous awards, including Best Ethnic Restaurant (1998 & 1999) and Best New Restaurant (1997) by the Gaslamp Quarter Association, and the Reader's Choice Winner (1998) by San Diego Home & Garden Magazine. More recently, the Zagat Survey recognized Bandar as one of the "Area's Top Restaurants" (1999). $$

Bandar

825 4th Avenue, San Diego, CA 92101 (619) 238-0101

SHISH KABOB (½ SERVING) ☺

Juicy marinated chunks of filet mignon, skewered and charbroiled to perfection with charbroiled vegetables. Served with basmati rice (not included, see analysis below). Analysis is for ½ of a full serving.

- ✓ CALORIES: Good Choice (365)
- ✓ FAT: Good Choice (15 g)
- ✓ CHOLESTEROL: Good Choice (130 mg)
- ✓✓ SODIUM: Excellent Choice (185 mg)**

EXCHANGES: 6 Meat, 1¾ Veg, ¼ Fat
PROTEIN: 45 g, CARBOHYDRATE: 11 g

ADAS POLO (½ SERVING)

Juicy chunks of charbroiled boneless chicken tenders marinated in a special sauce (saffron, onion, fresh lemon juice). Served with basmati rice mixed with lentils, black currant raisins, fresh dates and saffron (not included, see analysis below). Analysis is for ½ of a full serving.

- ✓✓ CALORIES: Excellent Choice (275)
- ✓✓ FAT: Excellent Choice (7 g)
- ✓ CHOLESTEROL: Good Choice (130 mg)
- ✓✓ SODIUM: Excellent Choice (165 mg)**

EXCHANGES: 6¾ Meat (extra lean), ½ Veg, ¼ Fat
PROTEIN: 48 g, CARBOHYDRATE: 3 g

FISH KABOB (½ SERVING) ☺

Fresh filet of white fish dipped in saffron sauce and charbroiled with vegetables. Served with basmati rice (not included, see analysis below). Analysis is for ½ of a full serving.

- ✓ CALORIES: Good Choice (440)
- ✓ FAT: Good Choice (17 g)*
- CHOLESTEROL: Moderate (175 mg)
- ✓✓ SODIUM: Excellent Choice (155 mg)**

EXCHANGES: 8 Meat, 1¾ Veg
PROTEIN: 57 g, CARBOHYDRATE: 11 g

GHEIMEH BADEMJAN (½ SERVING) ☺

A savory medley of eggplant, yellow split peas and a special tomato base, lightly spiced to perfection. Served with basmati rice (not included, see analysis below). Analysis is for ½ of a full serving.

- ✓✓ CALORIES: Excellent Choice (345)
- ✓✓ FAT: Excellent Choice (8 g)*
- ✓✓ CHOLESTEROL: Excellent Choice (0 mg)
- SODIUM: High (1470 mg)

EXCHANGES: 1 Meat (extra lean), 2 Bread, 4½ Veg, 1¼ Fat
PROTEIN: 17 g, CARBOHYDRATE: 58 g

BASMATI RICE (1 CUP)†

- CALORIES: Moderate (215)
- ✓✓ FAT: Excellent Choice (2 g)*
- ✓✓ CHOLESTEROL: Excellent Choice (0 mg)
- ✓✓ SODIUM: Excellent Choice (0 mg)

EXCHANGES: 3 Bread, ½ Fat
PROTEIN: 4 g, CARBOHYDRATE: 43 g

---

* Primarily unsaturated fat
** If you request no added salt

† Side dish guidelines are 1/3 of entree guidelines
Healthy Dining in San Diego **49**

"Inland North County's own lovely French gem," as mentioned in the 1999 Zagat Survey Guide. This multi-award winning restaurant features a full mahogany bar, two lovely dining rooms with large countryside murals, a wine cellar and two fireplaces, one in the outdoor covered patio. $$

Bernard'O Restaurant

12457 Rancho Bernardo Road, San Diego, CA 92128 (858) 487-7171

SAUTÉED SHRIMP & SCALLOP SKEWER ON RICE PILAF – SPECIAL REQUEST 🍎

Sautéed shrimp and scallops skewered and served on rice pilaf with stir-fried vegetables and a spicy citrus vinaigrette (vinaigrette not included in analysis). Request less oil (1 Tbs) and vinaigrette on the side.

✓ CALORIES: Good Choice (490) CHOLESTEROL: Moderate (195 mg)
✓ FAT: Good Choice (20 g)* ✓ SODIUM: Good Choice (455 mg)**
EXCHANGES: 3¼ Meat (extra lean), 2¼ Bread, 1¾ Veg, 3 Fat
PROTEIN: 45 g, CARBOHYDRATE: 43 g

ANGEL HAIR PASTA WITH TOMATOES, BASIL & GARLIC – SPECIAL REQUEST

Angel hair pasta with white wine tomato concasse. Request less oil (1 Tbs) and no butter.

✓ CALORIES: Good Choice (515) ✓ CHOLESTEROL: Good Choice (130 mg)
✓ FAT: Good Choice (18 g)* ✓✓ SODIUM: Excellent Choice (55 mg)**
EXCHANGES: 4 Bread, 1 Veg, 3¾ Fat
PROTEIN: 16 g, CARBOHYDRATE: 70 g

GRILLED SALMON AND ASPARAGUS SALAD – SPECIAL REQUEST 🍎

Grilled salmon and asparagus salad with lemon and dill sauce (dill sauce not included in analysis). Request less oil (½ Tbs).

✓✓ CALORIES: Excellent Choice (310) ✓✓ CHOLESTEROL: Excellent Choice (75 mg)
✓ FAT: Good Choice (16 g)* ✓✓ SODIUM: Excellent Choice (80 mg)**
EXCHANGES: 3½ Meat, 1½ Veg, 1¼ Fat
PROTEIN: 32 g, CARBOHYDRATE: 10 g

GRILLED SALMON WITH AVOCADO & TOMATO COULIS – SPECIAL REQUEST 🍎

served with fresh steamed vegetables. Request less oil (½ tsp).

✓ CALORIES: Good Choice (405) ✓ CHOLESTEROL: Good Choice (90 mg)
FAT: Moderate (23 g)* ✓✓ SODIUM: Excellent Choice (140 mg)**
EXCHANGES: 4¼ Meat, 1½ Veg, 2¼ Fat
PROTEIN: 41 g, CARBOHYDRATE: 10 g

🍎 at least 2 fruit/vegetable servings
✓ Good Choice ✓✓ Excellent Choice

At Bistro Yang, we specialize in exquisite Chinese cooking with a touch of European influence. We proudly bring you our cultural classics and our Bistro Specialties. We are able to prepare our dishes in accord with special dietary requirements, e.g., salt free, diabetic, etc. Please discuss your special needs with our staff. $$

Bistro Yang

4705 G Clairemont Dr., San Diego, CA 92117 (858) 483-6893

CHICKEN CLEOPATRA – SPECIAL REQUEST

Sliced breast of chicken prepared with snow peas, carrots, water chestnuts, blackwood mushrooms, green onions, garlic, tomato sauce and a light touch of soy sauce. Request less oil in preparation of chicken (¼ tsp).

✓ CALORIES: Good Choice (580)
✓✓ CHOLESTEROL: Excellent Choice (0 mg)
✓ FAT: Good Choice (11 g)
SODIUM: High (1300 mg)
EXCHANGES: 11 Meat (extra lean), ¼ Bread, 5¼ Veg, ¼ Fat
PROTEIN: 85 g, CARBOHYDRATE: 33 g

STIR-FRIED SEA BASS – SPECIAL REQUEST

Tender boneless filets of Chilean sea bass stir-fried with scallion, fresh mushrooms and sweet snow peas in a delicate white wine garlic sauce. Request less oil when preparing fish (¼ tsp).

✓✓ CALORIES: Excellent Choice (350)
✓ CHOLESTEROL: Good Choice (120 mg)
✓✓ FAT: Excellent Choice (7 g)*
SODIUM: High (1185 mg)
EXCHANGES: 7¾ Meat (extra lean), 2 Veg, ¼ Fat
PROTEIN: 58 g, CARBOHYDRATE: 11 g

CHI-YAO SHRIMP – SPECIAL REQUEST

Shrimp sautéed with broccoli, snow peas, carrots, fresh mushrooms and bamboo shoots in a white wine sauce. Request less oil (¼ tsp).

✓✓ CALORIES: Excellent Choice (300)
CHOLESTEROL: High (390 mg)
✓✓ FAT: Excellent Choice (4 g)*
SODIUM: High (1485 mg)
EXCHANGES: 5¾ Meat (extra lean), 3½ Veg, ¼ Fat
PROTEIN: 48 g, CARBOHYDRATE: 18 g

BUDDHA'S DELIGHT – SPECIAL REQUEST

A delightful combination of nine fresh vegetables lightly stir-fried in your choice of a brown garlic sauce or white wine sauce. Analysis for white wine sauce. Brown sauce adds 30 calories. Request less oil (¼ tsp).

✓✓ CALORIES: Excellent Choice (225)
✓✓ CHOLESTEROL: Excellent Choice (0 mg)
✓✓ FAT: Excellent Choice (3 g)*
SODIUM: High (4415 mg)
EXCHANGES: ¾ Bread, 6 Veg, ¼ Fat
PROTEIN: 11 g, CARBOHYDRATE: 44 g

* Primarily unsaturated fat
** If you request no added salt

Well known for their fabulous prime rib, Bully's also offers an exciting steak and seafood menu. Also featured are the famous Bully burger, baby back ribs, chicken sandwiches and salads. Bully's lunch menu includes all your favorite sandwiches, a varied selection of salads, and features a daily special. Bully's also offers a children's menu. This lively fun restaurant also features patio dining. If you want good food, good drink, and a memorable time for a reasonable price, Bully's is the place to be. $

Bully's East 2401 Camino Del Rio S., San Diego, CA 92108   (619) 291-2665

Bully's La Jolla 5755 La Jolla Blvd., La Jolla, CA 92037   (858) 459-2768

Bully's Del Mar 1404 Camino Del Mar, Del Mar, CA 92014   (858) 755-1660

Recommended side dishes: garden salad, baked potato (plain), rice pilaf (see analysis below) or sliced tomatoes.

BREAST OF CHICKEN
Served with teriyaki sauce (not included in analysis).

✓✓ CALORIES: Excellent Choice (335)   CHOLESTEROL: Moderate (175 mg)

✓✓ FAT: Excellent Choice (7 g)   ✓✓ SODIUM: Excellent Choice (150 mg)**

EXCHANGES: 9 Meat (extra lean)

PROTEIN: 63 g, CARBOHYDRATE: 0 g

SHRIMP SCAMPI

✓✓ CALORIES: Excellent Choice (300)   CHOLESTEROL: Moderate (275 mg)

✓ FAT: Good Choice (15 g)*   ✓ SODIUM: Good Choice (325 mg)**

EXCHANGES: 4¼ Meat (extra lean), ¾ Veg, 3 Fat

PROTEIN: 31 g, CARBOHYDRATE: 6 g

FRESH FISH OF THE DAY WITH MANGO CHUTNEY ☙
Request charbroiled, broiled or prepared with white wine and lemon.

✓ CALORIES: Good Choice (485)   ✓ CHOLESTEROL: Good Choice (80 mg)

✓✓ FAT: Excellent Choice (6 g)*   ✓✓ SODIUM: Excellent Choice (160 mg)**

EXCHANGES: 5 Meat (extra lean), 3½ Fruit

PROTEIN: 53 g, CARBOHYDRATE: 52 g

AUSTRALIAN LOBSTER
One tail. Analysis does not include butter.

✓✓ CALORIES: Excellent Choice (210)   CHOLESTEROL: Moderate (155 mg)

✓✓ FAT: Excellent Choice (1 g)*   SODIUM: Moderate (810 mg)**

EXCHANGES: 5¼ Meat (extra lean)

PROTEIN: 44 g, CARBOHYDRATE: 3 g

RICE PILAF† *(4 OZ)*

✓ CALORIES: Good Choice (160)   ✓✓ CHOLESTEROL: Excellent Choice (0 mg)

✓ FAT: Good Choice (4 g)   SODIUM: Moderate (285 mg)

EXCHANGES: 1¾ Bread, ¼ Veg, ¾ Fat

PROTEIN: 3 g, CARBOHYDRATE: 28 g

---

† Side dish guidelines are 1/3 of entree guidelines

☙ at least 2 fruit/vegetable servings

✓ Good Choice   ✓✓ Excellent Choice

Fine Indian Cuisine

Café India offers healthy and affordable Indian cuisine in a peaceful and cozy atmosphere - perfect for the casual date or family get-together. A buffet featuring four vegetable curries, rice, lentil soup, salad and bread is available for both lunch and dinner. In addition, the menu offers traditional chicken and lamb dishes, oven-baked breads and a large selection of vegetarian entrees. Café India has been given a 4-star rating by "Good Morning America," complimented by the San Diego Union- Tribune for its "authentic flavors and fire," and rewarded with a certificate from the San Diego Medical Society for "contributing to the health and well-being of the San Diego community." Open daily for lunch & dinner from 11 am to 10 pm Monday - Saturday, noon to 10 pm Sunday. Lunch buffet daily from 11 am to 3 pm. Dinner buffet Friday only 5 to 9 pm. Located in Sports Arena Village. $

Café India

3760-5 Sports Arena Blvd., San Diego, CA 92109   (619) 224-7500

TOFU JALFARAZI

Tofu sautéed with onion, bell pepper and vegetables.

✓✓ CALORIES: Excellent Choice (310)   ✓✓ CHOLESTEROL: Excellent Choice (0 mg)
✓✓ FAT: Excellent Choice (18 g)*   ✓✓ SODIUM: Excellent Choice (265 mg)**
EXCHANGES: 2¾ Meat, 2¼ Veg, 1¾ Fat
PROTEIN: 23 g, CARBOHYDRATE: 19 g

MOONG DAL

Sprouted moong lentils steam cooked, spiced and topped with fresh onions and cilantro leaves.

✓✓ CALORIES: Excellent Choice (130)   ✓✓ CHOLESTEROL: Excellent Choice (0 mg)
✓✓ FAT: Excellent Choice (7 g)*   ✓✓ SODIUM: Excellent Choice (15 mg)**
EXCHANGES: 2¼ Veg, 1½ Fat
PROTEIN: 4 g, CARBOHYDRATE: 14 g

BENGAN BHARTA

Tandoori (clay) oven baked eggplant sautéed with onions, garlic, tomatoes and peas.

✓✓ CALORIES: Excellent Choice (215)   ✓✓ CHOLESTEROL: Excellent Choice (0 mg)
✓✓ FAT: Excellent Choice (6 g)*   ✓✓ SODIUM: Excellent Choice (35 mg)**
EXCHANGES: ¼ Bread, 5 Veg, 1 Fat
PROTEIN: 6 g, CARBOHYDRATE: 39 g

ALOO SABZI

Potato curry

✓✓ CALORIES: Excellent Choice (320)   ✓✓ CHOLESTEROL: Excellent Choice (0 mg)
✓✓ FAT: Excellent Choice (10 g)*   ✓✓ SODIUM: Excellent Choice (140 mg)**
EXCHANGES: 2½ Bread, ¼ Veg, 1¼ Fat
PROTEIN: 7 g, CARBOHYDRATE: 51 g

VEGETABLE BIRYANI

Vegetables sautéed with onions and bell peppers, cooked with basmati rice, topped with raisins and nuts.

✓✓ CALORIES: Excellent Choice (250)   ✓✓ CHOLESTEROL: Excellent Choice (0 mg)
✓✓ FAT: Excellent Choice (7 g)*   ✓✓ SODIUM: Excellent Choice (40 mg)**
EXCHANGES: 2¼ Bread, 1¼ Veg, 1¼ Fat
PROTEIN: 6 g, CARBOHYDRATE: 42 g

* Primarily unsaturated fat

** If you request no added salt

Café Japengo's food and design express the cross cultural influences from East and West. The impressive combination of California cooking style with Asian ingredients and techniques merges to achieve a unique version of signature dishes. This progressive, high-energy restaurant has been the recipient of several awards from the San Diego Restaurant Association including "Best Asian Cuisine" six consecutive years and "Best Sushi Bar" in San Diego. The recent addition of an outdoor dining patio has added an exceptional flare to this unique, eclectic restaurant. Café Japengo's dedication to quality and consistency accompanied by a creative ambiance sets the stage for a memorable dining experience. $$

Café Japengo
8960 University Center Lane, San Diego, CA 92122 (858) 450-3355

PEPPER CRUSTED AHI ☺
*Seared black pepper crusted Ahi over fresh, thin egg noodles,
Chinese greens, coconut saffron, and sweet and spicy tomato chutney.*
✓ CALORIES: Good Choice (555)   ✓ CHOLESTEROL: Good Choice (90 mg)
✓ FAT: Good Choice (11 g)*   SODIUM: High (2600 mg)
EXCHANGES: 6¼ Meat (extra lean), 2 Bread, 3 Veg, 1¼ Fat
PROTEIN: 53 g, CARBOHYDRATE: 64 g

PAN ROASTED SALMON – SPECIAL REQUEST ☺
Salmon fillet filled with mushroom duxell and Thai green curry sauce. Served with stir-fried spinach and soba noodles. <u>Request no butter and for spinach to be prepared without oil.</u>
✓ CALORIES: Good Choice (520)   ✓ CHOLESTEROL: Good Choice (105 mg)
✓ FAT: Good Choice (20 g)*   ✓✓ SODIUM: Excellent Choice (245 mg)**
EXCHANGES: 5 Meat, 1¼ Bread, 2¼ Veg, ¼ Fruit, 1½ Fat
PROTEIN: 49 g, CARBOHYDRATE: 37 g

TAMARIND HONEY GLAZED SWORDFISH – SPECIAL REQUEST ☺
*Grilled center cut swordfish with citrus black bean sauce, wok vegetables and crispy leeks.
<u>Request less oil (1 tsp) and less of each glaze used (1 oz. each glaze).</u>
(Requesting plain fish without glazes will significantly reduce the sodium content.)*
✓ CALORIES: Good Choice (500)   ✓ CHOLESTEROL: Good Choice (95 mg)
✓ FAT: Good Choice (16 g)*   SODIUM: High (2390 mg)
EXCHANGES: 5 Meat, ¼ Bread, 2¼ Veg, 1¼ Fat
PROTEIN: 50 g, CARBOHYDRATE: 39 g

SHRIMP AND SCALLOPS – SPECIAL REQUEST ☺
*Shrimp and scallops wok fried with vegetables and rice stick noodles in peanut sauce.
<u>Request no peanuts and less peanut sauce (1 oz).</u>*
✓ CALORIES: Good Choice (545)   CHOLESTEROL: Moderate (230 mg)
✓ FAT: Good Choice (13 g)*   SODIUM: Moderate (860 mg)
EXCHANGES: 4¾ Meat (extra lean), 3 Bread, 2¼ Veg, 1¾ Fat
PROTEIN: 41 g, CARBOHYDRATE: 66 g

VEGETARIAN FRIED RICE ☺
Fresh vegetables sautéed with white rice.
CALORIES: Moderate (655)   ✓✓ CHOLESTEROL: Excellent Choice (0 mg)
✓ FAT: Good Choice (15 g)*   ✓ SODIUM: Good Choice (585 mg)**
EXCHANGES: 5½ Bread, 5¾ Veg, 3 Fat
PROTEIN: 18 g, CARBOHYDRATE: 113 g

☺ at least 2 fruit/vegetable servings
✓ Good Choice   ✓✓ Excellent Choice

CASA DE BANDINI
MEXICAN RESTAURANT

The magnificent historic hacienda of Juan Bandini, circa 1829, is the setting for traditional Mexican cuisine, seafood specialties and lively mariachis. Lush gardens and fountains surround the enchantingly beautiful dining patio. A lighter Mexican cuisine has been created for our health-conscious diners - low in calories, fat, cholesterol, and sodium, which maintain their flavor and nutritional value! $

Casa de Bandini

Bazaar del Mundo
Old Town San Diego State Historic Park
2754 Calhoun St., San Diego, CA 92110 (619) 297-8211

Hours: Mon-Sat 11 am - 9:30 pm
Sun 10 am - 9:30 pm
Summer to 10 pm daily

CHICKEN AND BLACK BEAN TOSTADA

Seasoned, shredded chicken, black beans, shredded lettuce, tomato and olives, spiced with salsa ranchera & sprinkled with parmesan cheese. Analysis does not include tostada shell.
- ✓✓ CALORIES: Excellent Choice (320)
- ✓✓ FAT: Excellent Choice (7 g)
- ✓✓ CHOLESTEROL: Excellent Choice (25 mg)
- SODIUM: Moderate (925 mg)**

EXCHANGES: 1¾ Meat, 1¾ Bread, 3 Veg, ½ Fat
PROTEIN: 23 g, CARBOHYDRATE: 44 g

BLACK BEAN BURRITO WITH TOMATILLO SAUCE

Delectable black beans stuffed in a large burrito & covered with tomatillo sauce. Garnished with lettuce & tomato & sprinkled with parmesan cheese. Served with a concha of rice (not included, see analysis for rice below).
- ✓ CALORIES: Good Choice (585)
- ✓ FAT: Good Choice (11 g)
- ✓✓ CHOLESTEROL: Excellent Choice (5 mg)
- SODIUM: Moderate (970 mg)**

EXCHANGES: ½ Meat, 5¼ Bread, 1¾ Veg, 1¼ Fat
PROTEIN: 28 g, CARBOHYDRATE: 97 g

FIESTA FAJITAS

All vegetable fajitas with eight kinds of fresh vegetables sautéed & seasoned with achiote sauce. Served with black beans & rice (not included, see analyses below) & tortillas (not included in analysis).
- ✓✓ CALORIES: Excellent Choice (195)
- ✓ FAT: Good Choice (15 g)*
- ✓✓ CHOLESTEROL: Excellent Choice (0 mg)
- ✓✓ SODIUM: Excellent Choice (45 mg)**

EXCHANGES: 2¼ Veg, ¼ Fruit, 2¾ Fat
PROTEIN: 3 g, CARBOHYDRATE: 16 g

ARROZ CON POLLO A LA MEXICANA

Choice morsels of chicken breast specially cooked with bell peppers, tomatoes & onions. Served with black beans & Mexican rice (not included, see analyses below) & tortillas (not included in analysis).
- ✓ CALORIES: Good Choice (365)
- ✓ FAT: Good Choice (18 g)
- ✓ CHOLESTEROL: Good Choice (110 mg)
- ✓✓ SODIUM: Excellent Choice (100 mg)**

EXCHANGES: 5¾ Meat (extra lean), 1¼ Veg, 2¾ Fat
PROTEIN: 41 g, CARBOHYDRATE: 8 g

FISH BURRITO

Tender chunks of grilled filet of cod wrapped in a flour tortilla, garnished with cabbage & Bandini's spicy vegetable sauce. Choice of black beans or Mexican rice (not included, see analyses below).
- ✓ CALORIES: Good Choice (435)
- ✓✓ FAT: Excellent Choice (9 g)
- ✓ CHOLESTEROL: Good Choice (85 mg)
- SODIUM: Moderate (705 mg)**

EXCHANGES: 5 Meat (extra lean), 2¾ Bread, 1¼ Veg, 1½ Fat
PROTEIN: 42 g, CARBOHYDRATE: 44 g

RICE *(5 oz)* - CAL: 193, FAT: 4 g*, CHOL: 0, SOD: 730 mg; EXCH: 2¼ Bread, ¼ Veg, ¾ Fat; PROT: 4 g, CARB: 33 g

BLACK BEANS *(5 oz)* - CAL: 183, FAT: 1 g*, CHOL: 0, SOD: 55 mg; EXCH: 2 Bread; PROT: 12 g, CARB: 33 g

* Primarily unsaturated fat
** If you request no added salt

CASA DE PICO
MEXICAN RESTAURANT

A beautiful courtyard atmosphere, strolling mariachis and fabulous Mexican food make Casa de Pico one of the most popular Mexican restaurants in town. A lighter cuisine has been created for our health-conscious diners - healthy entrees low in calories, fat, cholesterol, and sodium, which maintain flavor and nutrition. $

Casa de Pico

Bazaar del Mundo, Old Town San Diego State Historic Park   Hours: Daily 10 am - 9:30 pm
2754 Calhoun Street, San Diego, CA 92110 (619) 296-3267   Summer to 10 pm daily

---

CHICKEN AND BLACK BEAN TOSTADA ☙

Seasoned, shredded chicken, black beans, shredded lettuce, tomato and olives, spiced with salsa ranchera & sprinkled with parmesan cheese. Analysis does not include tostada shell.
- ✓✓ CALORIES: Excellent Choice (320)   ✓✓ CHOLESTEROL: Excellent Choice (25 mg)
- ✓✓ FAT: Excellent Choice (7 g)   SODIUM: Moderate (925 mg)**

EXCHANGES: 1¾ Meat, 1¾ Bread, 3 Veg, ½ Fat
PROTEIN: 23 g, CARBOHYDRATE: 44 g

BLACK BEAN BURRITO WITH TOMATILLO SAUCE ☙

Delectable black beans stuffed in a large burrito & covered with tomatillo sauce. Garnished with lettuce & tomato & sprinkled with parmesan cheese. Served with a concha of rice (not included, see analysis below).
- ✓ CALORIES: Good Choice (585)   ✓✓ CHOLESTEROL: Excellent Choice (5 mg)
- ✓ FAT: Good Choice (11 g)   SODIUM: Moderate (970 mg)**

EXCHANGES: ½ Meat, 5¼ Bread, 1¾ Veg, 1¼ Fat
PROTEIN: 28 g, CARBOHYDRATE: 97 g

ENCHILADAS VERDES DE POLLO ☙

Specially seasoned chicken wrapped in two corn tortillas & topped with tomatillo sauce. Sprinkled with parmesan cheese & served with black beans. Concha shell not included in analysis.
- ✓ CALORIES: Good Choice (440)   ✓✓ CHOLESTEROL: Excellent Choice (35 mg)
- ✓ FAT: Good Choice (14 g)   SODIUM: Moderate (790 mg)**

EXCHANGES: 1¾ Meat, 2¾ Bread, 1¾ Veg, 1¾ Fat
PROTEIN: 26 g, CARBOHYDRATE: 54 g

ARROZ CON POLLO A LA MEXICANA ☙

Choice morsels of chicken breast specially cooked with bell peppers, tomatoes & onions. Served with black beans & Mexican rice (not included, see analyses below).
- ✓ CALORIES: Good Choice (365)   ✓ CHOLESTEROL: Good Choice (110 mg)
- ✓ FAT: Good Choice (18 g)   ✓✓ SODIUM: Excellent Choice (100 mg)**

EXCHANGES: 5¾ Meat (extra lean), 1¼ Veg, 2¾ Fat
PROTEIN: 41 g, CARBOHYDRATE: 8 g

VEGETARIAN SOFT TACOS ☙

Steamed corn tortillas filled with black beans, pico de gallo, salsa ranchera picosa, green cabbage, chopped tomatoes & parmesan cheese. Served with Mexican rice (not included, see analysis below). Delicioso!
- ✓ CALORIES: Good Choice (445)   ✓✓ CHOLESTEROL: Excellent Choice (5 mg)
- ✓ FAT: Good Choice (12 g)   SODIUM: High (1030 mg)

EXCHANGES: ¼ Meat, 4 Bread, 1½ Veg, 1¾ Fat
PROTEIN: 20 g, CARBOHYDRATE: 68 g

BLACK BEANS *(5 oz)* - CAL: 183, FAT: 1 g*, CHOL: 0, SOD: 55 mg; EXCH: 2 Bread; PROT: 12 g, CARB: 33 g
RICE *(5 oz)* - CAL: 193, FAT: 4 g*, CHOL: 0, SOD: 730 mg; EX: 2¼ Bread, ¼ Veg, ¾ Fat; PROT: 4 g, CARB: 33 g

☙ at least 2 fruit/vegetable servings
✓ Good Choice   ✓✓ Excellent Choice

A beautiful courtyard atmosphere, strolling mariachis and fabulous Mexican food make Casa Guadalajara one of the most popular Mexican restaurants in town. A lighter cuisine has been created for our health-conscious diners - healthy entrees low in calories, fat, cholesterol, and sodium, which maintain flavor and nutrition. $

Casa Guadalajara Old Town

Bazaar del Mundo Old Town San Diego State Historic Park
4105 Taylor Street, San Diego, CA 92110 (619) 295-5111

FIESTA FAJITAS

Fresh vegetables sautéed and seasoned with achiote sauce. Served with Spanish rice (included in analysis) and black beans (not included, see analysis below). Guacamole and tortillas not included in analysis.

- ✓ CALORIES: Good Choice (365)
- ✓ FAT: Good Choice (17 g)*
- ✓✓ CHOLESTEROL: Excellent Choice (0 mg)
- SODIUM: High (1060 mg)

EXCHANGES: 1¼ Bread, 4¼ Veg, ¼ Fruit, 3¼ Fat
PROTEIN: 9 g, CARBOHYDRATE: 49 g

GRILLED CHICKEN AND BLACK BEAN TOSTADA - SPECIAL REQUEST

<u>Request dressing on the side</u>. Tostada shell and dressing not included in analysis.

- ✓ CALORIES: Good Choice (420)
- ✓ FAT: Good Choice (12 g)
- ✓ CHOLESTEROL: Good Choice (130 mg)
- ✓ SODIUM: Good Choice (300 mg)**

EXCHANGES: 7 Meat (extra lean), ¾ Bread, 2 Veg, 1¼ Fat
PROTEIN: 55 g, CARBOHYDRATE: 22 g

GRILLED FISH TACOS

Tender chunks of grilled cod in our homemade corn tortilla, garnished with our special sauce. Served with salsa fresca and cabbage with vinaigrette (both included in analysis), and black beans (not included, see analysis below).

- ✓ CALORIES: Good Choice (475)
- ✓ FAT: Good Choice (14 g)
- ✓ CHOLESTEROL: Good Choice (90 mg)
- SODIUM: Moderate (625 mg)**

EXCHANGES: 5 Meat (extra lean), 1¾ Bread, 1¾ Veg, 2½ Fat
PROTEIN: 41 g, CARBOHYDRATE: 45 g

POLLO ASADA

Grilled boneless breast of chicken marinated in a mild achiote sauce and covered with fresh grilled vegetables. Served with cabbage with vinaigrette (included in analysis) and black beans (not included, see analysis below).

- ✓ CALORIES: Good Choice (485)
- ✓ FAT: Good Choice (15 g)
- CHOLESTEROL: Moderate (175 mg)
- SODIUM: Moderate (865 mg)**

EXCHANGES: 9 Meat (extra lean), 2¾ Veg, ¼ Fruit, 1½ Fat
PROTEIN: 69 g, CARBOHYDRATE: 18 g

VEGETABLE BURRITO

Fresh colorful garden vegetables in a burrito topped with salsa verde. Served with cabbage with vinaigrette (included in analysis) and black beans (not included, see analysis below).

- ✓ CALORIES: Good Choice (565)
- FAT: Moderate (24 g)*
- ✓✓ CHOLESTEROL: Excellent Choice (<1 mg)
- SODIUM: High (2080 mg)

EXCHANGES: ¼ Meat, 2¾ Bread, 6½ Veg, ½ Fruit, 4½ Fat
PROTEIN: 18 g, CARBOHYDRATE: 78 g

BLACK BEANS: CAL: 138, FAT: 3 g*, CHOL: <1 mg, SOD: 310 mg; EXCH: ½ Meat, 1¼ Bread, ½ Fat; PROT: 8 g, CARB: 20 g

* Primarily unsaturated fat
** If you request no added salt

Chili's is an original -- with outstanding Southwest-style food in a casual, friendly, fun-feeling place. Come in and see why "no place else" has the food or feeling of Chili's. And now announcing our new "Guiltless Grill" menu items, which include low-fat and low-calorie versions of some of the restaurant's more popular offerings. We also serve 4 delicious low-fat salad dressings. All items are available to go. **Most locations now deliver and cater. $**

Chili's locations:

Escondido: 1105 W. Valley Parkway (off 15 Freeway, 1½ miles S. of 78 Frwy.)	(760) 737-5101
Encinitas: 1004 N. El Camino Real (at Olivenhain in Encinitas Ranch Shopping Center)	(760) 634-5488
La Mesa: 8285 Fletcher Parkway (1½ miles N. of 8 Frwy. at Jackson)	(619) 280-7996
Mission Valley: 4252 Camino del Rio N. (off 8 Frwy., 1 mile E. of Qualcomm Stadium)	(619) 656-2710
Rancho del Rey: 800 Paseo del Rey (1½ miles E. of 805 Frwy. on "H" St.)	(858) 634-5488
Sorrento Valley/Mira Mesa: 5969 Lusk Blvd. (1 mile off 805 Frwy. E. of La Jolla)	(858) 694-0099
Temecula: 27645 Ynez Rd. (Rancho California Rd. exit)	(909) 589-9890

GUILTLESS CHICKEN SALAD

Charbroiled chicken, mixed greens, pico de gallo, kidney beans, sprouts, green onions & no-fat Southwest dressing.

✓✓ CALORIES: Excellent Choice (270)   ✓✓ CHOLESTEROL: Excellent Choice (50 mg)
✓✓ FAT: Excellent Choice (5 g)   SODIUM: High (1475 mg)
PROTEIN: 29 g, CARBOHYDRATE: 27 g

GUILTLESS GRILLED CHICKEN SANDWICH

Charbroiled chicken with no-fat honey-mustard, lettuce, pickles & tomato. Served with fresh steamed veggies with Parmesan cheese & low-fat pasta salad (pasta salad not included in analysis).

✓ CALORIES: Good Choice (530)   ✓✓ CHOLESTEROL: Excellent Choice (45 mg)
✓✓ FAT: Excellent Choice (9 g)   SODIUM: High (2925 mg)
PROTEIN: 44 g, CARBOHYDRATE: 70 g

GUILTLESS GRILLED CHICKEN PLATTER

Chicken breast, charbroiled & served with rice, corn cobbette and fresh steamed veggies with Parmesan cheese.

✓ CALORIES: Good Choice (565)   ✓✓ CHOLESTEROL: Excellent Choice (60 mg)
✓✓ FAT: Excellent Choice (9 g)   SODIUM: High (3285 mg)
PROTEIN: 38 g, CARBOHYDRATE: 83 g

GUILTLESS PASTA PRIMAVERA

Fresh steamed veggies on penne pasta with tomato basil marinara sauce and Parmesan cheese

CALORIES: Moderate (680)   ✓ CHOLESTEROL: Good Choice (125 mg)
✓ FAT: Good Choice (15 g)   SODIUM: Moderate (760 mg)
PROTEIN: 34 g, CARBOHYDRATE: 102 g

GUILTLESS CHICKEN PASTA PRIMAVERA

Grilled chicken breast and fresh steamed veggies on penne pasta with tomato basil marinara and Parmesan cheese.

CALORIES: Moderate (785)   CHOLESTEROL: Moderate (170 mg)
✓ FAT: Good Choice (15 g)   SODIUM: High (1195 mg)
PROTEIN: 53 g, CARBOHYDRATE: 106 g

GUILTLESS CHICKEN PITA

Warm pita bread stuffed with grilled chicken, pico de gallo, lettuce, and our low-fat Southwest dressing. Served with black beans.

✓ CALORIES: Good Choice (595)   ✓✓ CHOLESTEROL: Excellent Choice (35 mg)
✓✓ FAT: Excellent Choice (9 g)   SODIUM: High (2370 mg)
PROTEIN: 42g, CARBOHYDRATE: 87g

Nutrition information supplied by Chili's.

at least 2 fruit/vegetable servings
✓ Good Choice   ✓✓ Excellent Choice

Chin's Restaurants have been voted "Best Chinese" for thirteen consecutive years and are honored by the public recognition and patronage. Our goal is to provide you with exceptional Chinese cuisine along with friendly service while surrounded by the unique ambiance of Chin's. Using only the freshest ingredients, all dishes are prepared to order to ensure quality. We are here to serve you. $-$$

CHIN'S SZECHWAN CUISINE

Chin's Szechwan Cuisine

Carlsbad: 2958 Madison St. (760) 434-7115 Oceanside: 2241 El Camino Real (760) 439-3600
Encinitas: 1506 Encinitas Bl. (760) 753-3903 Rancho Bernardo: 15721A Bernardo Ht. Pky. (858) 676-0166
Escondido: 445 N. Escondido Bl. (760) 480-4115 San Marcos: 631 S. Rancho Santa Fe Rd. (760) 591-9648
Oceanside: 4140 Oceanside Bl. (760) 631-4808 Scripps Ranch: 9978 Scripps Ranch Bl. (858) 566-0031
Vista: 600 E. Vista Way   (760) 732-3880

HUNAN CHICKEN STRIPS
Sliced chicken breast sautéed with green peppers and onions in a black bean sauce.
✓ CALORIES: Good Choice (385)   ✓ CHOLESTEROL: Good Choice (135 mg)
✓ FAT: Good Choice (14 g)   SODIUM: High (1040 mg)
EXCHANGES: 6¾ Meat (extra lean), 1½ Veg, 1½ Fat
PROTEIN: 51 g, CARBOHYDRATE: 13 g

IMPERIAL SHRIMP
✓✓ CALORIES: Excellent Choice (270)   CHOLESTEROL: Moderate (285 mg)
✓✓ FAT: Excellent Choice (10 g)*   SODIUM: High (1100 mg)
EXCHANGES: 4¼ Meat (extra lean), ¼ Bread, 1¾ Veg, 1¼ Fat
PROTEIN: 36 g, CARBOHYDRATE: 12 g

MA LA THREE FLAVOR
Jumbo shrimp, beef and chicken sautéed with baby corn, mushrooms, bamboo shoots and Chinese peas in a spicy hot sauce.
✓ CALORIES: Good Choice (415)   CHOLESTEROL: Moderate (190 mg)
✓ FAT: Good Choice (17 g)   SODIUM: Moderate (910 mg)**
EXCHANGES: 6½ Meat (extra lean), ½ Bread, 1¼ Veg, 1¾ Fat
PROTEIN: 51 g, CARBOHYDRATE: 14 g

SZECHWAN BRAISED STRING BEANS
A famous Szechwan dish! A fresh selection of string beans, dry braised with imported Chinese preserved cabbage in a Chef's spicy garlic sauce and stir-fried with or without ground pork. Analysis does not include ground pork.
✓✓ CALORIES: Excellent Choice (200)   ✓✓ CHOLESTEROL: Excellent Choice (0 mg)
✓✓ FAT: Excellent Choice (10 g)*   ✓✓ SODIUM: Excellent Choice (265 mg)**
EXCHANGES: 3 Veg, 2¾ Fat
PROTEIN: 9 g, CARBOHYDRATE: 18 g

SZECHWAN SHRIMP
✓✓ CALORIES: Excellent Choice (320)   CHOLESTEROL: Moderate (285 mg)
✓ FAT: Good Choice (11 g)*   SODIUM: Moderate (880 mg)**
EXCHANGES: 4¼ Meat (extra lean), 1¼ Bread, ¾ Veg, 1½ Fat
PROTEIN: 36 g, CARBOHYDRATE: 20 g

* Primarily unsaturated fat

** If you request no added salt

*The first Claim Jumper Restaurant opened in 1977 in the city of Los Alamitos, California. The menu features rotisserie barbecue chicken, baby back pork ribs, fresh fish, USDA Choice steaks and prime rib, salads, pastas, dinner-sized sandwiches and wood-fired pizzas. Baked goods and desserts are made fresh daily. The saloon features hand poured drinks, an excellent wine list and more than 70 domestic, imported and micro-brewed beer along with Claim Jumper's own Hefeweizen, Honey Blonde and Original Red Ales. In 2000, twenty-three years after the first restaurant opened, Claim Jumper's formula for success remains the same - **great food, friendly service and good value**. $$*

Claim Jumper Restaurant

Carlsbad: 5958 Avenida Encinas   (760) 431-0889   La Mesa: 5500 Grossmont Ctr. Dr. (619) 469-3927
Carmel Mtn. Rch: 12384 Carmel Mtn. Rd. (909) 929-3340   Temecula: 29540 Rancho Cal. Rd. (909) 694-6887
Laguna Hills (Orange County): 25332 McIntyre St. (949) 768-0662

NORTHERN HALIBUT DINNER

*Fresh Northern halibut lightly brushed with butter and garnished with fresh fruit.
Served with produce bar or soup and your choice of accompaniment (produce bar, soup,
accompaniment and tarter sauce not included in analysis). Other fresh fish are available.*

✓ CALORIES: Good Choice (475)   ✓ CHOLESTEROL: Good Choice (130 mg)
✓ FAT: Good Choice (19 g)   ✓✓ SODIUM: Excellent Choice (295 mg)**
EXCHANGES: 6 Meat (extra lean), ½ Fruit, 2¼ Fat
PROTEIN: 66 g, CARBOHYDRATE: 8 g

TURKEY BURGER – SPECIAL REQUEST 🍎

*Fresh ground turkey, roasted pepper and charbroiled tomatoes, spring greens,
and served with apple garnish. <u>Request no mayonnaise and no cheese</u>.*

CALORIES: Moderate (700)   ✓ CHOLESTEROL: Good Choice (110 mg)
✓ FAT: Good Choice (15 g)   SODIUM: Moderate (900 mg)**
EXCHANGES: 7¾ Meat (extra lean), 3½ Bread, ½ Veg, 1½ Fruit, 2¾ Fat
PROTEIN: 65 g, CARBOHYDRATE: 78 g

MAHI MAHI DINNER

*Fresh mahi mahi lightly brushed with butter, topped with tomato onion relish, and garnished with fresh fruit.
Served with produce bar or soup and your choice of accompaniment (produce bar, soup,
accompaniment and tarter sauce not included in analysis). Other fresh fish are available.*

✓ CALORIES: Good Choice (480)   CHOLESTEROL: Moderate (260 mg)
✓ FAT: Good Choice (19 g)   SODIUM: Moderate (730 mg)**
EXCHANGES: 5 Meat (extra lean), ½ Veg, ½ Fruit, 3¼ Fat
PROTEIN: 60 g, CARBOHYDRATE: 15 g

TOMATO BASIL PIZZA (½ PIZZA) – SPECIAL REQUEST

Basil, mozzarella and goat cheese. <u>Request less mozarella cheese</u> (2 oz). Analysis is for ½ of a pizza.

✓ CALORIES: Good Choice (560)   ✓✓ CHOLESTEROL: Excellent Choice (30 mg)
✓ FAT: Good Choice (20 g)   SODIUM: Moderate (740 mg)**
EXCHANGES: 1¼ Meat, 4½ Bread, ¼ Veg, 3¼ Fat
PROTEIN: 20 g, CARBOHYDRATE: 73 g

CHOPPED CHINESE CHICKEN SALAD (½ SALAD) – SPECIAL REQUEST 🍎

*Chopped mixed greens tossed with crispy angel hair pasta, almonds, scallions, cilantro and chicken breast.
<u>Request dressing on the side</u>. Analysis does not include dressing, fried wontons or cheese toast and is for ½ salad.*

✓ CALORIES: Good Choice (390)   ✓ CHOLESTEROL: Good Choice (110 mg)
✓ FAT: Good Choice (14 g)   ✓✓ SODIUM: Excellent Choice (245 mg)**
EXCHANGES: 6 Meat (extra lean), ½ Bread, 2 Veg, 1¾ Fat
PROTEIN: 47 g, CARBOHYDRATE: 20 g

🍎 at least 2 fruit/vegetable servings

     ✓ Good Choice   ✓✓ Excellent Choice

For family dining, Coco's Café & Bakery is in a class by itself, providing just the right setting: friendly service in a casual, comfortable atmosphere and a menu that emphasizes quality, freshness and value. Breakfast, lunch and dinner selections cover a wide range of choices, from fresh vegetable omelettes to terrific pastas and fresh fish. Fresh baked muffins, cakes, and a wide variety of fresh baked pies, including delicious no-sugar-added pies, are available all day long. Coco's Cafes & Bakeries are located throughout California. Hours vary by location. $

Coco's Café & Bakery
22 San Diego are locations

EGG WHITE OMELETTE – SPECIAL REQUEST
Stuffed with fresh spinach, tomato, onion, fresh basil and feta cheese, and served with fresh fruit. <u>Request no feta</u>.
- ✓ CALORIES: Good Choice (415)
- ✓✓ CHOLESTEROL: Excellent Choice (0 mg)
- ✓✓ FAT: Excellent Choice (4 g)
-   SODIUM: Moderate (740 mg)

EXCHANGES: 2½ Meat, 4 Bread, 1 Fruit
PROTEIN: 30 g, CARBOHYDRATE: 69 g

TURKEY BURGER
A seasoned turkey burger served on a whole-wheat bun with creamy roasted garlic dressing. Served with coleslaw.
- ✓ CALORIES: Good Choice (550)
- ✓ CHOLESTEROL: Good Choice (95 mg)
-   FAT: Moderate (32 g)
-   SODIUM: High (1380 mg)

EXCHANGES: 4 Meat, 2 Bread, 2 Fat
PROTEIN: 33 g, CARBOHYDRATE: 31 g

GARDEN BURGER
A vegetarian indulgence: meatless patty, red onion, tomato, avocado, lettuce and spicy horseradish sauce on a bakery bun. Served with coleslaw.
- ✓ CALORIES: Good Choice (565)
- ✓✓ CHOLESTEROL: Excellent Choice (45 mg)
-   FAT: Moderate (25 g)
-   SODIUM: High (1380 mg)

EXCHANGES: 1 Meat, 5 Bread, 1 Fat
PROTEIN: 17 g, CARBOHYDRATE: 72 g

SOUP & SALAD COMBO
Today's soup or Cream of Broccoli soup, green garden salad and freshly baked bread.
- ✓ CALORIES: Good Choice (375)
- ✓✓ CHOLESTEROL: Excellent Choice (20 mg)
- ✓ FAT: Good Choice (16 g)
-   SODIUM: High (1810 mg)

EXCHANGES: 1 Meat, 3 Bread, 1 Fat
PROTEIN: 12 g, CARBOHYDRATE: 43 g

SPAGHETTI
with marinara sauce.
-   CALORIES: Moderate (640)
- ✓✓ CHOLESTEROL: Excellent Choice (5 mg)
- ✓ FAT: Good Choice (14 g)
-   SODIUM: Moderate (930 mg)

EXCHANGES: 6½ Bread, 1 Veg, 2 Fat
PROTEIN: 20 g, CARBOHYDRATE: 108 g

FRESH FISH
glazed with teriyaki on sautéed spinach and served with rice and vegetables.
- ✓ CALORIES: Good Choice (560)
- ✓ CHOLESTEROL: Good Choice (90 mg)
- ✓✓ FAT: Excellent Choice (6 g)
-   SODIUM: High (1830 mg)

EXCHANGES: 5 Meat (extra lean), 5 Bread
PROTEIN: 49 g, CARBOHYDRATE: 78 g

Nutrition information supplied by Coco's.

* Primarily unsaturated fat
** If you request no added salt

When cardiac surgeon Pat Daily couldn't find a quick-service restaurant that prepared good-tasting, low-fat food -- the way he likes to eat -- he opened his own! All of Daily's menu items contain fewer than 10 grams of fat and/or less than 20% of the calories from fat. Voted <u>Best Healthy Restaurant</u> by Channel 8's Unknown Eater and the San Diego Reader, Daily's uses the freshest, highest quality ingredients and publishes the <u>nutritional content on all the menu items</u>. The menu includes an array of salads, sandwiches, hot pasta, grilled fish, fruit smoothies, and even low-fat desserts. Below are 6 of the most popular menu items. $

Daily's Restaurant

8915 Towne Centre Drive, San Diego, CA 92122   Ph. (858) 453-1112   Fax (858) 453-1393

3-BEAN & CORN CHILI (VEGETARIAN)
with brown rice, a dollop of yogurt, and green salad.

✓✓ CALORIES: Excellent Choice (285)   ✓✓ CHOLESTEROL: Excellent Choice (0 mg)
✓✓ FAT: Excellent Choice (3½ g)*   ✓ SODIUM: Good Choice (350 mg)
EXCHANGES: 3 Bread, ¾ Veg, ½ Fat
PROTEIN: 13 g, CARBOHYDRATE: 53 g

BAJA FLAVORS PASTA SALAD
Penne pasta, vegetables, kidney and black beans in a spicy Baja dressing.

✓✓ CALORIES:Excellent Choice (350)   ✓✓ CHOLESTEROL: Excellent Choice (0 mg)
✓✓ FAT: Excellent Choice (8 g)*   ✓ SODIUM: Good Choice (380 mg)
EXCHANGES: 3½ Bread, 1¼ Veg, 1¼ Fat
PROTEIN: 16 g, CARBOHYDRATE: 55 g

GARDEN VEGETABLE BURGER ☉
Served on a whole grain honey bun.

✓ CALORIES: Good Choice (390)   ✓✓ CHOLESTEROL: Excellent Choice (0 mg)
✓✓ FAT: Excellent Choice (7 g)*   ✓ SODIUM: Good Choice (440 mg)
EXCHANGES: 3 Bread, 3¼ Veg, 1 Fat
PROTEIN: 18 g, CARBOHYDRATE: 69 g

DAILY'S SPICY GRILLED CHICKEN PIZZA ☉
Grilled chicken & red onions, peppers, spicy tomato marinade with skim milk mozzarella cheese on our whole wheat pizza crust.

✓ CALORIES: Good Choice (465)   ✓✓ CHOLESTEROL: Excellent Choice (60 mg)
✓✓ FAT: Excellent Choice (9 g)   ✓ SODIUM: Good Choice (445 mg)
EXCHANGES: 2½ Meat, 3 Bread, 2 Veg, ½ Milk
PROTEIN: 38 g, CARBOHYDRATE: 53 g

CAJUN CATFISH
with black beans, brown rice and green salad.

✓ CALORIES: Good Choice (400)   ✓✓ CHOLESTEROL: Excellent Choice (70 mg)
✓✓ FAT: Excellent Choice (6 g)*   ✓ SODIUM: Good Choice (430 mg)
EXCHANGES: 2¾ Meat, 2 Bread, ½ Veg
PROTEIN: 33 g, CARBOHYDRATE: 47 g

DAILY'S FUDGY BROWNIE SUNDAE†
CALORIES: Moderate Choice (260)   ✓✓ CHOLESTEROL: Excellent Choice (15 mg)
✓✓ FAT: Excellent Choice (2 g)*   SODIUM: Moderate Choice (290 mg)
EXCHANGES: ½ Milk, 2 Bread, 1 Fruit, ¼ Fat
PROTEIN: 10 g, CARBOHYDRATE: 60 g

Nutrition information supplied by Daily's.

---

† Side dish guidelines are 1/3 of entree guidelines   ☉ at least 2 fruit/vegetable servings

          ✓ Good Choice ✓✓ Excellent Choice

When you are looking for traditional Mexican cuisine that focuses on the tastes of Mexico City and its surrounding regions, the place to go is El Callejon. At El Callejon, we feature family recipes that have been used for more than seven centuries. We also offer more than 380 brands of tequila to choose from for making your favorite margarita to enjoy on our spacious patio out back. $$

El Callejon Restaurant

345 South Coast Highway 101, Encinitas, CA 92024   (760) 634-2793   www.el-callejon.com

---

CAMARONES A LA MEXICANA

*Giant shrimp in a tomato sauce. Served with rice and salad
(not included in analysis, see analysis for rice below).*

✓✓ CALORIES: Excellent Choice (245) CHOLESTEROL: Moderate (295 mg)
✓✓ FAT: Excellent Choice (7 g)* SODIUM: High (1525 mg)
EXCHANGES: 4½ Meat (extra lean), 1½ Veg, 1 Fat
PROTEIN: 34 g, CARBOHYDRATE: 13 g

PESCADO ZARANDEADO

*Halibut marinated in a lime-chili sauce. Served with rice and a
salad (not included in analysis, see analysis for rice below).*

✓ CALORIES: Good Choice (390) ✓✓ CHOLESTEROL: Excellent Choice (70 mg)
✓ FAT: Good Choice (19 g)* SODIUM: High (1065 mg)
EXCHANGES: 5½ Meat (extra lean), 2¾ Fat
PROTEIN: 49 g, CARBOHYDRATE: 3 g

PESCADO A LA PARRILLA

Red snapper cooked on the grill. Served with rice (not included in analysis, see analysis for rice below)

✓✓ CALORIES: Excellent Choice (225) ✓ CHOLESTEROL: Good Choice (85 mg)
✓✓ FAT: Excellent Choice (3 g)* ✓✓ SODIUM: Excellent Choice (145 mg)**
EXCHANGES: 6¾ Meat (extra lean)
PROTEIN: 46 g, CARBOHYDRATE: 0 g

RICE *(6 OZ)*: CAL: 330, FAT: 3 g*, CHOL: 5 mg, SOD: 10 mg; EXCH: 4¾ Bread, ½ Fat; PROT: 8 g, CARB: 73 g

* Primarily unsaturated fat
** If you request no added salt

Since 1940 El Indio has been serving San Diego the best quality Mexican food at affordable prices. Ralph Romo Pesqueira, Sr. started his tiny tortilla factory, patting out by hand thirty dozen tortillas a day. El Indio's original location on India Street still remains, along with one additional location. $

El Indio Mexican Restaurant

3695 India Street, San Diego   (619) 299-0333
409 "F" St. *Gaslamp Quarter,* San Diego   (619) 239-8151

BEAN TOSTADA
Beans, lettuce, tomato, cheese and salsa.
Analysis does not include tostada shell, sour cream or guacamole.

✓✓ CALORIES: Excellent Choice (325)   ✓✓ CHOLESTEROL: Excellent Choice (30 mg)
✓ FAT: Good Choice (13 g)   SODIUM: Moderate (665 mg)
EXCHANGES: 1½ Meat, 2 Bread, ½ Veg, 1¾ Fat
PROTEIN: 18 g, CARBOHYDRATE: 33 g

BURRITO INDIO ⚘
A whole wheat tortilla filled with specialty seasoned zucchini, corn, onion, beans and jack cheese.

✓ CALORIES: Good Choice (490)   ✓✓ CHOLESTEROL: Excellent Choice (25 mg)
✓ FAT: Good Choice (17 g)   ✓ SODIUM: Good Choice (585 mg)
EXCHANGES: 1¼ Meat (extra lean), 4 Bread, 1 Veg, 2¾ Fat
PROTEIN: 20 g, CARBOHYDRATE: 65 g

VEGGIE TACO – SPECIAL REQUEST ⚘
A corn tortilla filled with seasoned fresh mashed potatoes, green onion and spices.
Garnished with lettuce, tomato and jack cheese. Request soft tortilla, not fried.

✓✓ CALORIES: Excellent Choice (245)   ✓✓ CHOLESTEROL: Excellent Choice (20 mg)
✓✓ FAT: Excellent Choice (8 g)   ✓✓ SODIUM: Excellent Choice (165 mg)**
EXCHANGES: ½ Meat, 2¼ Bread, ¾ Veg, 1¼ Fat
PROTEIN: 8 g, CARBOHYDRATE: 38 g

⚘ at least 2 fruit/vegetable servings
✓ Good Choice   ✓✓ Excellent Choice

Once known as Rock Lobster, Eva's has been remodeled to give a bright interior with colorful red and green accents, along with hand-painted flowers, murals, and handpicked decorations to add to the vibrant, warm, inviting atmosphere. Eva's offers traditional Mexican cuisine with a special California flair. Please visit us soon. $

Eva's Cocina & Cantina 6690 Mission Gorge Rd., San Diego, CA 92120 (619) 284-5874

CAMARONES RANCHEROS
Mouth watering shrimp, bell pepper, onions and tomatoes sautéed in our special ranchero salsa. Served with black beans and Mexican rice (see analyses below).
- ✓✓ CALORIES: Excellent Choice (235)
- ✓✓ FAT: Excellent Choice (7 g)*
- CHOLESTEROL: Moderate (275 mg)
- SODIUM: Moderate (680 mg)**

EXCHANGES: 4¼ Meat (extra lean), 1½ Veg, 1 Fat
PROTEIN: 32 g, CARBOHYDRATE: 11 g

CHICKEN AND BLACK BEAN TOSTADA
Chicken, black beans, lettuce, tomato, cilantro & salsa ranchero. Tortilla shell not included in analysis.
- ✓✓ CALORIES: Excellent Choice (315)
- ✓ FAT: Good Choice (12 g)
- ✓✓ CHOLESTEROL: Excellent Choice (45 mg)
- SODIUM: Moderate (945 mg)**

EXCHANGES: 2½ Meat, ¾ Bread, 1¾ Veg, ¾ Fat
PROTEIN: 26 g, CARBOHYDRATE: 27 g

CHICKEN ENCHILADAS VERDES
Chicken enchiladas topped with tomatillo salsa and garnished with lettuce and tomato. Served with black beans and Mexican rice (see analyses below).
- ✓✓ CALORIES: Excellent Choice (310)
- ✓ FAT: Good Choice (13 g)
- ✓✓ CHOLESTEROL: Excellent Choice (40 mg)
- SODIUM: Moderate (750 mg)**

EXCHANGES: 2 Meat, 1½ Bread, ¾ Veg, 1½ Fat
PROTEIN: 19 g, CARBOHYDRATE: 30 g

SHRIMP TACOS DE FRANCO PLATE
Two tacos stuffed with Franco's special sautéed shrimp, squash, celery, chiles and spices. Served with black beans and Mexican rice (see analyses below).
- ✓ CALORIES: Good Choice (470)
- ✓✓ FAT: Excellent Choice (9 g)*
- CHOLESTEROL: Moderate (250 mg)
- SODIUM: Moderate (975 mg)**

EXCHANGES: 3¾ Meat, 3¼ Bread, 1½ Veg, ¾ Fruit, 1¼ Fat
PROTEIN: 35 g, CARBOHYDRATE: 65 g

FISH TACO ESPECIALES
Two flaky white fillets wrapped into hot corn tortillas, then topped with shredded cabbage, tomatoes, cheese, and our own special sauce. Served with black beans and Mexican rice (see analyses below),.
- ✓ CALORIES: Good Choice (545)
- ✓ FAT: Good Choice (20 g)
- ✓✓ CHOLESTEROL: Excellent Choice (75 mg)
- SODIUM: Moderate (725 mg)**

EXCHANGES: 3½ Meat, 3½ Bread, 1 Veg, ¼ Milk, 3¼ Fat
PROTEIN: 34 g, CARBOHYDRATE: 60 g

VEGETARIAN TAMALES
Moist and tender tamales stuffed with fresh seasoned vegetables, topped with Eva's special ranchero salsa. Served with black beans and Mexican rice (see analyses below). Contains no lard!
- CALORIES: Moderate (650)
- ✓✓ FAT: Excellent Choice (10 g)*
- ✓✓ CHOLESTEROL: Excellent Choice (0 mg)
- SODIUM: Moderate (670 mg)**

EXCHANGES: 7½ Bread, 2 Veg, ¾ Fat
PROTEIN: 17 g, CARBOHYDRATE: 129 g

RICE *(4 oz)* CAL: 155, FAT: 4 g*, CHOL: <2 mg, SOD: 580 mg; EXC: 1¾ Br., ¼ Veg, ½ Fat; PROT: 3 g, CARB: 27 g
BLACK BEANS *(4 oz)* CAL: 295, FAT: 2 g*, CHOL: 0, SOD: 2 mg; EXC.: 1¼ Meat, 3½ Br.; PRO: 19 g, CARB: 52 g

* Primarily unsaturated fat

** If you request no added salt

Healthy Dining in San Diego **65**

The Fish Market - casual style dining in a clean and comfortable atmosphere. The freshness and quality of our fish speaks for itself. We also offer a retail market where you can select from our extensive variety of fresh fish and menu items for take out. Our entire staff is committed to providing you, our guest, with the utmost in courteous, attentive service and superior seafood knowledge. Your experience is our number one priority; you are the most important person in our restaurants! $$-$$$

The Fish Market

640 Via de la Valle, Del Mar, CA 92075   (858) 755-2277
750 N. Harbor Dr., San Diego, CA 92101   (619) 232-3474

PASTA ANGELICA WITH SEAFOOD – SPECIAL REQUEST ♨
Angel hair pasta tossed with scallops, pesto, garlic and tomatoes. <u>Request less oil (¼ oz) and no cheese.</u>
  CALORIES: Moderate (610)   ✓✓ CHOLESTEROL: Excellent Choice (40 mg)
  ✓ FAT: Good Choice (17 g)*   ✓ SODIUM: Good Choice (540 mg)**
EXCHANGES: 2¾ Meat (extra lean), 4¼ Bread, 2¼ Veg, 3 Fat
PROTEIN: 33 g, CARBOHYDRATE: 80 g

MAZATLAN PRAWNS – SPECIAL REQUEST ♨
Mesquite charbroiled shrimp with jalapeno peppers, onion, bell pepper and tomato. <u>Request less oil and butter (¼ oz each).</u>
✓ CALORIES: Good Choice (390)   CHOLESTEROL: High (350 mg)
✓ FAT: Good Choice (15 g)   SODIUM: Moderate (740 mg)**
EXCHANGES: 5 Meat (extra lean), 2¾ Veg, 3 Fat
PROTEIN: 38 g, CARBOHYDRATE: 15 g

FRESH BAJA HALIBUT – SPECIAL REQUEST
Mesquite charbroiled halibut with black beans, garlic, ginger and soy sauce. <u>Request less olive and sesame oils (¼ oz each).</u>
✓ CALORIES: Good Choice (505)   ✓ CHOLESTEROL: Good Choice (90 mg)
  FAT: Moderate (21 g)*   SODIUM: High (1780 mg)
EXCHANGES: 8 Meat (extra lean), ¼ Bread, ½ Veg, 2¾ Fat
PROTEIN: 63 g, CARBOHYDRATE: 12 g

GRILLED SWORDFISH WITH CILANTRO PESTO
Grilled swordfish served with cilantro pesto sauce.
✓ CALORIES: Good Choice (420)   ✓ CHOLESTEROL: Good Choice (95 mg)
  FAT: Moderate (24 g)*   ✓✓ SODIUM: Excellent Choice (255 mg)**
EXCHANGES: 5¼ Meat, 3 Fat
PROTEIN: 47 g, CARBOHYDRATE: 1 g

WARM SPINACH SALAD WITH FETA CHEESE – SPECIAL REQUEST ♨
<u>Request less oil(1 Tbs).</u>
✓✓ CALORIES: Excellent Choice (300)   ✓✓ CHOLESTEROL: Excellent Choice (25 mg)
  ✓ FAT: Good Choice (20 g)   SODIUM: High (1325 mg)
EXCHANGES: ½ Meat, ¾ Bread, 1¼ Veg, 3½ Fat
PROTEIN: 17 g, CARBOHYDRATE: 9 g

SHELLFISH MARINARA (½ ORDER) ♨
Linguine with clams topped with marinara sauce and grated romano cheese. Analysis is for ½ full order.
✓ CALORIES: Good Choice (480)   ✓✓ CHOLESTEROL: Excellent Choice (45 mg)
✓ FAT: Good Choice (13 g)   SODIUM: High (1445 mg)
EXCHANGES: 2 Meat (extra lean), 2¼ Bread, 4 Veg, 1½ Fat
PROTEIN: 26 g, CARBOHYDRATE: 63 g

♨ at least 2 fruit/vegetable servings for entrée, 1 for side dish

      ✓ Good Choice   ✓✓ Excellent Choice

The Fish Merchant was established in 1980 in San Diego's East County. Boasting the feel of a charming Boston style fish house, it has colorful salt-water aquariums to complement the nautical décor. Its casual atmosphere and beautiful bar attract diners of all ages. Specializing in fresh charbroiled fish, The Fish Merchant also offers wonderful salads, chicken, steak and prime rib. $$

The Fish Merchant

7005 Navajo Road, San Diego, CA 92119 (619) 462-3811

All dinners include choices of accompaniments (not included in analysis). We recommend homemade fish chowder or dinner salad, baked potato (plain) or sliced tomatoes and a fresh vegetable (steamed).

SEAFOOD BROCHETTE
Fresh fish, scallops and shrimp charbroiled on a skewer with fresh vegetables.
✓✓ CALORIES: Excellent Choice (285)   CHOLESTEROL: Moderate (170 mg)
✓✓ FAT: Excellent Choice (7 g)*   ✓ SODIUM: Good Choice (340 mg)**
EXCHANGES: 6½ Meat (extra lean), ½ Veg, ½ Fat
PROTEIN: 49 g, CARBOHYDRATE: 5 g

HAWAIIAN CHICKEN BROCHETTE
Tender white meat marinated in our teriyaki sauce and charbroiled with fresh vegetables.
✓ CALORIES: Good Choice (450)   ✓ CHOLESTEROL: Good Choice (150 mg)
✓✓ FAT: Excellent Choice (6 g)   SODIUM: High (3365 mg)
EXCHANGES: 7¾ Meat (extra lean), ½ Veg, 1¼ Fruit
PROTEIN: 58 g, CARBOHYDRATE: 38 g

SALMON MARINATED IN RED GINGER SOY VINAIGRETTE
Charbroiled fresh salmon marinated in a red ginger vinaigrette sauce.
✓✓ CALORIES: Excellent Choice (325)   ✓ CHOLESTEROL: Good Choice (110 mg)
✓ FAT: Good Choice (15 g)*   ✓ SODIUM: Good Choice (515 mg)**
EXCHANGES: 5 Meat, ½ Fat
PROTEIN: 40 g, CARBOHYDRATE: 3 g

CAPTAIN SALAD
Crabmeat, bay shrimp, artichoke heart, egg, tomato, bell pepper, carrots and olives on a bed of lettuce with your choice of dressing (dressing not included in analysis). Low calorie dressing available.
✓✓ CALORIES: Excellent Choice (350)   CHOLESTEROL: High (390 mg)
✓ FAT: Good Choice (11 g)   SODIUM: High (1475 mg)
EXCHANGES: 6¼ Meat (extra lean), 3½ Veg, 2¼ Fat
PROTEIN: 48 g, CARBOHYDRATE: 21 g

MANHATTAN FISH CHOWDER (CUP)†
✓✓ CALORIES: Excellent Choice (75)   ✓✓ CHOLESTEROL: Excellent Choice (15 mg)
✓✓ FAT: Excellent Choice (2 g)*   SODIUM: Moderate (380 mg)**
EXCHANGES: ¾ Meat (extra lean), 1 Veg, ¼ Fat
PROTEIN: 6 g, CARBOHYDRATE: 6 g

* Primarily unsaturated fat

** If you request no added salt

† Side dish guidelines are 1/3 of entree guidelines

Healthy Dining in San Diego **67**

We invite you to come and experience the Fortune Cookie Restaurant and its exquisite authentic Chinese cooking with a touch of French influence. We proudly bring you the most unique gourmet experience, specializing in Hunan and Szechuan cuisine. We are also able to prepare our dishes in accord with special dietary requirements. Just discuss your requests with our staff. $$

Fortune Cookie

16425 Bernardo Center Dr., San Diego 92128 (858) 451-8958

CLEOPATRA CHICKEN – SPECIAL REQUEST 🍎

Sliced chicken stir-fried with snow peas, carrots, blackwood mushrooms, bamboo shoots and water chestnuts in a rich tomato dynasty sauce with a touch of soy sauce. <u>Request less oil in preparation of chicken</u> (¼ tsp).

✓ CALORIES: Good Choice (580)   ✓✓ CHOLESTEROL: Excellent Choice (0 mg)
✓ FAT: Good Choice (11 g)   SODIUM: High (1300 mg)
EXCHANGES: 11 Meat (extra lean), ¼ Bread, 5¼ Veg, ¼ Fat
PROTEIN: 85 g, CARBOHYDRATE: 33 g

STIR-FRIED SEA BASS – SPECIAL REQUEST

Tender boneless filets of white sea bass stir-fried with sliced scallions, fresh mushrooms, sweet snow peas and ginger with a delicate white wine sauce and a kiss of fresh garlic. <u>Request less oil when preparing fish</u> (¼ tsp).

✓✓ CALORIES: Excellent Choice (350)   ✓ CHOLESTEROL: Good Choice (120 mg)
✓✓ FAT: Excellent Choice (7 g)*   SODIUM: High (1185 mg)
EXCHANGES: 7¾ Meat (extra lean), 2 Veg, ¼ Fat
PROTEIN: 58 g, CARBOHYDRATE: 11 g

CHI-YAO SHRIMP – SPECIAL REQUEST 🍎

Tender Gulf shrimp sautéed in a white garlic sauce with fresh broccoli, carrots and snow peas with a touch of white wine. <u>Request less oil</u> (¼ tsp).

✓✓ CALORIES: Excellent Choice (300)   CHOLESTEROL: High (390 mg)
✓✓ FAT: Excellent Choice (4 g)*   SODIUM: High (1485 mg)
EXCHANGES: 5¾ Meat (extra lean), 3½ Veg, ¼ Fat
PROTEIN: 48 g, CARBOHYDRATE: 18 g

BUDDHA'S DELIGHT – SPECIAL REQUEST 🍎

A delightful combination of nine fresh vegetables lightly stir-fried in your choice of a brown garlic sauce or white wine sauce. Analysis for white wine sauce. Brown sauce adds 30 calories. <u>Request less oil</u> (¼ tsp).

✓✓ CALORIES: Excellent Choice (225)   ✓✓ CHOLESTEROL: Excellent Choice (0 mg)
✓✓ FAT: Excellent Choice (3 g)*   SODIUM: High (4415 mg)
EXCHANGES: ¾ Bread, 6 Veg, ¼ Fat
PROTEIN: 11 g, CARBOHYDRATE: 44 g

MOO GOO GAI PAN – SPECIAL REQUEST 🍎

Tender slices of chicken stir-fried with fresh broccoli, snow peas, mushrooms and bamboo shoots in a light white wine sauce with a touch of garlic. <u>Request less oil</u> (¼ tsp).

✓ CALORIES: Good Choice (525)   CHOLESTEROL: Moderate (215 mg)
✓ FAT: Good Choice (11 g)   SODIUM: High (4420 mg)
EXCHANGES: 11 Meat (extra lean), 3¼ Veg, ¼ Fat
PROTEIN: 11 g, CARBOHYDRATE: 44 g

BEAN CURD WITH BROCCOLI – SPECIAL REQUEST 🍎

Sautéed bean curd stir-fried with fresh broccoli and bamboo shoots in a brown sauce. <u>Request steamed tofu</u>.

✓ CALORIES: Good Choice (415)   ✓✓ CHOLESTEROL: Excellent Choice (0 mg)
✓ FAT: Good Choice (17 g)   SODIUM: High (1795 mg)
EXCHANGES: 5¼ Meat, 1 Bread, 2 Veg
PROTEIN: 46 g, CARBOHYDRATE: 32 g

🍎 at least 2 fruit/vegetable servings
✓ Good Choice ✓✓ Excellent Choice

French Gourmet

960 Turquoise Street, San Diego, CA 92109 (858) 488-1725

GRILLED SALMON ☼

Grilled filet of fresh salmon, served with papaya salsa, steamed seasonal vegetables and herbed rice. Rice not included in analysis.

✓ CALORIES: Good Choice (385) ✓ CHOLESTEROL: Good Choice (105 mg)
✓ FAT: Good Choice (17 g)* ✓✓ SODIUM: Excellent Choice (205 mg)**
EXCHANGES: 5 Meat, 1½ Veg, ½ Fruit, 1 Fat
PROTEIN: 42 g, CARBOHYDRATE: 15 g

MEDITERRANEAN-STYLE CHICKEN SAUSAGE ☼

Chicken sausage with lots of Italian flavor - sun-dried tomatoes, pine nuts, basil, parsley, bell peppers and white wine, served with rosemary potatoes and steamed seasonal vegetables.

✓ CALORIES: Good Choice (475) CHOLESTEROL: Moderate (160 mg)
✓ FAT: Good Choice (15 g) SODIUM: High (2990 mg)
EXCHANGES: 6 Meat, 1¾ Bread, 1¼ Veg, 1 Fat
PROTEIN: 46 g, CARBOHYDRATE: 42 g

RATATOUILLE ☼

with steamed seasonal vegetables and your choice of herbed rice or couscous. Analysis is for rice; couscous similar.

✓ CALORIES: Good Choice (570) ✓✓ CHOLESTEROL: Excellent Choice (0 mg)
✓✓ FAT: Excellent Choice (9 g)* SODIUM: High (2010 mg)
EXCHANGES: 4¾ Bread, 7½ Veg, 1½ Fat
PROTEIN: 16 g, CARBOHYDRATE: 111 g

SEARED AHI ☼

Ahi tuna steak served with an Asian slaw, cucumber salad and wasabi dipping sauce (wasabi sauce not included in analysis).

✓ CALORIES: Good Choice (585) ✓ CHOLESTEROL: Good Choice (90 mg)
FAT: Moderate (30 g)* SODIUM: High (1320 mg)
EXCHANGES: 6¼ Meat (extra lean), ¼ Bread, 2 Veg, 5½ Fat
PROTEIN: 52 g, CARBOHYDRATE: 25 g

SALAD NICOISE ☼

Traaitional French salad - mixed greens tossed with potatoes, green beans, tuna, boiled egg and olives, topped with anchovies. Dressing not included in analysis.

✓ CALORIES: Good Choice (385) CHOLESTEROL: Moderate (300 mg)
✓ FAT: Good Choice (11 g) SODIUM: High (1030 mg)
EXCHANGES: 2 Meat (extra lean), 1¾ Bread, 1¾ Veg, ¾ Fat
PROTEIN: 27 g, CARBOHYDRATE: 43 g

* Primarily unsaturated fat
** If you request no added salt

French Market Grille is a charming bistro specializing in affordable French-country cooking. French Market Grille was awarded top honors in the 1999 Zagat guide, being described as a "French food haven" and a "distinctive romantic European bistro with the freshest ingredients." French Market Grille is open every day for lunch and dinner. A catering menu is also available, bringing award-winning bistro cuisine to the office, home and special events. $$

French Market Grille

15717 Bernardo Heights Parkway, San Diego, CA 92128 (858) 485-8055

VEGETABLE RAVIOLI WITH RATATOUILLE PROVENCALE ☙
Vegetable raviolis with ratatouille provencale.

✓ CALORIES: Good Choice (395)   ✓✓ CHOLESTEROL: Excellent Choice (60 mg)
✓✓ FAT: Excellent Choice (10 g)*   ✓✓ SODIUM: Excellent Choice (255 mg)**
EXCHANGES: 2½ Bread, 2¾ Veg, ¾ Fat
PROTEIN: 21 g, CARBOHYDRATE: 56 g

ROASTED SCALLOPS A LA NAGE WITH SPINACH – SPECIAL REQUEST ☙
Sea scallops and spinach with a red pepper coulis. Request less oil (1 tsp).

✓ CALORIES: Good Choice (595)   CHOLESTEROL: Moderate (215 mg)
✓ FAT: Good Choice (18 g)*   SODIUM: High (1005 mg)
EXCHANGES: 5½ Meat (extra lean), 5½ Veg, 1¾ Fat
PROTEIN: 89 g, CARBOHYDRATE: 32 g

PACIFIC COAST BOUILLABAISSE ☙
Traditional French seafood soup. Analysis is for soup only. Rouille Croustade not included in analysis.

✓ CALORIES: Good Choice (385)   CHOLESTEROL: Moderate (200 mg)
✓ FAT: Good Choice (14 g)*   ✓ SODIUM: Good Choice (400 mg)**
EXCHANGES: 4¼ Meat (extra lean), 1¼ Bread, ¾ Veg, 1½ Fat
PROTEIN: 41 g, CARBOHYDRATE: 28 g

SEABASS TAPENADE WITH FENNEL IN A CITRUS SAUCE ☙
Seabass baked with spinach and fennel in parchment paper.

✓ CALORIES: Good Choice (400)   ✓ CHOLESTEROL: Good Choice (95 mg)
✓ FAT: Good Choice (14 g)*   ✓✓ SODIUM: Excellent Choice (255 mg)**
EXCHANGES: 4 Meat (extra lean), 3½ Veg, 1¾ Fat
PROTEIN: 48 g, CARBOHYDRATE: 19 g

OVEN ROASTED FREE-RANGE CHICKEN
Oven roasted free-range chicken with chanterelles in natural juice.

✓✓ CALORIES: Excellent Choice (345)   ✓ CHOLESTEROL: Good Choice (135 mg)
✓ FAT: Good Choice (11 g)   ✓✓ SODIUM: Excellent Choice (145 mg)**
EXCHANGES: 6¾ Meat (extra lean), 2 Veg, 1 Fat
PROTEIN: 51 g, CARBOHYDRATE: 10 g

☙ at least 2 fruit/vegetable servings
✓ Good Choice   ✓✓ Excellent Choice

It is our love of the business and your satisfaction that bring our greatest reward. We are delighted to serve you, and our hospitality comes from our hearts. Our recipes are part of our family heritage, handed down through many generations. Your meals are prepared from the finest, freshest ingredients we can find, all meeting our highest standards of excellence. We're sure you will be delighted with this authentic dining experience, and we welcome you anytime! $

The Greek Palace

8878 Clairemont Mesa Boulevard, Suite A, San Diego, CA 92111 (858) 573-0155

TABOULEH SALAD

Chopped parsley, onions, tomatoes and bulgar wheat, mixed in a special dressing.

CALORIES: Moderate (705)
✓✓ CHOLESTEROL: Excellent Choice (0 mg)
✓ FAT: Good Choice (17 g)*
✓ SODIUM: Good Choice (400 mg)**
EXCHANGES: 7 Bread, 3 Veg, ¼ Fruit, 2¾ Fat
PROTEIN: 23 g, CARBOHYDRATE: 128 g

HUMMUS SANDWICH

Garbanzo beans whipped with garlic, lemon juice and tahini, served on a pita with lettuce, tomatoes and pickles.

✓ CALORIES: Good Choice (395)
✓✓ CHOLESTEROL: Excellent Choice (0 mg)
✓✓ FAT: Excellent Choice (6 g)*
SODIUM: High (1250 mg)
EXCHANGES: ½ Meat, 5¼ Bread, ½ Veg, 1 Fat
PROTEIN: 18 g, CARBOHYDRATE: 71 g

VEGETARIAN DOLMADES

Grape leaves rolled with rice and tomato, and then topped with tomato sauce. Analysis is for 5 stuffed leaves.

✓✓ CALORIES: Excellent Choice (255)
✓✓ CHOLESTEROL: Excellent Choice (0 mg)
✓✓ FAT: Excellent Choice (8 g)*
✓ SODIUM: Good Choice (565 mg)**
EXCHANGES: 1¾ Bread, 2½ Veg, 1½ Fat
PROTEIN: 5 g, CARBOHYDRATE: 42 g

FATTOOSH SALAD

Crisp lettuce, tomatoes, bell peppers, cucumbers, mint leaves and diced crispy pita tossed with our dressing.

✓✓ CALORIES: Excellent Choice (305)
✓✓ CHOLESTEROL: Excellent Choice (0 mg)
✓ FAT: Good Choice (15 g)*
SODIUM: Moderate (890 mg)**
EXCHANGES: 1¾ Bread, 2¼ Veg, ¼ Fruit, 3 Fat
PROTEIN: 8 g, CARBOHYDRATE: 38 g

CHICKEN SOUVLAKI

Marinated chicken tenders, charbroiled to perfection, served with vegetables on a bed of rice.

✓ CALORIES: Good Choice (565)
✓ CHOLESTEROL: Good Choice (115 mg)
✓✓ FAT: Excellent Choice (8 g)
✓ SODIUM: Good Choice (330 mg)**
EXCHANGES: 6 Meat (extra lean), 4¼ Bread, 1¼ Veg, ½ Fat
PROTEIN: 52 g, CARBOHYDRATE: 70 g

CHICKEN SALAD – SPECIAL REQUEST

Large Greek salad topped with marinated chicken tenders.
Request dressing on the side (not included in analysis).

✓ CALORIES: Good Choice (470)
CHOLESTEROL: Moderate (190 mg)
FAT: Moderate (21 g)
SODIUM: Moderate (840 mg)**
EXCHANGES: 8¼ Meat (extra lean), 1 Veg, 2½ Fat
PROTEIN: 61 g, CARBOHYDRATE: 8 g

* Primarily unsaturated fat
** If you request no added salt

Healthy Gourmet is a one-of-a-kind service that provides delicious, fresh meals for the home that free you of shopping, cooking and clean up. Award winning bakery goods made from scratch and extensive a la carte selections supplement a complete weekly menu of low-fat, low-sodium, and low-cholesterol items offered in three daily calorie levels. All meals are prepared for pick-up or delivery every Monday and Friday. $

Healthy Gourmet - Meals for the Home and Office

For information & to order call: 1-888-EZ-MEALS (396-3257)
Conveniently located pick-up throughout San Diego County!

ORIENTAL CHICKEN SALAD

Roasted breast of chicken, shredded cabbage and romaine lettuce, red bell pepper, mushroom slices, carrots and broccoli, garnished with pineapple chunks and roasted peanuts. Served with and Orange Thai Dressing.

✓✓ CALORIES: Excellent Choice (265) ✓✓ CHOLESTEROL: Excellent Choice (70 mg)
✓✓ FAT: Excellent Choice (7 g) ✓✓ SODIUM: Excellent Choice (300 mg)
PROTEIN: 31 g, CARBOHYDRATE: 20 g

HONEY THYME PORK

Roasted pork loin glazed with honey and seasoned with garlic, dijon, and thyme.

✓✓ CALORIES: Excellent Choice (325) ✓✓ CHOLESTEROL: Excellent Choice (55 mg)
✓✓ FAT: Excellent Choice (5 g) ✓✓ SODIUM: Excellent Choice (220 mg)
PROTEIN: 21 g, CARBOHYDRATE: 51 g

RASPBERRY CHICKEN

Mustard marinated grilled chicken breast with a fresh raspberry sauce over basil rice.

✓✓ CALORIES: Excellent Choice (285) ✓ CHOLESTEROL: Good Choice (95 mg)
✓✓ FAT: Excellent Choice (9 g) ✓✓ SODIUM: Excellent Choice (125 mg)
PROTEIN: 33 g, CARBOHYDRATE: 17 g

COD PROVENCAL

Fresh poached cod topped with a tomato, black olive, garlic, and basil sauce. Served over brown rice.

✓✓ CALORIES: Excellent Choice (210) ✓✓ CHOLESTEROL: Excellent Choice (60 mg)
✓✓ FAT: Excellent Choice (5 g) ✓✓ SODIUM: Excellent Choice (245 mg)
PROTEIN: 27 g, CARBOHYDRATE: 11 g

FAJITA CHICKEN WRAP

Grilled chicken breast, green peppers, and onions rolled in a fat free tortilla with a chipotle cream cheese spread. Served with a spicy Mexican Tomato Sauce.

✓✓ CALORIES: Excellent Choice (190) ✓✓ CHOLESTEROL: Good Choice (55 mg)
✓✓ FAT: Excellent Choice (5 g) ✓✓ SODIUM: Excellent Choice (300 mg)
PROTEIN: 26 g, CARBOHYDRATE: 10 g

LINGUINI WITH CILANTRO PESTO

Durum wheat semolina pasta tossed with a cilantro pesto and topped with diced tomatoes and fresh garlic.

✓✓ CALORIES: Excellent Choice (285) ✓✓ CHOLESTEROL: Good Choice (5 mg)
✓✓ FAT: Excellent Choice (7 g) ✓✓ SODIUM: Excellent Choice (95 mg)
PROTEIN: 11 g, CARBOHYDRATE: 48 g

Nutrition information supplied by Healthy Gourmet.

🍎 at least 2 fruit/vegetable servings
✓ Good Choice ✓✓ Excellent Choice

Step inside Il Fornaio and take a culinary journey through Italy. Early mornings bring rustic, crisp, crusted breads hot from the oven accompanied by the scent of fresh brewed espresso. During lunch and dinner hours, pastas and flavorful sauces simmer while meats and vegetables roast over hot coals. In the tradition of Italy's thousandfold trattorias, the sights, sounds and aromas of authentic Italian cuisine are recreated fresh everyday at the seventeen Il Fornaio restaurants with bakeries. $$

Il Fornaio

1333 First Street, Coronado, CA 92118 (619) 437-4911
1555 Camino Del Mar, #301, Del Mar, CA 92014 (858) 755-8876

PRIMIZIE DI FINE STAGIONE – SPECIAL REQUEST

Selection of mesquite-grilled winter vegetables. Request less oil (1 Tbs).

✓✓ CALORIES: Excellent Choice (190)   ✓✓ CHOLESTEROL: Excellent Choice (0 mg)
✓ FAT: Good Choice (14 g)*   ✓✓ SODIUM: Excellent Choice (175 mg)**
EXCHANGES: ¾ Bread, 1½ Veg, 2¾ Fat
PROTEIN: 3 g, CARBOHYDRATE: 17 g

PIZZA VEGETARIANA CHEESELESS

Grilled zucchini, squash, peppers, artichokes and tomato sauce.

CALORIES: Moderate (670)   ✓✓ CHOLESTEROL: Excellent Choice (0 mg)
✓ FAT: Good Choice (16 g)*   SODIUM: Moderate (970 mg)**
EXCHANGES: 6½ Bread, 2¾ Veg, 2¾ Fat
PROTEIN: 17 g, CARBOHYDRATE: 117 g

SALMONE – SPECIAL REQUEST

Grilled salmon with lemon sauce served with vegetables and potatoes.
Request no added oil. Request steamed vegetables and potatoes.

✓ CALORIES: Good Choice (515)   ✓ CHOLESTEROL: Good Choice (120 mg)
✓ FAT: Good Choice (18 g)*   ✓✓ SODIUM: Excellent Choice (280 mg)**
EXCHANGES: 5¾ Meat, 1¾ Bread, 1½ Veg, ½ Fruit, ¾ Fat
PROTEIN: 51 g, CARBOHYDRATE: 42 g

CAPELLINI AL POMODORO NATURALE – SPECIAL REQUEST

Capellini pasta topped with homemade marinara sauce and basil. Request less oil (1 Tbs).

✓ CALORIES: Good Choice (530)   ✓✓ CHOLESTEROL: Excellent Choice (0 mg)
✓ FAT: Good Choice (16 g)*   ✓✓ SODIUM: Excellent Choice (215 mg)**
EXCHANGES: 4¾ Bread, 1¼ Veg, 2¾ Fat
PROTEIN: 14 g, CARBOHYDRATE: 82 g

LINGUINI MARE CHIARO – SPECIAL REQUEST

Fresh mussels, clams, scallops and shrimp served over pasta with marinara sauce. Request less oil (½ Tbs).

CALORIES: Moderate (730)   CHOLESTEROL: Moderate (260 mg)
✓ FAT: Good Choice (13 g)*   SODIUM: Moderate (760 mg)**
EXCHANGES: 6¼ Meat (extra lean), 4½ Bread, 1¼ Veg, 1½ Fat
PROTEIN: 68 g, CARBOHYDRATE: 82 g

* Primarily unsaturated fat
** If you request no added salt

JACK IN THE BOX® *prepares food that not only tastes great, but also provides the nutritional balance that people are looking for. We cook with only 100% cholesterol-free vegetable oil, a soybean/cottonseed blend that contains no tropical oils and is low in saturated fat. And we're looking out for you with low fat milk, farm fresh vegetables in our sandwiches and salads, and reduced calorie dressing. JACK IN THE BOX® has only one mission: to continually create the most exciting, best tasting fast food anywhere. $*

CHICKEN TERIYAKI BOWL
Strips of teriyaki-marinated chicken breast, broccoli florets, carrots and teriyaki sauce, all served on a bed of steamed white rice.

CALORIES: Moderate (670)
✓✓ FAT: Excellent Choice (4 g)
✓✓ CHOLESTEROL: Excellent Choice (15 mg)
SODIUM: High (1730 mg)
EXCHANGES: ½+ Meat, 8 Bread, 1 Veg
PROTEIN: 26 g, CARBOHYDRATE: 128 g

CHICKEN FAJITA PITA
Tender chunks of all white meat chicken, natural cheddar cheese, tomatoes & lettuce. All in a pita pocket and all less than 300 calories. Guacamole and salsa not included in analysis.

✓✓ CALORIES: Excellent Choice (280)
✓✓ FAT: Excellent Choice (9 g)
✓✓ CHOLESTEROL: Excellent Choice (75 mg)
SODIUM: Moderate (840 mg)
EXCHANGES: 1 Meat, 2 Bread
PROTEIN: 24 g, CARBOHYDRATE: 25 g

GRILLED CHICKEN FILLET W/ BBQ SAUCE – SPECIAL REQUEST
Tender, boneless breast of chicken, lightly seasoned and grilled. Topped with tomatoes, lettuce and BBQ sauce on a toasted wheat bun <u>*Request BBQ sauce instead of mayo onion sauce and no cheese.*</u>

✓✓ CALORIES: Excellent Choice (340)
✓✓ FAT: Excellent Choice (7 g)
✓✓ CHOLESTEROL: Excellent Choice (45 mg)
SODIUM: Moderate (980 mg)
EXCHANGES: 3 Meat (extra lean), 3 Bread, 2½ Fat
PROTEIN: 25 g, CARBOHYDRATE: 45 g

GARDEN CHICKEN SALAD ☘
Iceberg & Romaine lettuce with strips of marinated chicken breast, natural cheddar cheese, fresh carrots and tomatoes. Dressing and croutons not included in analysis.

✓✓ CALORIES: Excellent Choice (200)
✓✓ FAT: Excellent Choice (9 g)
✓✓ CHOLESTEROL: Excellent Choice (65 mg)
✓ SODIUM: Good Choice (420 mg)
EXCHANGES: 2 Meat, 2 Veg, ½ Fat
PROTEIN: 23 g, CARBOHYDRATE: 8 g

HAMBURGER
A hot, delicious hamburger patty that's topped with 2 of America's favorite sauces (mustard and ketchup), and then a pickle slice is added to provide just a bit of crunch. This mainstream burger is served on a warm, toasted bun.

✓✓ CALORIES: Excellent Choice (250)
✓✓ FAT: Excellent Choice (9 g)
✓✓ CHOLESTEROL: Excellent Choice (30 mg)
SODIUM: Moderate (610 mg)
EXCHANGES: 1 Meat, 2 Bread, 1 Fat
PROTEIN: 12 g, CARBOHYDRATE: 30 g

Nutrition information supplied by JACK IN THE BOX®

☘ at least 2 fruit/vegetable servings
✓ Good Choice ✓✓ Excellent Choice

Jamba Juice is a leading retail purveyor of blended-to-order smoothies and fresh squeezed juices. Our mission is to enrich the daily experience of our customers, community and team members through the life nourishing qualities of fruits and vegetables. Also, try the new power source – Jambolas – delicious, highly nutritious breads that are perfect with a smoothie. $

Jamba Juice with 11 area locations in: Carmel Mountain, Del Mar, Hillcrest, Horton Plaza, La Jolla, La Mesa, Mira Mesa, Mission Valley, Pacific Beach, Point Loma, and UCSD La Jolla campus
Call 1-888-JAMBA12 for your nearest location.

All smoothies include one FREE Juice Boost and can be made non-dairy!

THE JAMBA POWERBOOST™ SMOOTHIE *(24 oz.)*
Powered from all 6 Juice Boosts, fresh squeezed orange juice, strawberries, raspberries, banana, nonfat Jamba sorbet and ice.
- ✓ CALORIES: Good Choice (455)
- ✓✓ FAT: Excellent Choice (2 g)
- ✓✓ CHOLESTEROL: Excellent Choice (0 mg)
- ✓✓ SODIUM: Excellent Choice (80 mg)

PROTEIN: 10 g, CARBOHYDRATE: 96 g

THE COLDBUSTER™ SMOOTHIE *(24 oz.)*
Orange juice, peaches, banana, orange sherbet, Coldbuster Boost and ice.
- ✓ CALORIES: Good Choice (430)
- ✓✓ FAT: Excellent Choice (3 g)
- ✓✓ CHOLESTEROL: Excellent Choice (10 mg)
- ✓✓ SODIUM: Excellent Choice (30 mg)

PROTEIN: 5 g, CARBOHYDRATE: 104 g

CARIBBEAN PASSION™ SMOOTHIE *(24 oz.)*
Passionfruit mango juice, peaches, strawberries, orange sherbet and ice.
- ✓ CALORIES: Good Choice (415)
- ✓✓ FAT: Excellent Choice (2 g)
- ✓✓ CHOLESTEROL: Excellent Choice (10 mg)
- ✓✓ SODIUM: Excellent Choice (70 mg)

PROTEIN: 4 g, CARBOHYDRATE: 105 g

RAZZMATAZZ™ SMOOTHIE *(24 oz.)*
Raspberry juice, strawberries, banana, orange sherbet and ice.
- ✓ CALORIES: Good Choice (440)
- ✓✓ FAT: Excellent Choice (2 g)
- ✓✓ CHOLESTEROL: Excellent Choice (10 mg)
- ✓✓ SODIUM: Excellent Choice (70 mg)

PROTEIN: 4 g, CARBOHYDRATE: 113 g

KIWI BERRY BURNER™ SMOOTHIE *(24 oz.)*
Kiwi juice, strawberries, peaches, nonfat Jamba sorbet, nonfat frozen yogurt, Burner Boost and ice.
- ✓ CALORIES: Good Choice (420)
- ✓✓ FAT: Excellent Choice (1 g)
- ✓✓ CHOLESTEROL: Excellent Choice (0 mg)
- ✓✓ SODIUM: Excellent Choice (95 mg)

PROTEIN: 5 g, CARBOHYDRATE: 112 g

BEYOND BROCCOLI SOUP
16 oz serving of soup with Souper Boost.
- ✓✓ CALORIES: Excellent Choice (160)
- ✓✓ FAT: Excellent Choice (1 g)
- ✓✓ CHOLESTEROL: Excellent Choice (<5 mg)
- SODIUM: High (1500 mg)

PROTEIN: 14 g, CARBOHYDRATE: 38 g

MIND-OVER BLUEBERRY JAMBOLA†
Delicious bread made with blueberries, lemon zest and raisins, boosted with Ginko Biloba.
- ✓ CALORIES: Good Choice (260)
- ✓✓ FAT: Excellent Choice (<1 g)
- ✓✓ CHOLESTEROL: Excellent Choice (<5 mg)
- SODIUM: Moderate (205 mg)

PROTEIN: 5 g, CARBOHYDRATE: 36 g

Nutrition information supplied by Jamba Juice.

* Primarily unsaturated fat
** If you request no added salt

† Side dish guidelines are 1/3 of entree guidelines

There are many reasons to eat in Jimbo's Kitchen, drink at our Java-Juice Bar or take food out. For one, we use whole foods - ingredients with all their nutrition intact. We also use as many organically grown ingredients in our deli dishes as are available. Our Java-Juice Bar offers exclusively organic coffee drinks and smoothies made from organically grown fruits and vegetables. Our meat dishes feature hormone and antibiotic-free meat and poultry. In addition, you'll find no additives, preservatives or anything artificial in any of our food. What you will find is delicious, nutritious dishes from around the world. Come see how tasty healthy dining can be at Jimbo's...Naturally! $

Jimbo's...Naturally!

Del Mar: 12853 El Camino Real, San Diego, CA 92130 (858) 793-7755
Escondido: 1633 S. Centre City Parkway, Escondido, CA 92025 (760) 489-7755

TOFU EGG-FREE SALAD (4 OZ)

✓✓ CALORIES: Excellent Choice (210) ✓✓ CHOLESTEROL: Excellent Choice (0 mg)
✓ FAT: Good Choice (15 g)* SODIUM: Moderate (640 mg)
EXCHANGES: 2¼ Meat, ¼ Veg, 1¾ Fat
PROTEIN: 16 g, CARBOHYDRATE: 6 g

WENDY'S ALTERNATIVE MAC AND SOY (8 OZ)

Macaroni served with a soy based cheese sauce.
CALORIES: Moderate (610) ✓✓ CHOLESTEROL: Excellent Choice (0 mg)
FAT: Moderate (25 g)* ✓ SODIUM: Good Choice (410 mg)
EXCHANGES: 2½ Meat, 3¾ Bread, ¼ Veg, ¼ Milk, 3¾ Fat
PROTEIN: 30 g, CARBOHYDRATE: 63 g

RED LENTIL LOAF

✓✓ CALORIES: Excellent Choice (280) ✓✓ CHOLESTEROL: Excellent Choice (0 mg)
✓✓ FAT: Excellent Choice (2 g)* ✓ SODIUM: Good Choice (480 mg)
EXCHANGES: ¾ Meat (extra lean), 3¼ Bread, ½ Veg
PROTEIN: 14 g, CARBOHYDRATE: 54 g

VEGAN MEATLESS MEATLOAF WITH GRAVY 🍎

with broccoli, carrots, mushrooms, bell pepper, tofu, hazelnuts, black olives, and spices.
✓ CALORIES: Good Choice (510) ✓✓ CHOLESTEROL: Excellent Choice (0 mg)
FAT: Moderate (32 g)* SODIUM: High (1385 mg)
EXCHANGES: 2¼ Meat, 1 Bread, 2 Veg, 6½ Fat
PROTEIN: 27 g, CARBOHYDRATE: 37 g

LILY ABOVE THE POND 🍎

Basmati rice, tofu, broccoli, burdock root, carrots, snow peas, mung beans & bamboo shoots, stir fried.
✓✓ CALORIES: Excellent Choice (290) ✓✓ CHOLESTEROL: Excellent Choice (0 mg)
✓✓ FAT: Excellent Choice (10 g)* ✓ SODIUM: Good Choice (460 mg)
EXCHANGES: ¾ Meat, 1¾ Bread, 2½ Veg, 1½ Fat
PROTEIN: 12 g, CARBOHYDRATE: 40 g

VEGETABLE SOUP (8 OZ)† 🍎

✓✓ CALORIES: Excellent Choice (90) ✓✓ CHOLESTEROL: Excellent Choice (0 mg)
✓✓ FAT: Excellent Choice (0 g) ✓✓ SODIUM: Excellent Choice (20 mg)
EXCHANGES: 1¼ Bread
PROTEIN: 3 g, CARBOHYDRATE: 20 g

† Side dish guidelines are 1/3 of entree guidelines
🍎 at least 2 fruit/vegetable servings for entrée, 1 for side dish
✓ Good Choice ✓✓ Excellent Choice

KABUL WEST

Since 1992, we at Kabul West Afghan Cuisine have taken pride in providing our customers with the best Afghan food possible. All entrees and pastries are prepared daily on our premises from scratch without artificial ingredients. Over the years, we have been reviewed by local newspapers and TV restaurant critics and have always been credited for the quality of our food and friendly services. Good quick serve restaurants are hard to find. You will be glad you found Kabul West where your satisfaction is our #1 priority. Catering available. $

Kabul West

9450 Scranton Road, #114G, San Diego, CA 92121 (858) 622-9500

SIRLOIN SAUTÉ ☺

Prepared with a base of fresh tomatoes, onions, bell peppers and a special blend of Middle Eastern spices, served with fresh garden salad, basmati rice and homemade bread.
- ✓ CALORIES: Good Choice (510)
- ✓ FAT: Good Choice (14 g)
- ✓ CHOLESTEROL: Good Choice (90 mg)
- SODIUM: High (1005 mg)

EXCHANGES: 4¼ Meat, 3¼ Bread, ½ Veg, 1¼ Fat
PROTEIN: 39 g, CARBOHYDRATE: 54 g

SHRIMP CURRY

Served with fresh garden salad, basmati rice and homemade bread.
- ✓ CALORIES: Good Choice (440)
- ✓✓ FAT: Excellent Choice (7 g)*
- CHOLESTEROL: Moderate (275 mg)
- SODIUM: Moderate (735 mg)**

EXCHANGES: 4¼ Meat (extra lean), 3 Bread, ¾ Veg, ¾ Fat
PROTEIN: 32 g, CARBOHYDRATE: 22 g

FISH KABOB

Grilled fish served with fresh garden salad, basmati rice and homemade bread.
- ✓ CALORIES: Good Choice (385)
- ✓✓ FAT: Excellent Choice (3 g)*
- ✓ CHOLESTEROL: Good Choice (105 mg)
- ✓ SODIUM: Good Choice (465 mg)**

EXCHANGES: 3¾ Meat (extra lean), 3¼ Bread, ½ Veg, ½ Fat
PROTEIN: 34 g, CARBOHYDRATE: 52 g

VEGETARIAN COMBO ☺

Served with fresh garden salad, basmati rice and homemade bread.
- ✓ CALORIES: Good Choice (410)
- ✓✓ FAT: Excellent Choice (7 g)*
- ✓✓ CHOLESTEROL: Excellent Choice (0 mg)
- ✓ SODIUM: Good Choice (390 mg)**

EXCHANGES: 4¼ Bread, 1¾ Veg, 1¼ Fat
PROTEIN: 12 g, CARBOHYDRATE: 76 g

GRILLED CHICKEN WRAP

Grilled chicken, cabbage, onion, lettuce, tomato, bell pepper wrapped in lavash.
- ✓ CALORIES: Good Choice (370)
- ✓✓ FAT: Excellent Choice (6 g)
- ✓ CHOLESTEROL: Good Choice (85 mg)
- ✓ SODIUM: Good Choice (425 mg)**

EXCHANGES: 4½ Meat (extra lean), 2¼ Bread, 1¼ Veg, ¼ Fat
PROTEIN: 39 g, CARBOHYDRATE: 42 g

JALAPENO SAUCE (1 OZ) - CAL: 5, FAT: 0 g, CHOL: 0 mg, SOD: 395 mg; EXCH: ¼ Veg; PROT: 0 g, CARB: 2 g

CILANTRO SAUCE (1 OZ) - CAL: 10 , FAT: 0 g, CHOL: 0 mg, SOD: 55 mg; EXCH: ; PROT: 1 g, CARB: 0 g

MUSTARD DRESSING (1 OZ) - CAL: 125, FAT: 13 g, CHOL: 0 mg, SOD: 285 mg; EXCH: 2¼ Fat; PROT: 1 g, CARB: 3 g

TOMATO SAUCE (1 OZ) - CAL: 5, FAT: 0 g, CHOL: 0 mg, SOD: 45 mg; EXCH: ¼ Veg; PROT: 0 g, CARB: 1 g

* Primarily unsaturated fat
** If you request no added salt

KC's Tandoor boasts the only Indian fast food in San Diego. Traditional Indian tandoor ovens lend an authentic flavor and aroma to an array of exceptional dishes, including vegetarian, chicken, fish and lamb, served as curries, kebabs, and tandoor style. Prices are reasonable and the atmosphere informal. Free samples are cheerfully offered before you place your order. Try the "Best Ethnic Food" in San Diego (Unknown Eater, 1993). $

KC's Tandoor

Sorrento Valley: 9450 Scranton Rd.   (858) 535-1941
Mission Valley: 5608 Mission Center Rd (619) 497-0751

BAINGAN BHARTHA
*Roasted eggplant cooked with tomatoes and onions, and
served with dal (lentils), rice and naan (bread, ½ piece).*
✓ CALORIES: Good Choice (540)   ✓✓ CHOLESTEROL: Excellent Choice (10 mg)
✓✓ FAT: Excellent Choice (9 g)*   ✓ SODIUM: Good Choice (410 mg)**
EXCHANGES: ½ Meat (extra lean), 5¼ Bread, 2¾ Veg, 1¾ Fat
PROTEIN: 19 g, CARBOHYDRATE: 97 g

KC'S SUPREME CHICKEN SALAD
*Marinated chunks of chicken breast served on a bed of romaine
with authentic Indian dressing, and served with naan (bread, ½ piece).*
✓ CALORIES: Good Choice (525)   ✓ CHOLESTEROL: Good Choice (95 mg)
✓ FAT: Good Choice (17 g)   ✓ SODIUM: Good Choice (545 mg)**
EXCHANGES: 4½ Meat (extra lean), 2½ Bread, 1¼ Veg, ¼ Fruit, 2½ Fat
PROTEIN: 40 g, CARBOHYDRATE: 53 g

PALAK PANEER (VEGETARIAN)
Curried spinach with Indian cheese cubes, and served with dal (lentils), rice and naan (bread, ½ piece).
CALORIES: Moderate (670)   ✓✓ CHOLESTEROL: Excellent Choice (15 mg)
✓ FAT: Good Choice (16 g)   SODIUM: Moderate (785 mg)**
EXCHANGES: ½ Meat, 5¼ Bread, 5 Veg, 3 Fat
PROTEIN: 26 g, CARBOHYDRATE: 109 g

KARAHI SHRIMP
*Shrimp sautéed with bell peppers, onions and tomatoes,
and served with dal (lentils), rice & naan (bread, ½ piece).*
CALORIES: Moderate (620)   CHOLESTEROL: Moderate (290 mg)
✓✓ FAT: Excellent Choice (9 g)*   SODIUM: Moderate (930 mg)**
EXCHANGES: 4¾ Meat (extra lean), 5¼ Bread, 1 Veg, 1½ Fat
PROTEIN: 46 g, CARBOHYDRATE: 85 g

TANDOORI CHICKEN
*Two pieces of chicken marinated in yogurt and spices, and cooked
in the Tandoor, and served with dal (lentils), rice and naan (bread, ½ piece).*
CALORIES: Moderate (675)   ✓ CHOLESTEROL: Good Choice (120 mg)
✓ FAT: Good Choice (14 g)   ✓ SODIUM: Good Choice (370 mg)**
EXCHANGES: 4¾ Meat (extra lean), 5¼ Bread, ¼ Veg, 1 Fat
PROTEIN: 51 g, CARBOHYDRATE: 82 g

at least 2 fruit/vegetable servings
✓ Good Choice   ✓✓ Excellent Choice

At Ki's, we serve an array of food and drinks made from high quality fruits, vegetables, grains, eggs, dairy, and poultry products. Our goal is to serve low fat, great tasting, healthy food and drinks at an affordable price. Along with this, we strive to have an atmosphere of friendliness while providing service in a quick and efficient manner. Every customer is special at Ki's. $

Ki's Restaurant & Juice Bar

2591 South Highway 101, Cardiff, CA 92007 (760) 436-5236

KIED RICE
Brown rice, fresh vegetables and tofu.
- ✓ CALORIES: Good Choice (440)
- ✓ FAT: Good Choice (14 g)*
- ✓✓ CHOLESTEROL: Excellent Choice (0 mg)
- ✓ SODIUM: Good Choice (520 mg)**

EXCHANGES: ½ Meat, 4¼ Bread, ¾ Veg, 2 Fat
PROTEIN: 13 g, CARBOHYDRATE: 68 g

TOFU SALAD SANDWICH
Tofu salad topped with sprouts and stuffed into a whole wheat pita.
- ✓✓ CALORIES: Excellent Choice (290)
- ✓ FAT: Good Choice (11 g)*
- ✓✓ CHOLESTEROL: Excellent Choice (5 mg)
- SODIUM: Moderate (690 mg)**

EXCHANGES: ½ Meat, 2¼ Bread, ¾ Veg, 2 Fat
PROTEIN: 10 g, CARBOHYDRATE: 41 g

GREEK PASTA SALAD
Pasta tossed with fresh vegetables, herbs and feta cheese.
- ✓✓ CALORIES: Excellent Choice (335)
- ✓✓ FAT: Excellent Choice (9 g)
- ✓✓ CHOLESTEROL: Excellent Choice (25 mg)
- SODIUM: High (1280 mg)

EXCHANGES: ½ Meat, 2½ Bread, 1¾ Veg, 1¼ Fat
PROTEIN: 12 g, CARBOHYDRATE: 51 g

TURKEY SLOPPY JOE'S
Ground turkey, onions, peppers and spices served on a sprouted bun.
- ✓✓ CALORIES: Excellent Choice (275)
- ✓✓ FAT: Excellent Choice (6 g)
- ✓✓ CHOLESTEROL: Excellent Choice (45 mg)
- ✓ SODIUM: Good Choice (560 mg)**

EXCHANGES: 1¼ Meat, 2¼ Bread, ½ Veg, ¼ Fat
PROTEIN: 15 g, CARBOHYDRATE: 38 g

BASIL PASTA PRIMAVERA
Tri-colored rotelli pasta sautéed with extra virgin olive oil, seasonal veggies, fresh basil, garlic, parmesan cheese and topped with chopped tomatoes.
- ✓ CALORIES: Good Choice (475)
- ✓✓ FAT: Excellent Choice (6 g)
- ✓✓ CHOLESTEROL: Excellent Choice (10 mg)
- ✓✓ SODIUM: Excellent Choice (285 mg)**

EXCHANGES: ¾ Meat, 4½ Bread, 2¼ Veg, ¾ Fat
PROTEIN: 21 g, CARBOHYDRATE: 84 g

TOFU BURRITO
Tofu, bell peppers, tomatoes and onion sautéed in tamari and spices, rolled in a whole wheat tortilla, and served with rice, beans and salsa. Guacamole not included in analysis.
- CALORIES: Moderate (620)
- ✓ FAT: Good Choice (12 g)*
- ✓✓ CHOLESTEROL: Excellent Choice (0 mg)
- SODIUM: High (3270 mg)

EXCHANGES: 1¼ Meat, 5½ Bread, 1½ Veg, 1¼ Fat
PROTEIN: 29 g, CARBOHYDRATE: 103 g

* Primarily unsaturated fat

** If you request no added salt

Koo Koo Roo California Kitchen features Original Skinless Flame-Broiled Chicken™ fresh oven-roasted turkey, garlic & country herb rotisserie chicken, salads, and 24 freshly prepared gourmet side dishes. Food is made fresh throughout the day and appeals to those who appreciate delicious, high quality, fresh food that can be enjoyed on the premises or as a home meal replacement. Catering available. $

Koo Koo Roo

Del Mar: 2690 Via de la Valle (858) 481-0500
La Jolla: 8650 Genesee Avenue (858) 625-9011
Mission Valley: 891 Camino de la Reina (619) 299-2270

HEALTHY DINING COMBO #1:
ORIGINAL CHICKEN BREAST, GREEN BEANS & MASHED POTATOES

✓ CALORIES: Good Choice (380)
✓ FAT: Good Choice (11 g)
✓ CHOLESTEROL: Good Choice (105 mg)
SODIUM: Moderate (880 mg)
EXCHANGES: 3¾ Meat (extra lean), 2 Bread, 1¼ Veg, 1½ Fat
PROTEIN: 31 g, CARBOHYDRATE: 41 g

HEALTHY DINING COMBO #2:
ORIGINAL CHICKEN BREAST & WING, CORN & YAM

✓ CALORIES: Good Choice (480)
✓✓ FAT: Excellent Choice (8 g)
✓✓ CHOLESTEROL: Excellent Choice (25 mg)
SODIUM: Moderate (705 mg)
EXCHANGES: 5 Meat, 4¼ Bread, ¼ Fruit
PROTEIN: 40 g, CARBOHYDRATE: 67 g

HEALTHY DINING COMBO #3: ORIGINAL CHICKEN LEG & THIGH, CUCUMBER SALAD & ROASTED GARLIC POTATOES

✓✓ CALORIES: Excellent Choice (320)
✓ FAT: Good Choice (11 g)
✓✓ CHOLESTEROL: Excellent Choice (55 mg)
SODIUM: Moderate (635 mg)
EXCHANGES: 3 Meat (extra lean), 1½ Bread, ½ Veg, ¼ Fruit, ½ Fat
PROTEIN: 24 g, CARBOHYDRATE: 32 g

HEALTHY DINING COMBO #4: ROTISSERIE CHICKEN BREAST & WING, BUTTERNUT SQUASH & TOMATO BASIL PASTA SALAD

✓ CALORIES: Good Choice (550)
✓ FAT: Good Choice (18 g)
✓ CHOLESTEROL: Good Choice (140 mg)
SODIUM: Moderate (905 mg)
EXCHANGES: 6¾ Meat, 2½ Bread, ½ Veg, ¾ Fat
PROTEIN: 54 g, CARBOHYDRATE: 43 g

HEALTHY DINING COMBO #5:
SLICED TURKEY BREAST, MASHED POTATOES & STEAMED VEGETABLES

✓ CALORIES: Good Choice (370)
✓✓ FAT: Excellent Choice (6 g)
✓ CHOLESTEROL: Good Choice (110 mg)
✓ SODIUM: Good Choice (445 mg)
EXCHANGES: 5 Meat (extra lean), 2 Bread, 1¼ Veg, 1 Fat
PROTEIN: 40 g, CARBOHYDRATE: 39 g

HEALTHY DINING COMBO #6:
½ TURKEY SANDWICH, TANGY TOMATO SALAD & FRESH FRUIT

✓ CALORIES: Good Choice (365)
✓✓ FAT: Excellent Choice (7 g)
✓✓ CHOLESTEROL: Excellent Choice (60 mg)
SODIUM: Moderate (845 mg)**
EXCHANGES: 3 Meat (extra lean), 1¾ Bread, 1½ Veg, ¼ Milk, 1 Fruit, 1¼ Fat
PROTEIN: 27 g, CARBOHYDRATE: 50 g

🍎 at least 2 fruit/vegetable servings

    ✓ Good Choice   ✓✓ Excellent Choice

The freshest of ingredients, innovative menus, and attentive service. All are part of La Costa Resort and Spa's award-winning dining experience. Our superb Spa cuisine, created by Executive Chef Josef Lageder, is served in each of our restaurants to maximize your dining options. Brasserie La Costa offers informal indoor dining plus an outdoor patio with sweeping views of the golf courses and is open daily for breakfast, lunch or dinner. Ristorante Figaro features classic Northern Italian cuisine in an elegant old-world dining room. Pisces, our signature restaurant, is renowned for its classic seafood presentations. $$$

La Costa Resort and Spa

Costa del Mar Road, Carlsbad, CA 92009   (760) 438-9111

MARINATED MUSHROOMS OVER CHICKEN

*Chicken breast and whole wheat pasta tossed with herb sauce
and marinated mushrooms, and served with seasonal vegetables.*

✓ CALORIES: Good Choice (375)   ✓✓ CHOLESTEROL: Excellent Choice (70 mg)
✓✓ FAT: Excellent Choice (5 g)   ✓✓ SODIUM: Excellent Choice (200 mg)**
EXCHANGES: 3¾ Meat, 2½ Bread, 2¼ Veg
PROTEIN: 36 g, CARBOHYDRATE: 49 g

ASPARAGUS AND ROASTED RED BELL PEPPER

Asparagus and roasted red bell peppers tossed with balsamic vinaigrette, and served with seasonal vegetables.

✓✓ CALORIES: Excellent Choice (215)   ✓✓ CHOLESTEROL: Excellent Choice (0 mg)
✓✓ FAT: Excellent Choice (2 g)*   ✓✓ SODIUM: Excellent Choice (160 mg)**
EXCHANGES: ½ Bread, 3¼ Veg
PROTEIN: 8 g, CARBOHYDRATE: 44 g

SALMON WITH HORSERADISH CRUST

Salmon prepared in a horseradish crust, and served with seasonal vegetables.

✓✓ CALORIES: Excellent Choice (255)   ✓✓ CHOLESTEROL: Excellent Choice (45 mg)
✓✓ FAT: Excellent Choice (7 g)*   ✓ SODIUM: Good Choice (315 mg)**
EXCHANGES: 2¼ Meat, ¾ Bread, 2¼ Veg, ¼ Fat
PROTEIN: 21 g, CARBOHYDRATE: 29 g

FILO WITH ARTICHOKE HEARTS, WILD MUSHROOMS AND SUNDRIED TOMATOES

*Filo dough stuffed with artichoke hearts, wild mushrooms and sundried tomatoes.
Served with seasonal vegetables. Analysis is for two filo pockets and vegetables.*

✓✓ CALORIES: Excellent Choice (300)   ✓✓ CHOLESTEROL: Excellent Choice (75 mg)
✓✓ FAT: Excellent Choice (3 g)*   SODIUM: High (1355 mg)
EXCHANGES: 1¾ Meat (extra lean), 2¼ Bread, 2½ Veg, ¼ Fat
PROTEIN: 20 g, CARBOHYDRATE: 44 g

BEEF TENDERLOIN STUFFED WITH ARTICHOKE & PIMENTOS

*Tender beef tenderloin stuffed with artichoke hearts and pimentos covered
with a wild mushroom sauce, and served with seasonal vegetables.*

✓✓ CALORIES: Excellent Choice (270)   ✓✓ CHOLESTEROL: Excellent Choice (65 mg)
✓✓ FAT: Excellent Choice (8 g)   ✓✓ SODIUM: Excellent Choice (240 mg)**
EXCHANGES: 3 Meat, ¼ Bread, 3 Veg
PROTEIN: 27 g, CARBOHYDRATE: 23 g

RASPBERRY GLAZED TURKEY BREAST

Raspberry glazed turkey breast, served with seasonal vegetables.

✓✓ CALORIES: Excellent Choice (250)   ✓✓ CHOLESTEROL: Excellent Choice (75 mg)
✓✓ FAT: Excellent Choice (1 g)   ✓✓ SODIUM: Excellent Choice (105 mg)**
EXCHANGES: 4 Meat (extra lean), ¾ Bread, 2 Veg, ½ Fruit
PROTEIN: 30 g, CARBOHYDRATE: 30 g

---

* Primarily unsaturated fat
** If you request no added salt

For a fresh alternative to fast food and pizza, discover Ladles. All of our soups, salads, specialty sandwiches and topped focaccias are made from scratch, just like you'd prepare if you had more time. Let us do the cooking for your family! $

Ladles

Encinitas: 1070 N. El Camino Real (760) 634-5006
Poway: 12265 Scripps Poway Parkway B-111 (858) 684-3101

ENSALADA AZTECA

✓✓ CALORIES: Excellent Choice (350)   ✓✓ CHOLESTEROL: Excellent Choice (40 mg)
FAT: Moderate (22 g)   SODIUM: Moderate (720 mg)
PROTEIN: 14 g, CARBOHYDRATE: 24 g

WATERCRESS ORANGE SALAD

✓✓ CALORIES: Excellent Choice (190)   ✓✓ CHOLESTEROL: Excellent Choice (0 mg)
✓ FAT: Good Choice (14 g)*   ✓ SODIUM: Good Choice (320 mg)
PROTEIN: 2 g, CARBOHYDRATE: 15 g

SPINACH MANDARIN SALAD

✓✓ CALORIES: Excellent Choice (190)   ✓✓ CHOLESTEROL: Excellent Choice (0 mg)
✓ FAT: Good Choice (13 g)*   ✓ SODIUM: Good Choice (320 mg)
PROTEIN: 3 g, CARBOHYDRATE: 15 g

CALIFORNIA CHOPPED SALAD

✓✓ CALORIES: Excellent Choice (290)   ✓✓ CHOLESTEROL: Excellent Choice (40 mg)
FAT: Moderate (21 g)   SODIUM: Moderate (720 mg)
PROTEIN: 13 g, CARBOHYDRATE: 12 g

ROASTED VEGETABLE SALAD

✓✓ CALORIES: Excellent Choice (250)   ✓✓ CHOLESTEROL: Excellent Choice (10 mg)
FAT: Moderate (21 g)*   SODIUM: Moderate (690 mg)
PROTEIN: 4 g, CARBOHYDRATE: 11 g

LADLES' HOUSE CHILI (1 CUP)†

✓ CALORIES: Good Choice (230)   ✓ CHOLESTEROL: Good Choice (35 mg)
✓ FAT: Good Choice (5 g)   SODIUM: High (780 mg)
PROTEIN: 19 g, CARBOHYDRATE: 26 g

TORTILLA & CHICKEN SOUP (1 CUP)†

✓ CALORIES: Good Choice (150)   ✓ CHOLESTEROL: Good Choice (30 mg)
✓✓ FAT: Excellent Choice (3 g)   SODIUM: High (990 mg)
PROTEIN: 13 g, CARBOHYDRATE: 16 g

Nutrition information supplied by Ladles.

---

† Side dish guidelines are 1/3 of entree guidelines   🍎 at least 2 fruit/vegetable servings
82 *Healthy Dining in San Diego*   ✓ Good Choice ✓✓ Excellent Choice

Inspired by the famous street taquerias of Mexico City, La Salsa has grown to be Southern California's favorite family of Mexican Restaurants. We serve only the freshest, most healthfully prepared gourmet food. All of our meat is 95% fat-free, and we use only canola and peanut oils.

We make more than 1 ton of fresh salsa daily and can accommodate most requests. Customize your dish with the unique flavors found on our fresh salsa bar. Every La Salsa restaurant also features an enthusiastic staff that wants to share the wonderful Mexican tradition of food and hospitality. $

San Diego La Salsa locations:

Coronado: 1360 Orange Ave.	(619) 435-7778	La Mesa: 4990 Baltimore Dr.	(619) 589-6696
Downtown: 415 Horton Plaza	(619) 234-6906	Mira Mesa: 9172 Mira Mesa Blvd.	(858) 530-0607
Downtown: 3707 N. Harbor Dr.	(619) 296-3789	Pacific Beach: 980 Grand Ave.	(858) 483-1007
La Jolla: 8750 Genesee Ave.	(858) 455-7229	Hillcrest: 1010 University Ave.	(619) 543-0777

CHICKEN TACOS LA SALSA WITH CHOPPED SALAD

Two soft corn tortillas filled with charbroiled chicken, cheese, lettuce and tomatoes. Served with our favorite chopped salad of greens, jicama, toasted corn, garbanzo beans, roma tomatoes and fresh basil topped with Salsa Mexicana.

✓ CALORIES: Good Choice (555) ✓ CHOLESTEROL: Good Choice (90 mg)
✓ FAT: Good Choice (17 g) SODIUM: Moderate (755 mg)**
EXCHANGES: 4½ Meat, 3¼ Bread, 1½ Veg, 1¼ Fat
PROTEIN: 37 g, CARBOHYDRATE: 58 g

STEAK TACOS LA SALSA WITH CHOPPED SALAD

Two soft corn tortillas filled with charbroiled steak, cheese, lettuce and tomatoes. Served with our favorite chopped salad of greens, jicama, toasted corn, garbanzo beans, roma tomatoes and fresh basil topped with Salsa Mexicana.

✓ CALORIES: Good Choice (585) ✓ CHOLESTEROL: Good Choice (90 mg)
✓ FAT: Good Choice (18 g) SODIUM: Moderate (655 mg)**
EXCHANGES: 4¾ Meat, 3¼ Bread, 1½ Veg, 1½ Fat
PROTEIN: 41 g, CARBOHYDRATE: 57 g

SONORA STYLE FISH TACOS WITH CHOPPED SALAD

Two flour tortillas filled with grilled Mahi Mahi, lettuce, tomatoes and cheese. Topped by our Sonora sauce and a squeeze of lime. Served with our favorite chopped salad of fresh greens, jicama, toasted corn, garbanzo beans, roma tomatoes and fresh basil topped with Salsa Mexicana.

✓ CALORIES: Good Choice (440) ✓ CHOLESTEROL: Good Choice (95 mg)
✓ FAT: Good Choice (14 g) SODIUM: Moderate (895 mg)**
EXCHANGES: 2¾ Meat (extra lean), 2¼ Bread, 1¼ Veg, ¼ Fruit, 2¼ Fat
PROTEIN: 34 g, CARBOHYDRATE: 42 g

BEAN, CHEESE & CHICKEN BURRITO WITH CHOPPED SALAD

Black beans, cheese and chicken in a warm flour tortilla served with our favorite chopped salad of fresh greens, jicama, toasted corn, garbanzo beans, roma tomatoes and fresh basil and topped with Salsa Mexicana.

CALORIES: Moderate (800) ✓✓ CHOLESTEROL: Excellent Choice (80 mg)
✓ FAT: Good Choice (24 g) SODIUM: High (1335 mg)
EXCHANGES: 4¾ Meat (extra lean), 6 Bread, 1 Veg, 2½ Fat
PROTEIN: 51 g, CARBOHYDRATE: 99 g

* Primarily unsaturated fat
** If you request no added salt

Pizzeria & Italian Restaurant

Leucadia Pizzeria is located in Encinitas on Hwy 101, in Rancho Santa Fe in the Del Rayo Village Center, and in La Jolla in the La Jolla Colony Plaza. Leucadia Pizzeria is a full Italian restaurant and is known for its specialty gourmet pizzas and pastas. We have a large selection of salads and low fat salad dressing for you to enjoy. Any pizza or calzone can be made with non-fat mozzarella cheese! The ambiance is upscale casual, appropriate for either a quick lunch or friendly dinner. Both indoor and patio dining are available. The full menu is available for delivery to most of Coastal North County. Reservations are not required but are accepted for large parties. $

Leucadia Pizzeria

Encinitas: 315 S. Coast Hwy. 101   (760) 942-2222
La Jolla: 7748 Regents Rd.   (858) 597-2222
Rancho Santa Fe: 16085 San Dieguito Rd.   (858) 759-2222

LITE PIZZA - 9 INCH (½ PIZZA) – SPECIAL REQUEST
Delicious and nutritious pizza with feta cheese, fresh broccoli, spinach and red onions.
<u>Request non-fat mozzarella</u>. Analysis is for ½ of a 9 inch pizza.
- ✓ CALORIES: Good Choice (510)
- ✓✓ CHOLESTEROL: Excellent Choice (15 mg)
- ✓✓ FAT: Excellent Choice (4 g)
- ✓ SODIUM: Good Choice (565 mg)**

EXCHANGES: 1¼ Meat (extra lean), 5¾ Bread, ½ Veg, ¾ Fat
PROTEIN: 23 g, CARBOHYDRATE: 93 g

CHICKEN CACCIATORE
Grilled pieces of chicken with sautéed vegetables and potatoes in a red sauce, on top of a bed of linguine.
- ✓ CALORIES: Good Choice (565)
- ✓ CHOLESTEROL: Good Choice (85 mg)
- ✓ FAT: Good Choice (11 g)
- SODIUM: Moderate (720 mg)**

EXCHANGES: 4½ Meat (extra lean), 3¾ Bread, 1½ Veg, 1¼ Fat
PROTEIN: 43 g, CARBOHYDRATE: 69 g

TOMATO-BASIL ANGEL HAIR PASTA – SPECIAL REQUEST
Angel hair pasta mixed with a light tomato basil sauce and a touch of garlic. <u>Request no butter</u>.
- ✓ CALORIES: Good Choice (435)
- ✓✓ CHOLESTEROL: Excellent Choice (0 mg)
- ✓ FAT: Good Choice (13 g)*
- ✓ SODIUM: Good Choice (565 mg)**

EXCHANGES: 3¾ Bread, 1½ Veg, 2½ Fat
PROTEIN: 12 g, CARBOHYDRATE: 65 g

PASTA WITH MARINARA SAUCE
Homemade marinara sauce served over your choice of hot pasta.
- ✓✓ CALORIES: Excellent Choice (335)
- ✓✓ CHOLESTEROL: Excellent Choice (0 mg)
- ✓✓ FAT: Excellent Choice (6 g)*
- ✓✓ SODIUM: Excellent Choice (220 mg)**

EXCHANGES: 3¾ Bread, ¼ Veg, 1 Fat
PROTEIN: 10 g, CARBOHYDRATE: 58 g

GRILLED CHICKEN SALAD (ENTRÉE SIZE) – SPECIAL REQUEST ☙
Charbroiled breast of chicken on a bed of mixed greens topped with feta cheese, tomatoes, olives and red onions. <u>Request dressing on the side</u> (not included in analysis).
- ✓ CALORIES: Good Choice (390)
- ✓ CHOLESTEROL: Good Choice (125 mg)
- ✓ FAT: Good Choice (17 g)
- SODIUM: Moderate (840 mg)**

EXCHANGES: 5¼ Meat (extra lean), 2¼ Veg, 2¼ Fat
PROTEIN: 41 g, CARBOHYDRATE: 16 g

FRESH BROCCOLI PIZZA - 9 INCH (½ PIZZA)
Fresh broccoli and mozzarella cheese (no sauce).
- ✓ CALORIES: Good Choice (505)
- ✓✓ CHOLESTEROL: Excellent Choice (20 mg)
- ✓✓ FAT: Excellent Choice (8 g)
- ✓ SODIUM: Good Choice (305 mg)**

EXCHANGES: ¾ Meat, 5¾ Bread, ¼ Veg, 1 Fat
PROTEIN: 17 g, CARBOHYDRATE: 91 g

☙ at least 2 fruit/vegetable servings

✓ Good Choice   ✓✓ Excellent Choice

A romantic Italian hideaway nestled in the vibrant courtyard of Bazaar del Mundo. Enjoy delicious Italian pastas, veal, chicken, and seafood specialties.

Flavorful dining in the best of health! A lighter Italian cuisine has been created for our health-conscious diners. These healthy entrees maintain their flavor and nutritional values, while being lower in calories, fat, cholesterol, and sodium. Hours: 11 am - 9:30 pm, summer to 10 pm. $

Lino's Italian Restaurant Bazaar del Mundo
Old Town San Diego State Historic Park
2754 Calhoun Street, San Diego, CA 92110 (619) 299-7124

CAPPELLINI ALLA POMMOROLA
Delicate angel hair pasta prepared with a sauce of fresh tomatoes and olive oil.
Parmesan cheese not included in analysis.

✓ CALORIES: Good Choice (595) ✓✓ CHOLESTEROL: Excellent Choice (0 mg)
✓ FAT: Good Choice (16 g)* ✓✓ SODIUM: Excellent Choice (20 mg)**
EXCHANGES: 5¼ Bread, 3¼ Veg, 2¾ Fat
PROTEIN: 17 g, CARBOHYDRATE: 98 g

LINGUINI PRIMAVERA
Spinach pasta and fresh vegetables prepared with olive oil, basil, garlic and chicken broth.
Parmesan cheese not included in analysis.

✓ CALORIES: Good Choice (570) ✓✓ CHOLESTEROL: Excellent Choice (<1 mg)
✓ FAT: Good Choice (16 g)* ✓✓ SODIUM: Excellent Choice (100 mg)**
EXCHANGES: 5½ Bread, ¾ Veg, 2¾ Fat
PROTEIN: 17 g, CARBOHYDRATE: 88 g

CAPELLINI ALLA MARINARA
Delicate angel hair pasta with a sauce of fresh tomatoes, basil, garlic and olive oil.

✓ CALORIES: Good Choice (580) ✓✓ CHOLESTEROL: Excellent Choice (0 mg)
✓ FAT: Good Choice (17 g)* ✓ SODIUM: Good Choice (565 mg)**
EXCHANGES: 5¼ Bread, 2 Veg, 2¾ Fat
PROTEIN: 16 g, CARBOHYDRATE: 93 g

LASAGNA VEGETARIANA
✓ CALORIES: Good Choice (520) ✓ CHOLESTEROL: Good Choice (85 mg)
FAT: Moderate (32 g) SODIUM: High (1125 mg)**
EXCHANGES: 2¾ Meat, 2 Bread, 1¾ Veg, 4¼ Fat
PROTEIN: 26 g, CARBOHYDRATE: 34 g

* Primarily unsaturated fat
** If you request no added salt

Los Cabos, located on the tip of the Baja California peninsula, is famous for its world class fishing and seafood. We combine the flavors and casual dining traditions of Baja with mainland Mexico's mesquite grilled cooking. We use only olive and canola oils, lean beef, and skinless boneless chicken breast. Unlike traditional Mexican fare, we have taken the influences of Mexico and combined them with the freshness and flair of San Diego, which is not only unique but delicious as well. $

Los Cabos 12955 El Camino Real, Ste. G-7, San Diego, CA 92130 (858) 792-2226
(in the Del Mar Highlands Towncenter across from the Edwards Cinema)

SEAFOOD ENCHILADAS ☙
Lobster, shrimp, scallops with leeks, roasted bell peppers and tomatoes, topped with traditional salsa. Served with choice of accompaniments (see below).
- ✓✓ CALORIES: Excellent Choice (315)
- ✓✓ FAT: Excellent Choice (3 g)*
- ✓ CHOLESTEROL: Good Choice (115 mg)
- ✓ SODIUM: Good Choice (480 mg)**

EXCHANGES: 3 Meat (extra lean), 1¾ Bread, 1¾ Veg, ½ Fat
PROTEIN: 26 g, CARBOHYDRATE: 39 g

CABOS CATCH
Yellowfin grilled over mesquite, with choice of salsa of the day and tortillas (2 corn tortillas included in analysis). Served with choice of accompaniments (see below).
- ✓ CALORIES: Good Choice (450)
- ✓✓ FAT: Excellent Choice (10 g)*
- ✓ CHOLESTEROL: Good Choice (100 mg)
- ✓✓ SODIUM: Excellent Choice (95 mg)**

EXCHANGES: 7¼ Meat (extra lean), 1¾ Bread, ¼ Veg, 1½ Fat
PROTEIN: 55 g, CARBOHYDRATE: 28 g

CHICKEN PALMILLA
A marinated skinless chicken breast charbroiled, sliced and served with corn salsa and tortillas (2 corn tortillas included in analysis). Served with choice of accompaniments (see below).
- ✓ CALORIES: Good Choice (545)
- ✓ FAT: Good Choice (17 g)
- ✓ CHOLESTEROL: Good Choice (150 mg)
- ✓ SODIUM: Good Choice (305 mg)**

EXCHANGES: 7¾ Meat (extra lean), 2 Bread, ½ Veg, 2 Fat
PROTEIN: 58 g, CARBOHYDRATE: 35 g

CABOS FISH TACO PLATE
Two wahoo fish tacos mesquite grilled and topped with Mexican cole slaw and salsa fresca. Served with choice of accompaniments (see below).
- ✓✓ CALORIES: Excellent Choice (285)
- ✓✓ FAT: Excellent Choice (8 g)*
- ✓✓ CHOLESTEROL: Excellent Choice (60 mg)
- ✓✓ SODIUM: Excellent Choice (295 mg)**

EXCHANGES: 1¼ Meat (extra lean), 1¾ Bread, ¾ Veg, 1½ Fat
PROTEIN: 19 g, CARBOHYDRATE: 29 g

RICE *(6 oz)*
CAL: 180, FAT: 3 g*, CHOL: 0 mg, SOD: 250 mg; EXCH: 2 Bread, ½ Veg, ½ Fat; PROT: 4 g, CARB: 34 g

WHITE BEANS *(4 oz)*
CAL: 160, FAT: 0 g, CHOL: 0 mg, SOD: 505 mg; EXCH: ¾ Meat, 1¾ Bread; PROT: 11 g, CARB: 29 g

BLACK BEANS *(4 oz)*
CAL: 145, FAT: 1 g*, CHOL: 0 mg, SOD: 500 mg; EXCH: ¾ Meat, 1¾ Bread; PROT: 10 g, CARB: 26 g

MEXICAN COLE SLAW *(6 oz)* ☙
CAL: 95, FAT: 7 g*, CHOL: 0 mg, SOD: 295 mg; EXCH: 1½ Veg, 1¼ Fat; PROT: 2 g, CARB: 8 g

☙ at least 2 fruit/vegetable servings for entrée, 1 for side dish
✓ Good Choice ✓✓ Excellent Choice

Pancho Marty and Jeff Dugger, owners of the fabulous Montanas American Grill, have been at it for over nine years now, which in restaurant business means you're a success. Key elements that contribute to the phenomenon that is Montanas are Western regional cuisine, hardwood grilled and smoked meats and fish, exceptional pastas, outrageous desserts, West Coast microbrewery beers, and a notable wine list. With a combination of superb contemporary cuisine, a stylish atmosphere, and great service, Montanas must be considered among the elite dining establishments in the county. $$

Montanas American Grill

1421 University Avenue, San Diego, CA 92103 (619) 297-0722

TURKEY MEATLOAF – SPECIAL REQUEST

Grilled lean ground turkey meatloaf. <u>Request steamed potatoes and no chipotle cream sauce</u>.

✓✓ CALORIES: Excellent Choice (295) ✓ CHOLESTEROL: Good Choice (135 mg)
✓✓ FAT: Excellent Choice (9 g) SODIUM: Moderate (675 mg)**

EXCHANGES: 3½ Meat, 1½ Bread, ½ Veg
PROTEIN: 27 g, CARBOHYDRATE: 27 g

GRILLED POLENTA AND VEGETABLES – SPECIAL REQUEST

Grilled polenta and vegetables with smoked tomato and red pepper sauce. <u>Request less oil when grilling vegetables</u> (1 Tbs).

✓ CALORIES: Good Choice (395) ✓✓ CHOLESTEROL: Excellent Choice (5 mg)
✓ FAT: Good Choice (17 g)* ✓ SODIUM: Good Choice (600 mg)**

EXCHANGES: 1½ Bread, 6½ Veg, 2¾ Fat
PROTEIN: 13 g, CARBOHYDRATE: 55 g

VINE RIPENED TOMATOES WITH GRILLED ASPARAGUS – SPECIAL REQUEST

Vine ripened tomatoes and grilled asparagus with homemade balsamic vinaigrette dressing. <u>Request less dressing</u> (2 Tbs).

✓✓ CALORIES: Excellent Choice (315) ✓✓ CHOLESTEROL: Excellent Choice (0 mg)
✓ FAT: Good Choice (19 g)* ✓✓ SODIUM: Excellent Choice (265 mg)**

EXCHANGES: ¼ Bread, 1½ Veg, 3½ Fat
PROTEIN: 6 g, CARBOHYDRATE: 29 g

FUSILLI PASTA WITH BABY SPINACH AND SUNDRIED TOMATOES

Pasta with baby spinach and sundried tomatoes tossed with lemon olive oil dressing.

✓ CALORIES: Good Choice (490) ✓✓ CHOLESTEROL: Excellent Choice (0 mg)
✓ FAT: Good Choice (11 g)* ✓✓ SODIUM: Excellent Choice (90 mg)**

EXCHANGES: 4 Bread, 3¾ Veg, 1¾ Fat
PROTEIN: 17 g, CARBOHYDRATE: 80 g

BBQ SALMON – SPECIAL REQUEST

BBQ salmon, served with grilled vegetables and potatoes. <u>Request steamed potatoes</u>.

✓ CALORIES: Good Choice (410) ✓ CHOLESTEROL: Good Choice (90 mg)
✓ FAT: Good Choice (16 g)* ✓ SODIUM: Good Choice (340 mg)**

EXCHANGES: 4¼ Meat, 1½ Bread, ¾ Veg, 1 Fat
PROTEIN: 37 g, CARBOHYDRATE: 30 g

* Primarily unsaturated fat
** If you request no added salt

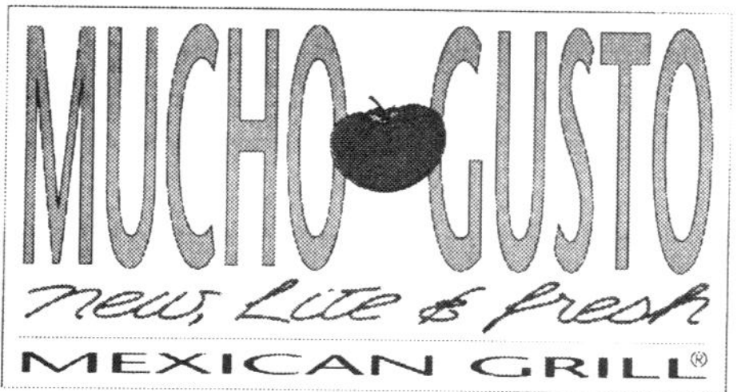

Mucho Gusto has been recognized by the Unknown Eater and awarded the 1994 "Favorite Burrito" by the San Diego Union-Tribune food critics. The selections are fresh, lite and delicious, with a choice of indoor or outdoor seating and reasonable prices. Don't be surprised if the owners, who boast an impressive international background and seven foreign languages, warmly welcome you! Once you try Mucho Gusto, you'll return again and again! $

Mucho Gusto 2668 Del Mar Heights Rd., Suite B, Del Mar, CA 92014 (858) 259-6855

5660 Balboa Avenue, San Diego, CA 92117   (858) 505-4111

Analyses for items below do not include tortilla chips.

PESCADO TACO AL CARBON

Soft mini tortilla with charbroiled snapper, served 'Baja Style' with chopped onions, cilantro and salsa.

✓✓ CALORIES: Excellent Choice (145)   ✓✓ CHOLESTEROL: Excellent Choice (20 mg)

✓✓ FAT: Excellent Choice (2 g)*   ✓ SODIUM: Good Choice (320 mg)**

EXCHANGES: 1½ Meat (extra lean), 1 Bread, 1¼ Veg

PROTEIN: 13 g, CARBOHYDRATE: 20 g

POLLO TACO AL CARBON

Soft mini tortilla with charbroiled chicken breast, served 'Baja Style' with chopped onions, cilantro and salsa.

✓✓ CALORIES: Excellent Choice (150)   ✓✓ CHOLESTEROL: Excellent Choice (30 mg)

✓✓ FAT: Excellent Choice (2 g)   ✓ SODIUM: Good Choice (320 mg)**

EXCHANGES: 1¾ Meat (extra lean), 1 Bread, ¾ Veg

PROTEIN: 14 g, CARBOHYDRATE: 18 g

VEGGIE TACO AL CARBON

Soft mini tortilla with beans, rice & peppers, served 'Baja Style' with chopped onions, cilantro and salsa.

✓✓ CALORIES: Excellent Choice (180)   ✓✓ CHOLESTEROL: Excellent Choice (0 mg)

✓✓ FAT: Excellent Choice (1 g)*   ✓✓ SODIUM: Excellent Choice (130 mg)**

EXCHANGES: ¼ Meat, 2¼ Bread, ¾ Veg, ¼ Fat

PROTEIN: 8 g, CARBOHYDRATE: 36 g

PESCADOR FISH BURRITO 🍎

Charbroiled red snapper with melted jack cheese, salsa fresca, fresh shredded cabbage and cilantro, wrapped in a warm Sonora flour tortilla.

✓ CALORIES: Good Choice (525)   ✓✓ CHOLESTEROL: Excellent Choice (60 mg)

✓ FAT: Good Choice (14 g)   SODIUM: High (1270 mg)

EXCHANGES: 4 Meat (extra lean), 3½ Bread, 1¾ Veg, 2 Fat

PROTEIN: 39 g, CARBOHYDRATE: 60 g

VEGETARIANO BURRITO 🍎

Red and green peppers, zucchini and onions sautéed in fresh garlic, with jack cheese and black or pinto beans and rice, hot or mild salsa, wrapped in a warm Sonora flour tortilla.

CALORIES: Moderate (610)   ✓✓ CHOLESTEROL: Excellent Choice (15 mg)

✓ FAT: Good Choice (13 g)   SODIUM: Moderate (920 mg)**

EXCHANGES: 1 Meat, 6½ Bread, 1½ Veg, 2 Fat

PROTEIN: 24 g, CARBOHYDRATE: 101 g

RICE *(4 oz.)* **-** CAL: 105, FAT: 0 g, CHOL: 0, SOD: 139 mg; EXCH: 1½ Bread, ¼ Veg; PROT: 2 g, CARB: 23 g

BEANS *(4 oz.)* **-** CAL: 150, FAT: 1 g, CHOL: 0, SOD: 117 mg; EXCH: ¾ Meat, 1¾ Bread; PROT: 10 g, CARB: 27 g

🍎 at least 2 fruit/vegetable servings

✓ Good Choice   ✓✓ Excellent Choice

Nicolosi's is a well-established San Diego tradition. Family owned and operated, the health and satisfaction of customers and staff have been primary goals. Our methods of preparation and the use of the finest ingredients have been constant for approximately fifty years. We feel a responsibility to continually research and add new menu items that will enable the customer to make healthy choices, with no compromise on flavor. $

Nicolosi's Italian Restaurant

5351 Adobe Falls Road, San Diego, CA 92120   (619) 287-5757

SPAGHETTI WITH MUSHROOM SAUCE

✓ CALORIES: Good Choice (560)   ✓✓ CHOLESTEROL: Excellent Choice (5 mg)
✓✓ FAT: Excellent Choice (7 g)   SODIUM: High (1855 mg)**
EXCHANGES: 5¼ Bread, 4½ Veg, ¼ Fruit, 1 Fat
PROTEIN: 19 g, CARBOHYDRATE: 108 g

SPAGHETTI WITH MARINARA SAUCE

✓ CALORIES: Good Choice (530)   ✓✓ CHOLESTEROL: Excellent Choice (0 mg)
✓✓ FAT: Excellent Choice (3 g)*   SODIUM: High (2500 mg)
EXCHANGES: 5¼ Bread, 4¾ Veg, ¼ Fruit, ¼ Fat
PROTEIN: 18 g, CARBOHYDRATE: 111g

PENNE PASTA - SPECIAL REQUEST

Fresh garlic, mushrooms, onions, basil and broccoli sautéed in olive oil.
Request less oil (½ oz.) and cheese on the side (not included in analysis).
✓ CALORIES: Good Choice (520)   ✓✓ CHOLESTEROL: Excellent Choice (30 mg)
✓ FAT: Good Choice (16 g)*   ✓✓ SODIUM: Excellent Choice (70 mg)**
EXCHANGES: 4¼ Bread, 2½ Veg, 2¾ Fat
PROTEIN: 16 g, CARBOHYDRATE: 79 g

CAPELLINI DI POMODORO AL FRESO - SPECIAL REQUEST

Request less oil (½ oz.) and no butter.
✓ CALORIES: Good Choice (505)   ✓✓ CHOLESTEROL: Excellent Choice (20 mg)
✓ FAT: Good Choice (17 g)*   ✓✓ SODIUM: Excellent Choice (75 mg)**
EXCHANGES: 3¼ Bread, 4¼ Veg, ¼ Fruit, 2¾ Fat
PROTEIN: 13 g, CARBOHYDRATE: 77 g

CHARBROILED CHICKEN SALAD - SPECIAL REQUEST

Mixed lettuce, red cabbage, walnuts, marinated chicken breast, served with balsamic vinegar dressing. Request cheese on side and use sparingly (not included in analysis).
✓ CALORIES: Good Choice (450)   ✓ CHOLESTEROL: Good Choice (110 mg)
FAT: Moderate (23 g)   ✓✓ SODIUM: Excellent Choice (145 mg)**
EXCHANGES: 5¾ Meat (extra lean), ½ Veg, 3½ Fat
PROTEIN: 44 g, CARBOHYDRATE: 16 g

* Primarily unsaturated fat

** If you request no added salt

For more than a generation, families and friends have been coming to Old Spaghetti Factories, located across the United States, to enjoy our delicious food, charming atmosphere and friendly service. We invite you to dine amidst old world antiques, collected from around the world, while savoring perfectly cooked pasta and spaghetti sauces, freshly made using only the finest ingredients. $

The Old Spaghetti Factory

275 Fifth Avenue, San Diego, CA 92101 (619) 233-4323
111 North Twin Oaks Valley Road, San Marcos, CA 92069 (760) 471-0155

Analyses below do not include bread, salad and ice cream served with the entrée.

SPAGHETTI WITH TOMATO SAUCE
Italians would say "Marinara."
✓ CALORIES: Good Choice (450)   ✓✓ CHOLESTEROL: Excellent Choice (0 mg)
✓✓ FAT: Excellent Choice (6 g)*   SODIUM: Moderate (820 mg)**
EXCHANGES: 5 Bread, 1¾ Veg, ¾ Fat
PROTEIN: 14 g, CARBOHYDRATE: 85 g

SPAGHETTI WITH MUSHROOM SAUCE
Fresh tender mushrooms, swimming in authentic Italian tomato sauce.
✓ CALORIES: Good Choice (455)   ✓✓ CHOLESTEROL: Excellent Choice (0 mg)
✓✓ FAT: Excellent Choice (7 g)*   SODIUM: Moderate (625 mg)**
EXCHANGES: 4¾ Bread, 1¾ Veg, 1 Fat
PROTEIN: 14 g, CARBOHYDRATE: 84 g

SPINACH & CHEESE RAVIOLI
Tender pillows of pasta stuffed with spinach and three kinds of cheese, topped with our savory tomato sauce.
✓ CALORIES: Good Choice (450)   ✓✓ CHOLESTEROL: Excellent Choice (60 mg)
✓ FAT: Good Choice (13 g)   SODIUM: Moderate (935 mg)**
EXCHANGES: 2 Meat, 3¾ Bread, 1 Veg, 2½ Fat
PROTEIN: 21 g, CARBOHYDRATE: 63 g

SPINACH TORTELLINI WITH MUSHROOM SAUCE – SPECIAL REQUEST
Hat shaped pasta, stuffed with a delicious blend of meat & cheese. Request Mushroom Sauce instead of Alfredo.
✓ CALORIES: Good Choice (560)   ✓✓ CHOLESTEROL: Excellent Choice (55 mg)
✓ FAT: Good Choice (14 g)   SODIUM: High (1420 mg)
EXCHANGES: 1 Meat, 5¼ Bread, 1 Veg, 2 Fat
PROTEIN: 24 g, CARBOHYDRATE: 84 g

SPAGHETTI WITH RICH MEAT SAUCE
For purists – our recipe comes straight from Naples.
✓ CALORIES: Good Choice (505)   ✓✓ CHOLESTEROL: Excellent Choice (25 mg)
✓✓ FAT: Excellent Choice (10 g)   SODIUM: Moderate (955 mg)**
EXCHANGES: ¾ Meat, 5 Bread, 1¼ Veg, 1¼ Fat
PROTEIN: 19 g, CARBOHYDRATE: 83 g

HOUSE SALAD WITH HONEY MUSTARD FAT FREE DRESSING† ☺
✓✓ CALORIES: Excellent Choice (50)   ✓✓ CHOLESTEROL: Excellent Choice (0 mg)
✓✓ FAT: Excellent Choice (0 g)*   ✓ SODIUM: Good Choice (170 mg)**
EXCHANGES: ½ Veg, ½ Fruit
PROTEIN: 1 g, CARBOHYDRATE: 11 g

---

† Side dish guidelines are 1/3 of entree guidelines   ☺ at least 2 fruit/vegetable servings, 1 for side dish

                ✓ Good Choice   ✓✓ Excellent Choice

The whimsical dining room of the Pacific Coast Grill, with its industrial feel and artistic decor, sets the stage for beyond-the-ordinary cuisine. The culinary staff draws its inspiration from the deliciously diverse elements of Pacific Coast Cuisine, which can be tasted in house specialties such as lobster tacos and turkey breast meatloaf. The hip double-curved bar offers an excellent selection of classic cocktails, Pacific Coast wines and 10 microbrewed beers on tap. Open for lunch and dinner daily and Sunday brunch. $

Pacific Coast Grill

437 South Highway 101, Solana Beach, CA 92075   (858) 764-4632

LEMON THYME PENNE – SPECIAL REQUEST

Fresh pasta with grilled squash, chopped roma tomatoes, fennel and pesto topped with parmesan cheese.
<u>Request less oil</u> (1 Tbs. in pesto and ½ Tbs. in preparation of dish).

✓ CALORIES: Good Choice (485)   ✓ CHOLESTEROL: Good Choice (120 mg)
✓ FAT: Good Choice (19 g)*   ✓✓ SODIUM: Excellent Choice (270 mg)**
EXCHANGES: ½ Meat, 3½ Bread, 2 Veg, 3½ Fat
PROTEIN: 18 g, CARBOHYDRATE: 64 g

GRILLED CHICKEN STIR FRY WITH BASMATI RICE AND VEGETABLES

Marinated grilled chicken breast stir-fried with broccoli, carrots, snow peas and Napa cabbage.
Served with basmati rice (not included in analysis).

✓ CALORIES: Good Choice (550)   ✓ CHOLESTEROL: Good Choice (85 mg)
✓ FAT: Good Choice (18 g)*   SODIUM: High (1260 mg)
EXCHANGES: 4½ Meat (extra lean), 2¼ Bread, 2 Veg, 2¾ Fat
PROTEIN: 40 g, CARBOHYDRATE: 49 g

CORIANDER SEARED AHI – SPECIAL REQUEST

Ahi seared with coriander, served with a cucumber and roma tomato salad.
<u>Request dressing on the side</u> (not included in analysis).

✓ CALORIES: Good Choice (365)   ✓✓ CHOLESTEROL: Excellent Choice (50 mg)
✓ FAT: Good Choice (16 g)*   SODIUM: Moderate (680 mg)**
EXCHANGES: 3½ Meat (extra lean), 3¼ Veg, 2 Fat
PROTEIN: 37 g, CARBOHYDRATE: 26 g

LOBSTER TACOS

with roasted corn salsa, black beans and tortillas. Analysis includes 4 corn tortillas.

✓ CALORIES: Good Choice (500)   ✓ CHOLESTEROL: Good Choice (80 mg)
✓✓ FAT: Excellent Choice (4 g)*   SODIUM: High (1280 mg)
EXCHANGES: 3¼ Meat (extra lean), 4¾ Bread, 1 Veg, ½ Fat
PROTEIN: 38 g, CARBOHYDRATE: 80 g

TURKEY BREAST MEATLOAF

with sundried tomato pesto, red mashed potatoes and steamed vegetables.

✓ CALORIES: Good Choice (500)   ✓✓ CHOLESTEROL: Excellent Choice (45 mg)
✓ FAT: Good Choice (20 g)   SODIUM: High (1360 mg)
EXCHANGES: 3 Meat (extra lean), 2¾ Bread, 1¾ Veg, 3¾ Fat
PROTEIN: 32 g, CARBOHYDRATE: 53 g

* Primarily unsaturated fat
** If you request no added salt

Consistently chosen as San Diego's and Orange County's most popular Chinese restaurants, Pick Up Stix prepares food with minimal oil in exhibition kitchens using only the finest ingredients. These Chinese bistros <u>freshly</u> wok each order without MSG or the usual heavy and/or salty sauces. Pick Up Stix specializes in take out but also offers casual service dining rooms for your enjoyment. $

Pick Up Stix: Carlsbad, Del Mar, Encinitas, Hillcrest, La Jolla, La Mesa, Pacific Beach, Scripps Ranch, Mission Valley. Visit us at www.pickupstix.com for the location nearest you.

GARLIC SHRIMP (½ SERVING)

Plump shrimp stir-fried with zucchini, broccoli, onions, mushrooms and water chestnuts in our special garlic sauce. Analysis is for ½ of a dinner portion serving.

✓✓ CALORIES: Excellent Choice (225) CHOLESTEROL: Moderate (195 mg)
✓✓ FAT: Excellent Choice (2 g)* ✓ SODIUM: Good Choice (440 mg)
EXCHANGES: 3 Meat (extra lean), 1 Bread, 1¾ Veg
PROTEIN: 24 g, CARBOHYDRATE: 28 g

CHICKEN WITH VEGETABLES (½ SERVING)

Chicken breast meat with broccoli, carrots, zucchini, mushrooms and water chestnuts in a sauce of white wine, garlic and soy. Analysis is for ½ of a dinner portion serving.

✓✓ CALORIES: Excellent Choice (295) ✓ CHOLESTEROL: Good Choice (80 mg)
✓✓ FAT: Excellent Choice (4 g) ✓✓ SODIUM: Excellent Choice (295 mg)
EXCHANGES: 4 Meat (extra lean), 1 Bread, 2½ Veg
PROTEIN: 32 g, CARBOHYDRATE: 32 g

BEEF & BROCCOLI (½ SERVING)

*Beef combined with broccoli and carrots in a delicious sauce of garlic and soy.
Analysis is for ½ of a dinner portion serving.*

✓ CALORIES: Good Choice (420) ✓✓ CHOLESTEROL: Excellent Choice (70 mg)
✓ FAT: Good Choice (14 g) ✓ SODIUM: Good Choice (335 mg)
EXCHANGES: 5½ Meat, 1 Bread, 2¼ Veg
PROTEIN: 44 g, CARBOHYDRATE: 29 g

SZECHWAN VEGETABLES (½ SERVING)

Seared red chili peppers wok'd with fresh broccoli, zucchini, carrots, celery, mushrooms, water chestnuts and green & white onions, in a zesty szechwan sauce. Analysis is for ½ of a dinner portion serving.

✓✓ CALORIES: Excellent Choice (165) ✓✓ CHOLESTEROL: Excellent Choice (<2 mg)
✓✓ FAT: Excellent Choice (2 g)* ✓✓ SODIUM: Excellent Choice (295 mg)
EXCHANGES: 1 Bread, 2¾ Veg, ¼ Fat
PROTEIN: 5 g, CARBOHYDRATE: 34 g

SZECHWAN SHRIMP (½ SERVING)

*Seared red chili peppers are wok'd with shrimp, celery, carrots and green & white onions.
Analysis is for ½ of a dinner portion serving.*

✓✓ CALORIES: Excellent Choice (215) CHOLESTEROL: Moderate (195 mg)
✓✓ FAT: Excellent Choice (2 g)* ✓ SODIUM: Good Choice (510 mg)
EXCHANGES: 3 Meat (extra lean), ½ Bread, 2½ Veg
PROTEIN: 24 g, CARBOHYDRATE: 25 g

CHINESE CHICKEN SALAD – SPECIAL REQUEST

Oven-roasted chicken breast over fresh greens, sprinkled with sunflower seeds. Served with 4 oz. fat-free Spicy Lime Cilantro dressing served on the side (included in analysis). <u>Request no Chinese croutons</u>.

✓ CALORIES: Good Choice (495) ✓✓ CHOLESTEROL: Excellent Choice (75 mg)
✓✓ FAT: Excellent Choice (10 g) SODIUM: High (1125 mg)
EXCHANGES: 4¼ Meat (extra lean), 2¼ Bread, 2¼ Veg, 1 Fat
PROTEIN: 39 g, CARBOHYDRATE: 66 g

 at least 2 fruit/vegetable servings
✓ Good Choice ✓✓ Excellent Choice

Pizza Nova is the gourmet pizza restaurant that has everybody talking. When people taste our incredibly delicious wood-fired California pizzas, scrumptious salads, rotisserie, and pastas, they can't wait to tell their friends how wonderfully delicious it is. Pizza Nova uses only the finest ingredients and creates each menu selection with dedicated attention to detail. The results keep Pizza Nova customers coming back for more. Try us for lunch or dinner. We're sure you'll agree. $

Pizza Nova

Hillcrest: 3955 Fifth Avenue (Village Hillcrest)	(619) 296-6682
Point Loma: 5120 North Harbor Drive (On the Bay)	(619) 226-0268
Solana Beach: 945 Lomas Santa Fe Drive	(858) 259-0666

WHITE BEAN AND VEGETABLE SOUP – SPECIAL REQUEST
Fresh vegetable soup with white beans and pesto. Request no parmesan cheese.
✓✓ CALORIES: Excellent Choice (155) ✓✓ CHOLESTEROL: Excellent Choice (10 mg)
✓✓ FAT: Excellent Choice (9 g)* ✓✓ SODIUM: Excellent Choice (285 mg)**
EXCHANGES: ¾ Bread, 1 Veg, 1½ Fat
PROTEIN: 6 g, CARBOHYDRATE: 17 g

SUNDRIED TOMATO LINGUINE (½ ORDER) – SPECIAL REQUEST
Linguine topped with fresh sundried tomato pesto. Request no butter.
✓ CALORIES: Good Choice (450) ✓✓ CHOLESTEROL: Excellent Choice (5 mg)
✓ FAT: Good Choice (11 g)* ✓✓ SODIUM: Excellent Choice (190 mg)**
EXCHANGES: ¼ Meat, 4½ Bread, ¼ Veg, 1¾ Fat
PROTEIN: 16 g, CARBOHYDRATE: 73 g

ROCK SHRIMP WITH CILANTRO (½ ORDER) – SPECIAL REQUEST
Linguine and shrimp topped with cilantro pesto. Request no added butter.
✓ CALORIES: Good Choice (455) CHOLESTEROL: Moderate (235 mg)
✓✓ FAT: Excellent Choice (9 g) ✓ SODIUM: Good Choice (505 mg)**
EXCHANGES: 2½ Meat (extra lean), 3¼ Bread, ½ Veg, 1 Fat
PROTEIN: 30 g, CARBOHYDRATE: 58 g

MARGHERITA PIZZA (½ PIZZA)
Sliced roma tomatoes, fresh basil, garlic, mozzarella and fontina cheese.
Can be prepared without cheese, upon request. Analysis for ½ of a whole pizza.
✓ CALORIES: Good Choice (420) ✓✓ CHOLESTEROL: Excellent Choice (25 mg)
✓ FAT: Good Choice (17 g) SODIUM: Moderate (630 mg)**
EXCHANGES: ¾ Meat, 3 Bread, ¾ Veg, 2¾ Fat
PROTEIN: 13 g, CARBOHYDRATE: 54 g

VEGETARIAN PIZZA - CHEESELESS (½ PIZZA) 🍎
Grilled eggplant, broccoli, onions, mushrooms, sundried tomatoes,
fresh oregano and our homemade tomato sauce. Analysis for ½ of a whole pizza.
✓✓ CALORIES: Excellent Choice (350) ✓✓ CHOLESTEROL: Excellent Choice (0 mg)
✓✓ FAT: Excellent Choice (7 g)* SODIUM: High (1060 mg)
EXCHANGES: 3 Bread, 2¼ Veg, 1¼ Fat
PROTEIN: 10 g, CARBOHYDRATE: 64 g

BROCCOLI WITH PENNE 🍎
Broccoli, fresh herbs, garlic, sundried tomatoes, extra virgin olive oil and parmesan cheese.
✓ CALORIES: Good Choice (485) ✓✓ CHOLESTEROL: Excellent Choice (10 mg)
✓ FAT: Good Choice (19 g)* ✓ SODIUM: Good Choice (330 mg)**
EXCHANGES: ¾ Meat, 3½ Bread, 2 Veg, 3 Fat
PROTEIN: 18 g, CARBOHYDRATE: 62 g

* Primarily unsaturated fat
** If you request no added salt

Prego Ristorante   1370 Frazee Road, San Diego, CA 92108   (619) 294-4700

PESCE SPADA ALL'AMALFITANA

Marinated thinly sliced Pacific swordfish with baby French green beans, carrots, celery, daikon sprouts and capers.

✓✓ CALORIES: Excellent Choice (275)   ✓✓ CHOLESTEROL: Excellent Choice (55 mg)
✓✓ FAT: Excellent Choice (10 g)*   ✓ SODIUM: Good Choice (505 mg)**
EXCHANGES: 4¼ Meat (extra lean), 2½ Veg, ¾ Fat
PROTEIN: 32 g, CARBOHYDRATE: 14 g

CAPELLINI ALLA CHECCA

Angel hair pasta, chopped Roma tomato, garlic, basil and extra virgin olive oil.

✓ CALORIES: Good Choice (585)   ✓✓ CHOLESTEROL: Excellent Choice (0 mg)
✓ FAT: Good Choice (16 g)*   ✓✓ SODIUM: Excellent Choice (25 mg)**
EXCHANGES: 5¼ Bread, 1¾ Veg, 2¾ Fat
PROTEIN: 17 g, CARBOHYDRATE: 94 g

PIATTO MISTO DI VERDURE

Seasonal grilled vegetables drizzled with extra virgin olive oil and herbs.

✓✓ CALORIES: Excellent Choice (320)   ✓✓ CHOLESTEROL: Excellent Choice (0 mg)
✓ FAT: Good Choice (16 g)*   ✓ SODIUM: Good Choice (460 mg)**
EXCHANGES: ¾ Bread, 3 Veg, 3 Fat
PROTEIN: 9 g, CARBOHYDRATE: 43 g

PESCE FRESCO

Fresh fish of the day grilled with fresh herbs and served with steamed seasonal vegetables. Analysis for halibut; other fish similar.

✓ CALORIES: Good Choice (435)   ✓ CHOLESTEROL: Good Choice (95 mg)
✓ FAT: Good Choice (14 g)*   ✓✓ SODIUM: Excellent Choice (205 mg)**
EXCHANGES: 8¼ Meat, 1¾ Veg, ¼ Fruit, 1½ Fat
PROTEIN: 66 g, CARBOHYDRATE: 12 g

SPAGHETTINI AI POMODORI SECCHI E ASPARAGI

Thin spaghetti, sundried tomatoes, asparagus, olive oil, garlic and Pecorino cheese.

CALORIES: Moderate (765)   ✓✓ CHOLESTEROL: Excellent Choice (30 mg)
FAT: Moderate (21 g)*   SODIUM: High (1540 mg)
EXCHANGES: 1¼ Meat, 5¼ Bread, 2¼ Veg, 3 Fat
PROTEIN: 33 g, CARBOHYDRATE: 115 g

at least 2 fruit/vegetable servings
✓ Good Choice   ✓✓ Excellent Choice

A feeling of warmth and subdued elegance, rich wood paneling, intimate leather booths, and comfortable groupings of tables adorned with crisp white linens. The chef is pleased to accommodate your special dietary requirements when preparing any of the dishes. $$$

Rainwater's   1202 Kettner Blvd., San Diego, CA 92101   (619) 233-5757

PETITE FILET MIGNON
Served with basmati rice. Bernaise sauce not included in analysis.
- ✓ CALORIES: Good Choice (590)   CHOLESTEROL: Moderate (170 mg)
- FAT: Moderate (24 g)   ✓ SODIUM: Good Choice (335 mg)**

EXCHANGES: 8¼ Meat, 2 Bread, 1¼ Fat
PROTEIN: 62 g, CARBOHYDRATE: 30 g

LIVE MAINE LOBSTER
Served with basmati rice. Butter not included in analysis.
- CALORIES: Moderate (770)   CHOLESTEROL: High (425 mg)
- ✓✓ FAT: Excellent Choice (10 g)*   SODIUM: High (2465 mg)

EXCHANGES: 14¾ Meat (extra lean), 2 Bread, 1¼ Fat
PROTEIN: 126 g, CARBOHYDRATE: 38 g

SALMON IN PARCHMENT
Roasted in paper with julienne vegetables and fresh herbs in a white wine sauce, and served with basmati rice.
- ✓ CALORIES: Good Choice (515)   ✓ CHOLESTEROL: Good Choice (105 mg)
- ✓ FAT: Good Choice (18 g)*   ✓ SODIUM: Good Choice (305 mg)**

EXCHANGES: 5 Meat, 2 Bread, 1¼ Veg, 1½ Fat
PROTEIN: 43 g, CARBOHYDRATE: 37 g

FILET OF RARE AHI – SPECIAL REQUEST
Served on charred onions with basmati rice. Request burgandy wine sauce on the side (not included in analysis).
- ✓ CALORIES: Good Choice (475)   ✓ CHOLESTEROL: Good Choice (90 mg)
- ✓ FAT: Good Choice (12 g)*   ✓✓ SODIUM: Excellent Choice (280 mg)**

EXCHANGES: 6¼ Meat (extra lean), 2 Bread, 1¼ Veg, 2 Fat
PROTEIN: 51 g, CARBOHYDRATE: 37 g

GRILLED BREAST OF SHELTON CHICKEN – SPECIAL REQUEST
Grilled chicken breast, served with spinach, onions, mushrooms and basmati rice. Request less oil (1 tsp).
- CALORIES: Moderate (605)   CHOLESTEROL: Moderate (170 mg)
- ✓ FAT: Good Choice (18 g)   ✓ SODIUM: Good Choice (445 mg)**

EXCHANGES: 9 Meat (extra lean), 2 Bread, 1½ Veg, 2¼ Fat
PROTEIN: 71 g, CARBOHYDRATE: 37 g

GAZPACHO†
Fresh vegetable soup, served cold.
- ✓✓ CALORIES: Excellent Choice (90)   ✓✓ CHOLESTEROL: Excellent Choice (0 mg)
- ✓ FAT: Good Choice (5 g)*   ✓ SODIUM: Good Choice (350 mg)**

EXCHANGES: 1¾ Veg, 1 Fat
PROTEIN: 2 g, CARBOHYDRATE: 10 g

* Primarily unsaturated fat
** If you request no added salt

† Side dish guidelines are 1/3 of entree guidelines
Healthy Dining in San Diego **95**

The "Days of the Dons" and vaqueros (Mexican cowboys) was an exciting time in early California history! Now Rancho el Nopal captures the romance and lively atmosphere in a rancho setting. Great Mexican food and Southwest specialties provide one of Old Town's most delightful dining experiences. The bright, colorful Cantina has famous margaritas, a light lunch menu, weekday happy hour and entertainment Fri and Sat nights. Open Mon - Thurs 11 am - 9:30 pm (summer to 10 pm); Fri - Sat 11 am - midnight; Sun 10 am - 10 pm. $

Rancho el Nopal Restaurant & Cantina
Bazaar del Mundo Old Town San Diego State Historic Park
2754 Calhoun St., San Diego, CA 92110 (619) 295-0584

CHICKEN CHILI
Chicken chili like you have never tasted before! Mildly spiced with chunks of chicken, onions, & red & green peppers. Served with green salad & toasted cheese bread (not included in analysis).

✓✓ CALORIES: Excellent Choice (190) ✓✓ CHOLESTEROL: Excellent Choice (65 mg)
✓✓ FAT: Excellent Choice (3 g) SODIUM: High (1575 mg)
EXCHANGES: 2¼ Meat (extra lean), ¼ Bread, 1½ Veg
PROTEIN: 22 g, CARBOHYDRATE: 18 g

CHICKEN AND BLACK BEAN TOSTADA ☺
Seasoned, shredded chicken, black beans, shredded lettuce, tomato and olives, spiced with salsa ranchera & sprinkled with parmesan cheese. Analysis does not include tostada shell.

✓✓ CALORIES: Excellent Choice (320) ✓✓ CHOLESTEROL: Excellent Choice (25 mg)
✓✓ FAT: Excellent Choice (7 g) SODIUM: Moderate (925 mg)**
EXCHANGES: 1¾ Meat, 1¾ Bread, 3 Veg, ½ Fat
PROTEIN: 23 g, CARBOHYDRATE: 44 g

CHICKEN FAJITA SALAD ☺
Fresh salad greens & sautéed chicken fajitas with tomatoes, onions & salsa picante. Guacamole & salad shell not included in analysis.

✓✓ CALORIES: Excellent Choice (330) ✓✓ CHOLESTEROL: Excellent Choice (35 mg)
✓ FAT: Good Choice (20 g) SODIUM: Moderate (605 mg)**
EXCHANGES: 1¼ Meat, 3¾ Veg, 3¼ Fat
PROTEIN: 16 g, CARBOHYDRATE: 25 g

BLACK BEAN BURRITO WITH TOMATILLO SAUCE ☺
Delectable black beans stuffed in a large burrito & covered with tomatillo sauce. Garnished with lettuce & tomato & sprinkled with Parmesan cheese. Served with a concha of rice (not included, see analysis for rice below).

✓ CALORIES: Good Choice (585) ✓✓ CHOLESTEROL: Excellent Choice (5 mg)
✓ FAT: Good Choice (11 g) SODIUM: Moderate (970 mg)**
EXCHANGES: ½ Meat, 5¼ Bread, 1¾ Veg, 1¼ Fat
PROTEIN: 28 g, CARBOHYDRATE: 97 g

FIESTA FAJITAS ☺
All vegetable fajitas with six kinds of fresh vegetables sautéed & seasoned with achiote sauce. Served with black beans & rice (not included, see analyses below) & tortillas (not included in analysis).

✓✓ CALORIES: Excellent Choice (175) ✓✓ CHOLESTEROL: Excellent Choice (0 mg)
✓ FAT: Good Choice (15 g)* ✓✓ SODIUM: Excellent Choice (35 mg)**
EXCHANGES: 1½ Veg, ¼ Fruit, 2¾ Fat
PROTEIN: 3 g, CARBOHYDRATE: 11 g

BLACK BEANS *(4 oz)* - CAL: 147, FAT: 1 g*, CHOL: 0, SOD: 44 mg; EXCH: 1¾ Bread; PROT: 10 g, CARB: 26 g
RICE *(4 oz)* - CAL: 155, FAT: 3 g*, CHOL: 0, SOD: 584 mg; EXCH: 1¾ Bread, ¼ Veg, ¾ Fat; PROT: 3 g, CARB: 27 g

☺ at least 2 fruit/vegetable servings
✓ Good Choice ✓✓ Excellent Choice

"Natural-Mex" Ranchos food is made fresh daily with the finest ingredients. We use olive or veggie oil, organic milk, and skinless chicken breast. Our nondairy smoothies are made with fruit only. We also feature fresh fish daily. We strive to provide you with only organic fruit and vegetables. Our beans and rice are prepared 100% vegetarian. We hope you will try "Natural - Mex" at Ranchos Cocina soon! $

Ranchos Cocina

1830 Sunset Cliffs Blvd., #H, Ocean Beach   (619) 226-7619
4705 Point Loma Ave., Ocean Beach   (619) 224-9815

STEAMED VEGGIE PLATE – SPECIAL REQUEST

Fresh vegetables steamed and grilled with a special seasoning, and served with rice and beans. Request brown rice and black beans.

- ✓ CALORIES: Good Choice (485)
- ✓✓ FAT: Excellent Choice (10 g)*
- ✓✓ CHOLESTEROL: Excellent Choice (0 mg)
- ✓ SODIUM: Good Choice (315 mg)**

EXCHANGES: ½ Meat (extra lean), 4¼ Bread, 3¼ Veg, 1½ Fat
PROTEIN: 19 g, CARBOHYDRATE: 86 g

EGGPLANT ENCHILADAS – SPECIAL REQUEST

Two corn tortillas filled with fresh eggplant, covered with homemade sauces and cheese, and served with rice and beans. Request brown rice and black beans.

- ✓ CALORIES: Good Choice (420)
- ✓✓ FAT: Excellent Choice (7 g)
- ✓✓ CHOLESTEROL: Excellent Choice (10 mg)
- ✓ SODIUM: Good Choice (455 mg)**

EXCHANGES: 1 Meat, 4¼ Bread, 2 Veg, ¾ Fat
PROTEIN: 18 g, CARBOHYDRATE: 75 g

MUSHROOM RANCHERO – SPECIAL REQUEST

Two corn tortillas filled with mushrooms and topped with our special sauces, and served with rice and beans. Request brown rice and black beans.

- ✓ CALORIES: Good Choice (375)
- ✓✓ FAT: Excellent Choice (3 g)*
- ✓✓ CHOLESTEROL: Excellent Choice (0 mg)
- ✓ SODIUM: Good Choice (380 mg)**

EXCHANGES: ½ Meat (extra lean), 4¼ Bread, 2¼ Veg, ¼ Fat
PROTEIN: 16 g, CARBOHYDRATE: 75 g

RANCHOS SIETE MARES

Hot, fresh seafood soup served with two corn tortillas.

- ✓✓ CALORIES: Excellent Choice (300)
- ✓✓ FAT: Excellent Choice (6 g)*
- ✓ CHOLESTEROL: Good Choice (150 mg)
- ✓ SODIUM: Good Choice (500 mg)**

EXCHANGES: 3½ Meat (extra lean), 1½ Bread, 1 Veg, ¼ Fat
PROTEIN: 30 g, CARBOHYDRATE: 30 g

PESCADO FRESCO – SPECIAL REQUEST

Fresh fish of the day served with rice and beans.
Request brown rice, black beans, and less oil (½ Tbs). Analysis for halibut, other fish similar.

- ✓ CALORIES: Good Choice (475)
- ✓✓ FAT: Excellent Choice (9 g)*
- ✓✓ CHOLESTEROL: Excellent Choice (70 mg)
- ✓✓ SODIUM: Excellent Choice (235 mg)**

EXCHANGES: 6¾ Meat (extra lean), 2½ Bread, ½ Fat
PROTEIN: 56 g, CARBOHYDRATE: 41 g

VEGGIE FAJITAS WITH TOFU – SPECIAL REQUEST

Fresh vegetables with tofu wrapped into two corn tortillas and served with rice and beans. Request brown rice, black beans, and no guacamole.

- ✓ CALORIES: Good Choice (435)
- ✓✓ FAT: Excellent Choice (7 g)*
- ✓✓ CHOLESTEROL: Excellent Choice (0 mg)
- ✓✓ SODIUM: Excellent Choice (265 mg)**

EXCHANGES: 1¼ Meat, 4¼ Bread, 1¾ Veg, ½ Fat
PROTEIN: 22 g, CARBOHYDRATE: 77 g

* Primarily unsaturated fat

** If you request no added salt

With over 80 restaurants nationwide, Rock Bottom Breweries provide an excellent avenue for great beer and pub style steak houses. In the San Diego locations of La Jolla and the Gaslamp district, Rock Bottom is serving comfort style foods and homemade libations to Southern California year round. From fresh light salads such as the seared Ahi tuna salad, to more substantial dishes such as our smoked tenderloin with Jack Daniel's Gorgonzola cream sauce, Rock Bottom Restaurants are sure to please. Additional room for banquets of all sizes makes meetings and gatherings a sure hit at Rock Bottom Restaurant and Brewery. $-$$

Rock Bottom Restaurant & Brewery

8980 Villa La Jolla Drive, La Jolla, CA 92037 (858) 450-9277
619 G Street (in the Gaslamp), San Diego, CA 92101 (619) 231-7000

ANGEL HAIR PASTA WITH SMOKED TOMATOES (½ SERVING) ☺

Pasta smothered with smoked roma tomatoes, onions, basil, roasted garlic and Asiago cheese. Analysis for ½ of a serving. Analysis does not include bread.

✓ CALORIES: Good Choice (400) ✓✓ CHOLESTEROL: Excellent Choice (<2 mg)
✓ FAT: Good Choice (19 g)* ✓ SODIUM: Good Choice (525 mg)**
EXCHANGES: ¼ Meat, 2¾ Bread, 1¼ Veg, 3¼ Fat
PROTEIN: 10 g, CARBOHYDRATE: 50 g

SALMON B.L.T. – SPECIAL REQUEST

Salmon fillet, alder smoked and char-grilled, topped with romaine and tomato on a multi-grain bun, and served with fresh fruit. Request no butter, no bacon and less oil (½ Tbs). Remoulade sauce not included in analysis.

✓ CALORIES: Good Choice (555) ✓✓ CHOLESTEROL: Excellent Choice (60 mg)
✓ FAT: Good Choice (17 g)* ✓ SODIUM: Good Choice (530 mg)**
EXCHANGES: 2¾ Meat, 3¾ Bread, ¼ Veg, ¾ Fruit, 1¼ Fat
PROTEIN: 33 g, CARBOHYDRATE: 66 g

TURKEY BURGER – SPECIAL REQUEST ☺

Garlic and black pepper seasoned ground turkey, char-grilled and served on a multi-grain bun with a sweet and tangy red onion confit and served with fresh fruit. Request no butter.

CALORIES: Moderate (625) ✓ CHOLESTEROL: Good Choice (105 mg)
✓ FAT: Good Choice (20 g) SODIUM: High (1010 mg)
EXCHANGES: 4¼ Meat (extra lean), 3½ Bread, 1 Veg, ¾ Fruit, 3½ Fat
PROTEIN: 41 g, CARBOHYDRATE: 70 g

TAOS CHICKEN SALAD – SPECIAL REQUEST ☺

Spice-rubbed, grilled and chilled chicken breast, with crisp greens, roasted corn, green chilies, fire-roasted tomatoes and black beans. Request less dressing (2 oz). Analysis does not include corn chips or croutons.

✓ CALORIES: Good Choice (500) ✓ CHOLESTEROL: Good Choice (95 mg)
FAT: Moderate (21 g) SODIUM: Moderate (850 mg)**
EXCHANGES: 4¾ Meat (extra lean), 1½ Bread, 1¼ Veg, 3¼ Fat
PROTEIN: 42 g, CARBOHYDRATE: 32 g

SEARED AHI SALAD – SPECIAL REQUEST ☺

Marinated fresh ahi, flash-seared with black pepper and sesame, served chilled over Wasabi slaw with warm, grilled shrimp and a tangy mango salsa. Request less dressing (1 oz).

✓ CALORIES: Good Choice (595) CHOLESTEROL: High (380 mg)
✓ FAT: Good Choice (19 g)* SODIUM: Moderate (810 mg)**
EXCHANGES: 8¼ Meat (extra lean), ½ Bread, 2¼ Veg, ¾ Fruit, 2 Fat
PROTEIN: 66 g, CARBOHYDRATE: 40 g

☺ at least 2 fruit/vegetable servings
✓ Good Choice ✓✓ Excellent Choice

Roppongi, awarded San Diego Restaurant Association's "Gold Medallion Award for Best New Restaurant" in 1999, serves a lunch and dinner menu of Asian-fusion cuisine - blends of Japanese, Chinese, Vietnamese, Thai, and Indian flavors using European cooking techniques. $$-$$$

Roppongi Restaurant, Bar & Café

875 Prospect Street, La Jolla, CA 92037 (858) 551-5252

GRILLED CHICKEN SALAD – SPECIAL REQUEST ☙

Romaine, organic greens, peppers, tomato, mango, cucumber and spicy cashew nut mint vinaigrette. <u>Request no bean thread noodles. Request dressing on the side.</u> Analysis does not include bean thread noodles or dressing.

✓ CALORIES: Good Choice (515)   CHOLESTEROL: Moderate (170 mg)
FAT: Moderate (22 g)   ✓✓ SODIUM: Excellent Choice (165 mg)**
EXCHANGES: 9 Meat (extra lean), 1¼ Veg, ¼ Fruit, 2¾ Fat
PROTEIN: 66 g, CARBOHYDRATE: 12 g

AHI POKI

Ahi marinated in soy and red pepper flakes. Analysis does not include fried won tons.

✓ CALORIES: Good Choice (525)   ✓ CHOLESTEROL: Good Choice (150 mg)
✓✓ FAT: Excellent Choice (8 g)*   SODIUM: High (2550 mg)
EXCHANGES: 10¾ Meat (extra lean), ½ Bread, ½ Veg, ¼ Fat
PROTEIN: 89 g, CARBOHYDRATE: 18 g

POLYNESIAN DUNGENESS CRAB STACK

Mango, pea shoots, cucumber, tomato, avocado and peanuts served with spicy ginger lime dressing.

✓✓ CALORIES: Excellent Choice (280)   ✓✓ CHOLESTEROL: Excellent Choice (45 mg)
✓✓ FAT: Excellent Choice (10 g)*   SODIUM: Moderate (780 mg)**
EXCHANGES: 2 Meat (extra lean), 1 Bread, ¾ Veg, ¼ Fruit, 1¾ Fat
PROTEIN: 18 g, CARBOHYDRATE: 33 g

HIBACHI GRILLED HALIBUT – SPECIAL REQUEST ☙

Grilled halibut with roasted vegetables and ponzu sauce. <u>Request less oil (1 Tbs) and no butter with vegetables</u>.

✓ CALORIES: Good Choice (530)   ✓✓ CHOLESTEROL: Excellent Choice (55 mg)
✓ FAT: Good Choice (20 g)*   SODIUM: Moderate (945 mg)**
EXCHANGES: 4¼ Meat (extra lean), 1¼ Bread, 2¾ Veg, ½ Fruit, 2¾ Fat
PROTEIN: 44 g, CARBOHYDRATE: 47 g

TERIYAKI GLAZED MAHI MAHI FILET – SPECIAL REQUEST ☙

Teriyaki glazed mahi mahi with mango sprout salad. Analysis does not include potatoes. <u>Request less oil (1 tsp)</u>.

✓ CALORIES: Good Choice (490)   ✓✓ CHOLESTEROL: Excellent Choice (60 mg)
✓✓ FAT: Excellent Choice (8 g)*   SODIUM: High (2940 mg)
EXCHANGES: 5 Meat (extra lean), ¼ Bread, 1¼ Veg, 2¼ Fruit, ½ Fat
PROTEIN: 51 g, CARBOHYDRATE: 57 g

SEA SCALLOP SATAY WITH TOBIKO CAVIAR – SPECIAL REQUEST

Sea scallops served on skewers with miso ginger vinaigrette and teriyaki drizzle. <u>Request tobiko caviar sauce on the side</u> (not included in analysis).

✓✓ CALORIES: Excellent Choice (245)   ✓✓ CHOLESTEROL: Excellent Choice (50 mg)
✓✓ FAT: Excellent Choice (9 g)*   SODIUM: High (1470 mg)
EXCHANGES: 1¾ Meat (extra lean), ½ Bread, ½ Veg, 1½ Fat
PROTEIN: 23 g, CARBOHYDRATE: 17 g

INDONESIAN TIGER SHRIMP SKEWERS ☙

Skewered tiger prawns served with tomato horseradish sauce and mango salsa.

✓ CALORIES: Good Choice (390)   CHOLESTEROL: Moderate (250 mg)
✓ FAT: Good Choice (20 g)*   SODIUM: Moderate (830 mg)**
EXCHANGES: 3¾ Meat (extra lean), ¼ Bread, 2¾ Veg, ½ Fruit, 2¾ Fat
PROTEIN: 30 g, CARBOHYDRATE: 23 g

* Primarily unsaturated fat

** If you request no added salt

We offer pizzas with a variety of sauces, a blend of three real cheeses, superior meats, fresh vegetables, and dough made fresh in our restaurants. Round Table Pizza offers many locations in San Diego County for your convenience. $

Round Table Pizza locations: Casa de Oro, Chula Vista, Clairemont, Encinitas, Escondido, La Jolla, La Mesa, Oceanside, Pacific Beach, Poway, Rancho Bernardo, Rancho Penasquitos, Rancho San Diego, Santee, Solana Beach, Tierrasanta, University City, Vista

---

Analyses below are for thin crust pizza; pan crust adds approx. ½ g fat & 50 calories per slice.

GUINEVERE'S GARDEN DELIGHT® PIZZA (2 SLICES)

Our classic red sauce, three cheeses, mushrooms, black olives, Roma tomatoes, yellow onions, and green peppers. Analysis for 2 slices large pizza.

✓✓ CALORIES: Excellent Choice (300)   ✓✓ CHOLESTEROL: Excellent Choice (30 mg)
✓ FAT: Good Choice (11 g)   ✓ SODIUM: Good Choice (500 mg)
PROTEIN: 14 g, CARBOHYDRATE: 36 g

GOURMET VEGGIE™ PIZZA (2 SLICES)

Creamy garlic sauce, three cheeses, artichoke hearts, zucchini, spinach, mushrooms, Roma tomatoes, red & green onions, Italian herb seasoning & lots of chopped garlic. Analysis for 2 slices large pizza.

✓✓ CALORIES: Excellent Choice (320)   ✓✓ CHOLESTEROL: Excellent Choice (30 mg)
✓ FAT: Good Choice (13 g)   ✓ SODIUM: Good Choice (400 mg)
PROTEIN: 14 g, CARBOHYDRATE: 36 g

CHICKEN & GARLIC GOURMET™ PIZZA (2 SLICES)

Creamy garlic sauce, three cheeses, roasted chicken, mushrooms, Roma tomatoes, red & green onions, Italian herb seasoning & lots of chopped garlic. Analysis for 2 slices large pizza.

✓✓ CALORIES: Excellent Choice (340)   ✓✓ CHOLESTEROL: Excellent Choice (50 mg)
✓ FAT: Good Choice (14 g)   ✓ SODIUM: Good Choice (560 mg)
PROTEIN: 18 g, CARBOHYDRATE: 34 g

SALUTÉ VEGGIE™ PIZZA (2 SLICES)#

Creamy garlic sauce, three cheeses, artichoke hearts, zucchini, spinach, mushrooms, Roma tomatoes, red & green onions and lots of chopped garlic. Topped with Italian herb seasoning, shredded Parmesan cheese & roasted red peppers. Analysis for 2 slices large pizza.

✓✓ CALORIES: Excellent Choice (280)   ✓✓ CHOLESTEROL: Excellent Choice (20 mg)
✓✓ FAT: Excellent Choice (9 g)   ✓ SODIUM: Good Choice (340 mg)
PROTEIN: 12 g, CARBOHYDRATE: 38 g

SALUTÉ CHICKEN & GARLIC™ PIZZA (2 SLICES)#

Creamy garlic sauce, three cheeses, roasted chicken, mushrooms, Roma tomatoes, red and green onions & lots of chopped garlic. Topped with Italian herb seasoning, shredded Parmesan cheese & roasted red peppers. Analysis for 2 slices large pizza.

✓✓ CALORIES: Excellent Choice (300)   ✓✓ CHOLESTEROL: Excellent Choice (40 mg)
✓ FAT: Good Choice (11 g)   ✓ SODIUM: Good Choice (500 mg)
PROTEIN: 16 g, CARBOHYDRATE: 36 g

 # Saluté selections available at participating locations only.
Nutrition information supplied by Round Table Pizza.

☘ at least 2 fruit/vegetable servings
✓ Good Choice   ✓✓ Excellent Choice

Royal Thai -- award-winning exotic cuisine and beautiful ambiance. Extensive menu features authentic Thai dishes from recipes handed down through the Tila family for generations. You'll enjoy a wide selection of delights to please your taste, either hot or mild. Let Royal Thai cater to you -- there's something to please everyone. $

Royal Thai Cuisine

467 Fifth Avenue, San Diego, Ca 92101 (619) 230-THAI
737 Pearl Street, La Jolla, CA 92307 (858) 551-THAI

NAKED SHRIMP (½ SERVING)
*Grilled, medium rare shrimp seasoned with lime, nampla and chili mingled
with lemon grass (hot and spicy). Analysis is for ½ of a full serving.*
- ✓✓ CALORIES: Excellent Choice (200)
- ✓✓ FAT: Excellent Choice (2 g)*
- ✓ CHOLESTEROL: Good Choice (105 mg)
- SODIUM: High (1140 mg)

EXCHANGES: 1 Meat (extra lean), ½ Bread, 1½ Veg, 1 Fruit
PROTEIN: 15 g, CARBOHYDRATE: 31 g

HOT BASIL WITH OYSTER MUSHROOMS (½ SERVING) - SPECIAL REQUEST
*Served with bell peppers, onions, mushrooms, chili and garlic sauce (hot and spicy).
Request less oil (2 Tbs). Analysis for ½ of a full serving.*
- ✓✓ CALORIES: Excellent Choice (250)
- ✓ FAT: Good Choice (15 g)*
- ✓✓ CHOLESTEROL: Excellent Choice (<5 mg)
- SODIUM: Moderate (750 mg)**

EXCHANGES: ¼ Bread, 4¼ Veg, ¼ Fruit, 2¾ Fat
PROTEIN: 6 g, CARBOHYDRATE: 28 g

STEAMED FRESH CATCH OF THE DAY WITH SPICY THAI SAUCE - SPECIAL REQUEST
Request steamed. Analysis is for sea bass; other fish similar.
- ✓ CALORIES: Good Choice (450)
- ✓✓ FAT: Excellent Choice (7 g)*
- ✓ CHOLESTEROL: Good Choice (120 mg)
- SODIUM: High (3915 mg)

EXCHANGES: 5 Meat (extra lean), 1½ Bread, 1¾ Veg
PROTEIN: 61 g, CARBOHYDRATE: 51 g

ROYAL YACHT (½ SERVING)
*A combination of seafood carefully prepared with cabbage, celery and silver noodles,
blended with spices and served in a royal yacht. Analysis is for ½ of a full serving.*
- ✓ CALORIES: Good Choice (495)
- ✓ FAT: Good Choice (15 g)*
- ✓ CHOLESTEROL: Good Choice (140 mg)
- SODIUM: High (1400 mg)

EXCHANGES: 1½ Meat (extra lean), 3¾ Bread, 2 Veg, 2¾ Fat
PROTEIN: 17 g, CARBOHYDRATE: 75 g

CHICKEN WITH EGGPLANT & BAMBOO SHOOTS (½ SERVING) - SPECIAL REQUEST
*Asian eggplant, chicken and bamboo shoots in sweet basil and chili sauce.
Request less oil (2 Tbs). Analysis for ½ of a full serving.*
- ✓✓ CALORIES: Excellent Choice (280)
- ✓ FAT: Good Choice (17 g)
- ✓✓ CHOLESTEROL: Excellent Choice (55 mg)
- ✓ SODIUM: Good Choice (500 mg)**

EXCHANGES: 2¾ Meat, ¼ Bread, 1 Veg, ¼ Fruit, 2¾ Fat
PROTEIN: 22 g, CARBOHYDRATE: 11 g

SOM TOM (GREEN PAPAYA SALAD)
- ✓ CALORIES: Good Choice (365)
- ✓✓ FAT: Excellent Choice (4 g)*
- ✓✓ CHOLESTEROL: Excellent Choice (0 mg)
- SODIUM: High (1290 mg)

EXCHANGES: ¼ Bread, 6 Veg, 2½ Fruit, ¾ Fat
PROTEIN: 15 g, CARBOHYDRATE: 74 g

* Primarily unsaturated fat
** If you request no added salt

Ruby's Diner

5630 Paseo del Norte, Ste. 130, Carlsbad 92008   (760) 931-RUBY
1640 Camino del Rio N., #360P, San Diego 92108   (619) 294-RUBY
1 Pierview Way, Oceanside 92054   (760) 433-RUBY

DELIGHTFUL FRESH ROAST TURKEY

Fresh oven-roasted turkey with lettuce, cranberry sauce and fat-free mayo on a soft RubyRoll.
Served with your choice of fresh fruit salad or our very popular Skinny Fries (see analyses below).

CALORIES: Moderate (610)   ✓ CHOLESTEROL: Good Choice (120 mg)
✓✓ FAT: Excellent Choice (7 g)   SODIUM: Moderate (715 mg)**
EXCHANGES: 6¼ Meat (extra lean), 3¾ Bread, 1¾ Fruit, 1¼ Fat
PROTEIN: 52 g, CARBOHYDRATE: 83 g

DELIGHTFUL CHICKEN RUBYBURGER

with a tender boneless, skinless chicken breast on a whole wheat burger bun with fat-free mayo.
Served with your choice of fresh fruit salad or our very popular Skinny Fries (see analyses below).

✓ CALORIES: Good Choice (495)   ✓ CHOLESTEROL: Good Choice (130 mg)
✓✓ FAT: Excellent Choice (10 g)   SODIUM: High (1055 mg)
EXCHANGES: 6¾ Meat (extra lean), 2½ Bread, ¼ Fruit, ¾ Fat
PROTEIN: 55 g, CARBOHYDRATE: 44 g

DELIGHTFUL VEGGIE RUBYBURGER

A tasty Gardenburger patty with lettuce, tomato and fat-free mayo on a grilled RubyBun.
Served with your choice of fresh fruit salad or our very popular Skinny Fries (see analyses below).

✓ CALORIES: Good Choice (430)   ✓✓ CHOLESTEROL: Excellent Choice (5 mg)
✓✓ FAT: Excellent Choice (8 g)*   SODIUM: Moderate (675 mg)**
EXCHANGES: ¼ Meat, 4¾ Bread, ¼ Fruit, ¾ Fat
PROTEIN: 19 g, CARBOHYDRATE: 72 g

DELIGHTFUL TLT SANDWICH COMBO

Fresh oven-roasted turkey with lettuce, tomato and fat-free mayo on a soft RubyRoll.
Served with your choice of fresh fruit salad or our very popular Skinny Fries (see analyses below).

✓ CALORIES: Good Choice (530)   ✓ CHOLESTEROL: Good Choice (120 mg)
✓✓ FAT: Excellent Choice (7 g)   SODIUM: Moderate (705 mg)**
EXCHANGES: 6¼ Meat, 3¾ Bread, ¼ Fruit, 1¼ Fat
PROTEIN: 52 g, CARBOHYDRATE: 62 g

DELIGHTFUL VEGGIE SOFT TACOS ☙

Two whole wheat tortillas filled with fresh lettuce, sprouts, cheese, Rancho beans,
olives and salsa. Served with fresh fruit salad (see analysis below).

✓ CALORIES: Good Choice (525)   ✓✓ CHOLESTEROL: Excellent Choice (15 mg)
✓ FAT: Good Choice (18 g)   SODIUM: High (1520 mg)
EXCHANGES: ¾ Meat, 4 Bread, 1¼ Veg, 3½ Fat
PROTEIN: 14 g, CARBOHYDRATE: 67 g

DELIGHTFUL TURKEY RUBYBURGER

A ⅛ lb. ground turkey patty with lettuce, tomato and fat-free mayo on a
grilled RubyBun. Served with fresh fruit salad (see analysis below).

✓ CALORIES: Good Choice (475)   ✓ CHOLESTEROL: Good Choice (130 mg)
✓ FAT: Good Choice (18 g)   ✓ SODIUM: Good Choice (575 mg)**
EXCHANGES: 3½ Meat, 2¾ Bread, ¼ Fruit, 1½ Fat
PROTEIN: 32 g, CARBOHYDRATE: 45 g

☙ **SKINNY FRIES:** CAL: 250, FAT: 8 g, CHOL: 0, SOD: 390 mg; EXCH: 2½ Br., 1¾ Fat; PROT: 5 g, CARB: 38 g

☙ **FRESH FRUIT SALAD:** CAL: 60, FAT: 0 g, CHOL: 0, SOD: 10 mg; EXCH: 1 Fruit; PROT: 1 g, CARB: 15 g

☙ at least 2 fruit/vegetable servings for entrée, 1 for side dish

     ✓ Good Choice   ✓✓ Excellent Choice

Fresh...Simple...Homemade. That's been our philosophy since the early 1970s when we first opened our doors to this community. It is this commitment to freshness, quality, and even a surprise or two that has kept St. Germain's Cafe on the forefront of the California dining experience. Open 7 am - 4 pm daily. Dinner Fridays and Saturdays until 10 pm. $

St. Germain's Cafe 1010 S. Hwy. 101, Encinitas, CA 92024 (760) 753-5411

EGG BEATERS BIG SCRAMBLE - SPECIAL REQUEST

With mushrooms, onion, tomato and bell pepper. Includes two slices of toast (dry) and fresh fruit. Request Egg Beaters and dry toast.

- ✓ CALORIES: Good Choice (375)
- ✓✓ FAT: Excellent Choice (5 g)*
- ✓✓ CHOLESTEROL: Excellent Choice (0 mg)
- SODIUM: Moderate (695 mg)**

EXCHANGES: 2½ Meat (extra lean), 2½ Bread, ½ Veg, 1 Fruit, ½ Fat
PROTEIN: 27 g, CARBOHYDRATE: 59 g

EGG BEATERS SPANISH OMELETTE - SPECIAL REQUEST

Topped with mild Spanish sauce. Includes two slices of toast (dry) and fresh fruit. Request Egg Beaters, no cheese and dry toast.

- ✓ CALORIES: Good Choice (370)
- ✓✓ FAT: Excellent Choice (5 g)*
- ✓✓ CHOLESTEROL: Excellent Choice (0 mg)
- SODIUM: Moderate (815 mg)**

EXCHANGES: 2½ Meat (extra lean), 2½ Bread, ½ Veg, 1 Fruit, ½ Fat
PROTEIN: 27 g, CARBOHYDRATE: 59 g

EGG BEATERS SPINACH & MUSHROOM OMELETTE - SPECIAL REQUEST

Fresh spinach and mushrooms sautéed. Includes two slices of toast (dry) and fresh fruit. Request toast dry and Egg Beaters with no cheese (cheese adds 110 calories and 9 g fat).

- ✓ CALORIES: Good Choice (385)
- ✓✓ FAT: Excellent Choice (5 g)*
- ✓✓ CHOLESTEROL: Excellent Choice (0 mg)
- SODIUM: Moderate (740 mg)**

EXCHANGES: 2½ Meat (extra lean), 2½ Bread, 1 Veg, 1 Fruit, ½ Fat
PROTEIN: 29 g, CARBOHYDRATE: 61 g

FAMOUS VEGETARIAN BURGER

Made from lentils, walnuts, onions and delicious spices, and topped with lettuce, tomato and onion. Served with fresh fruit and cafe potatoes. Analysis does not include potatoes or cheese.

- ✓ CALORIES: Good Choice (580)
- ✓ FAT: Good Choice (14 g)*
- ✓✓ CHOLESTEROL: Excellent Choice (40 mg)
- SODIUM: Moderate (995 mg)**

EXCHANGES: 1 Meat, 5½ Bread, 1 Veg, ½ Fruit, 2¼ Fat
PROTEIN: 26 g, CARBOHYDRATE: 94 g

TERIYAKI CHICKEN SANDWICH

Marinated in our own teriyaki sauce, crowned with pineapple, and topped with lettuce and tomato. Analysis includes fresh fruit.

- ✓ CALORIES: Good Choice (600)
- ✓✓ FAT: Excellent Choice (9 g)
- ✓ CHOLESTEROL: Good Choice (130 mg)
- SODIUM: High (1190 mg)

EXCHANGES: 6¾ Meat (extra lean), 4 Bread, ¾ Fruit, ½ Fat
PROTEIN: 60 g, CARBOHYDRATE: 72 g

WEST INDIES CHICKEN SANDWICH

Spiced with our unique cajun spices and charbroiled. Analysis includes fresh fruit.

- ✓ CALORIES: Good Choice (595)
- ✓✓ FAT: Excellent Choice (9 g)
- ✓ CHOLESTEROL: Good Choice (130 mg)
- SODIUM: High (1260 mg)

EXCHANGES: 6¾ Meat (extra lean), 4 Bread, ½ Fruit, ½ Fat
PROTEIN: 61 g, CARBOHYDRATE: 71 g

* Primarily unsaturated fat

** If you request no added salt

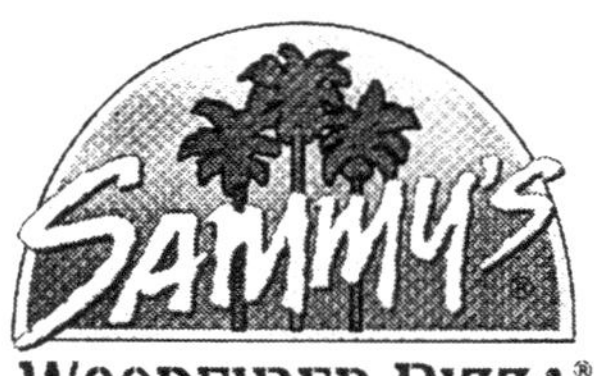

Winner of San Diego's Best Pizza Award 1989 - 2000. Serving gourmet woodfired pizza, heaping salads, fresh pastas, and specialty entrees in a lovely garden atmosphere, Sammy's is known for its imaginative combinations, generous portions, reasonable prices, and exemplary service. Local favorites include Garlic Chicken and Jamaican Shrimp pizzas, Shrimp Angel Hair pasta and Thai pasta. Come enjoy the best! $

Sammy's Woodfired Pizza

Carlsbad: 5970 Avenida Encinas (935) 438-1212 La Jolla: 702 Pearl St. (858) 456-5222
Costa Verde: 8650 Genessee Ave. (858) 404-9898 Mission Valley: 1620 Camino de la Reina
Del Mar: 12925 El Camino Real (858) 259-6600 (619) 298-8222
Downtown: 770 4th Ave. (619) 230-8888 Scripps Ranch: 10785 Scripps Poway Pky., #A
(858) 695-0900

HEALTHY DINING VEGETARIAN PIZZA (½ PIZZA)

Grilled eggplant, onions, bell peppers, fontina, garlic, zucchini and roma tomatoes with fat-free mozzarella. Analysis is for ½ of a pizza.

CALORIES: Moderate (885) ✓✓ CHOLESTEROL: Excellent Choice (20 mg)
FAT: Moderate (21 g)* SODIUM: High (2110 mg)
EXCHANGES: 2¾ Meat, 7¾ Bread, 1¼ Veg, 3½ Fat
PROTEIN: 38 g, CARBOHYDRATE: 130 g

HEALTHY DINING TOMATO ANGEL HAIR PASTA

Roma tomatoes, fresh basil and garlic.

CALORIES: Moderate (650) ✓✓ CHOLESTEROL: Excellent Choice (15 mg)
✓ FAT: Good Choice (18 g)* ✓✓ SODIUM: Excellent Choice (65 mg)**
EXCHANGES: 5¾ Bread, 2 Veg, 2¾ Fat
PROTEIN: 22 g, CARBOHYDRATE: 105 g

HEALTHY DINING GRILLED VEGETABLE PENNE

Seasonal grilled vegetables with spinach, olive oil, balsamic vinegar and Romano cheese.

CALORIES: Moderate (610) ✓✓ CHOLESTEROL: Excellent Choice (30 mg)
✓ FAT: Good Choice (20 g)* SODIUM: Moderate (685 mg)**
EXCHANGES: 1 Meat, 4¼ Bread, 2 Veg, 3½ Fat
PROTEIN: 24 g, CARBOHYDRATE: 84 g

HEALTHY DINING GRILLED SHRIMP WRAP

Bean sprouts, julienne vegetables, Asian greens and Thai dressing.

✓ CALORIES: Good Choice (560) CHOLESTEROL: Moderate (275 mg)
✓ FAT: Good Choice (19 g)* SODIUM: Moderate (965 mg)**
EXCHANGES: 4¼ Meat (extra lean), 3 Bread, 2 Veg, 3½ Fat
PROTEIN: 41 g, CARBOHYDRATE: 57 g

HEALTHY DINING CHINESE CHICKEN SALAD

Chinese greens, bell peppers, sesame seeds, cilantro, scallions, mandarin oranges and fat-free Oriental dressing.

✓ CALORIES: Good Choice (480) ✓ CHOLESTEROL: Good Choice (85 mg)
✓ FAT: Good Choice (13 g) SODIUM: High (2455 mg)
EXCHANGES: 4½ Meat (extra lean), ½ Bread, 3½ Veg, ¾ Fruit, ¾ Fat
PROTEIN: 42 g, CARBOHYDRATE: 49 g

HEALTHY DINING CHOPPED CHICKEN SALAD

Chicken breast, lettuce, tomatoes, olives, fat-free mozzarella, basil and fat-free dressing.

✓ CALORIES: Good Choice (395) ✓ CHOLESTEROL: Good Choice (90 mg)
✓ FAT: Good Choice (11 g) SODIUM: High (3130 mg)
EXCHANGES: 6¾ Meat (extra lean), 1¼ Veg, ¼ Fruit, 1¼ Fat
PROTEIN: 52 g, CARBOHYDRATE: 20 g

at least 2 fruit/vegetable servings

✓ Good Choice ✓✓ Excellent Choice

Sandy Crabbe, owner of The SandCrab Cafe, offers seafood with a difference. A California version of an East Coast Crab House, various seafood combinations are offered, as well as a la carte, including stone crab claws, mussels, and seafood gumbo. Open for lunch & dinner 7 days: Sun.-Thurs. 11 am - 9 pm, Fri.-Sat. 11 am - 10 pm. A different way to dine for the whole family. $$

SandCrab Cafe 2229 Micro Place, Escondido, CA 92029 (760) 480-CRAB (2722)

Directions: From Hwy 78 exit Nordahl south to Mission, turn right onto Mission, then first left onto Barham, left on Opper, then another left onto Micro Place.

SEAFOOD GUMBO

Spicy!

✓✓ CALORIES: Excellent Choice (255) ✓✓ CHOLESTEROL: Excellent Choice (70 mg)
✓✓ FAT: Excellent Choice (6 g)* ✓✓ SODIUM: Excellent Choice (255 mg)**
EXCHANGES: 2½ Meat (extra lean), 1¾ Bread, ½ Veg, 1 Fat
PROTEIN: 21 g, CARBOHYDRATE: 30 g

SNOW CRAB CLUSTERS

One pound. Cooked in our own special broth of savory spices. Analysis does not include butter.

✓✓ CALORIES: Excellent Choice (145) ✓✓ CHOLESTEROL: Excellent Choice (70 mg)
✓✓ FAT: Excellent Choice (1 g)* SODIUM: High (1970 mg)
EXCHANGES: 4¼ Meat (extra lean)
PROTEIN: 31 g, CARBOHYDRATE: 1 g

STONE CRAB CLAWS

Cooked in our own special broth of savory spices. Analysis does not include butter.

✓✓ CALORIES: Excellent Choice (195) ✓ CHOLESTEROL: Good Choice (95 mg)
✓✓ FAT: Excellent Choice (1 g)* SODIUM: High (2625 mg)
EXCHANGES: 5½ Meat (extra lean)
PROTEIN: 42 g, CARBOHYDRATE: 1 g

ALL CRAB COMBO

Snow crab, blue crab, stone crab claws, king crab leg, new potatoes and corn on the cob. Sausage and bread not included in analysis.

✓ CALORIES: Good Choice (360) ✓✓ CHOLESTEROL: Excellent Choice (65 mg)
✓✓ FAT: Excellent Choice (3 g)* SODIUM: High (3615 mg)
EXCHANGES: 2 Meat (extra lean), 5¾ Bread
PROTEIN: 28 g, CARBOHYDRATE: 58 g

FISHERMAN'S SAMPLER (½ SERVING)

Shrimp, clams, snow crab clusters, crawfish, New Zealand mussels, stone crab claws, lobster tail, new potatoes and corn on the cob all cooked in our own special broth of savory spices. Analysis for ½ of one large serving. Sausage and bread not included in analysis.

✓ CALORIES: Good Choice (395) CHOLESTEROL: High (300 mg)
✓✓ FAT: Excellent Choice (4 g)* SODIUM: High (2965 mg)
EXCHANGES: 7½ Meat (extra lean), 3 Bread
PROTEIN: 58 g, CARBOHYDRATE: 31 g

* Primarily unsaturated fat

** If you request no added salt

Please join Dan and Susan Sbicca for breakfast, lunch or dinner and savor contemporary American cuisine at it's most creative and flavorful. Enjoy ocean view terrace dining, cocktails, fine wines and good friends at Sbicca in the village of Del Mar. $$

Sbicca

215 15th Street, Del Mar, CA 92014   (858) 481-1101   www.sbiccabistro.com

GRILLED POLENTA (½ SERVING)† ☺

with wild mushrooms, artichoke hearts, sun dried tomato and ricotta salata. Analysis is for ½ of an appetizer portion.

✓ CALORIES: Good Choice (140)   ✓✓ CHOLESTEROL: Excellent Choice (<5 mg)
✓✓ FAT: Excellent Choice (3 g)*   ✓ SODIUM: Good Choice (165 mg)
EXCHANGES: ½ Bread, 2 Veg, ½ Fat
PROTEIN: 5 g, CARBOHYDRATE: 22 g

VEGETABLE LASAGNA ROULADES (½ SERVING)

Spinach, artichoke heart and mixed mushrooms with parmesan and marinara. Analysis is for ½ of a full serving.

✓ CALORIES: Good Choice (400)   ✓ CHOLESTEROL: Good Choice (100 mg)
✓ FAT: Good Choice (15 g)   SODIUM: Moderate (765 mg)**
EXCHANGES: 2½ Meat, 2 Bread, 1¼ Veg, 1½ Fat
PROTEIN: 26 g, CARBOHYDRATE: 40 g

SPICY CAJUN PENNE PASTA ☺

with rock shrimp, chicken andouille sausage, corn, roasted bell peppers and tomato-garlic sauce.

CALORIES: Moderate (655)   CHOLESTEROL: Moderate (265 mg)
✓ FAT: Good Choice (19 g)   SODIUM: High (1850 mg)
EXCHANGES: 7¼ Meat, 3½ Bread, 1¼ Veg, 1 Fat
PROTEIN: 58 g, CARBOHYDRATE: 65 g

CHEF'S WHITE OMELETTE – SPECIAL REQUEST

Omelette with artichoke hearts, grilled chicken, dill, green onion and Swiss cheese. <u>Request egg whites</u>. Served only on weekends.

✓ CALORIES: Good Choice (405)   ✓ CHOLESTEROL: Good Choice (95 mg)
✓ FAT: Good Choice (17 g)   SODIUM: Moderate (630 mg)**
EXCHANGES: 6¾ Meat, ¾ Veg, 1¾ Fat
PROTEIN: 51 g, CARBOHYDRATE: 9 g

SALMON & AVOCADO SALSA

Grilled salmon with corn, avocado-caper salsa and black bean sauce.

✓ CALORIES: Good Choice (380)   ✓ CHOLESTEROL: Good Choice (95 mg)
✓ FAT: Good Choice (17 g)*   ✓ SODIUM: Good Choice (405 mg)**
EXCHANGES: 4¾ Meat, ¾ Bread, 1 Fat
PROTEIN: 39 g, CARBOHYDRATE: 16 g

---

† Side dish guidelines are 1/3 of entree guidelines   ☺ at least 2 fruit/vegetable servings for entrée, 1 for side dish

            ✓ Good Choice   ✓✓ Excellent Choice

Sizzler is famous for affordable, delicious and comfortable family dining. Our grill menu features fresh, lean steaks and boneless skinless breast of chicken that is marinated and grilled to perfection. Our salad bar offers even more variety. From fresh fruit, crisp vegetables and tasty salads to hot, steaming soups and fresh baked bread, our salad bar offers an endless variety of delicious, healthy items that you can select to suit your tastes and nutritional needs. At Sizzler, delicious healthy dining sounds good. $

Participating Sizzler Locations:

1030 Fletcher Pkwy., El Cajon	(619) 596-1695	3805 Plaza Dr., Oceanside	(760) 630-1551
355 N. Escondido Blvd., Escondido	(760) 741-2568	2855 Midway Dr., San Diego	(619) 224-3347
	3755 Murphy Canyon Rd., San Diego	(858) 278-6988	

GARDEN BURGER – SPECIAL REQUEST

The classic meatless burger topped with grilled mushrooms, crisp lettuce, fresh sliced tomato and red onion. Served with choice of sides, not included in analysis. Request less margarine (¼ oz).

- ✓ CALORIES: Good Choice (500)
- ✓ FAT: Good Choice (14 g)
- ✓✓ CHOLESTEROL: Excellent Choice (5 mg)
- SODIUM: Moderate (895 mg)**

EXCHANGES: ¼ Meat, 4¾ Bread, ½ Veg, 2¼ Fat
PROTEIN: 18 g, CARBOHYDRATE: 74 g

RAINBOW TROUT – SPECIAL REQUEST

Trout with lemon pepper seasoning, served with steamed vegetables. Request butter on the side. Served with choice of sides, not included in analysis. Butter sauce and cheese toast not included in analysis.

- ✓ CALORIES: Good Choice (390)
- ✓ FAT: Good Choice (17 g)
- ✓ CHOLESTEROL: Good Choice (120 mg)
- ✓ SODIUM: Good Choice (440 mg)**

EXCHANGES: 6¼ Meat (extra lean), 1¾ Veg, ¾ Fat
PROTEIN: 47 g, CARBOHYDRATE: 11 g

SIZZLIN' GARLIC HERB CHICKEN – SPECIAL REQUEST

Seasoned chicken served with grilled vegetables and cheese toast (cheese toast not included in analysis). Request less garlic margarine (½ oz).

- ✓ CALORIES: Good Choice (575)
- ✓ FAT: Good Choice (20 g)
- CHOLESTEROL: Moderate (215 mg)
- SODIUM: Moderate (755 mg)**

EXCHANGES: 11¼ Meat (extra lean), 2¼ Veg, 2¼ Fat
PROTEIN: 81 g, CARBOHYDRATE: 13 g

DOUBLE HIBACHI CHICKEN DINNER – SPECIAL REQUEST

Chicken breast, 10 oz., broiled and basted with Hibachi sauce and served with fresh broccoli and cheese toast. Cheese toast not included in analysis. Request steamed broccoli.

- ✓ CALORIES: Good Choice (575)
- ✓ FAT: Good Choice (14 g)
- CHOLESTEROL: Moderate (215 mg)
- SODIUM: High (1160 mg)

EXCHANGES: 11¼ Meat (extra lean), 2 Veg, ¼ Fruit, 1 Fat
PROTEIN: 85 g, CARBOHYDRATE: 25 g

SIZZLIN' GRILLED SHRIMP SKEWERS

Grilled shrimp served on skewers. Served on a bed of vegetables with melted margarine. Request no margarine on vegetables and less margarine in preparation (½ oz).

- ✓ CALORIES: Good Choice (430)
- ✓ FAT: Good Choice (16 g)*
- CHOLESTEROL: High (385 mg)
- SODIUM: Moderate (465 mg)**

EXCHANGES: 7¼ Meat (extra lean), 2¼ Veg, 2½ Fat
PROTEIN: 55 g, CARBOHYDRATE: 16 g

* Primarily unsaturated fat
** If you request no added salt

Souplantation™
The Salad Buffet Restaurant

As one of the original salad buffet restaurants, Souplantation has maintained freshness as a way of life since 1978. We serve only the finest greens and produce and never use fresheners. All of our salad dressings are made from our own original recipes. All our soups and chilies are made from scratch each day, and our made-from-scratch muffins and breads are served warm from the oven. $

Souplantation Locations:

Carlsbad: 1860 Marron Rd.   (760) 434-9100   Mira Mesa: 8105 Mira Mesa Blvd.   (858) 566-1172
Del Mar: 3804 Valley Centre Dr.   (858) 481-3225   Mission Gorge: 6171 Mission Gorge Rd. (619) 280-7087
Kearny Mesa: 7095 Clmnt. Mesa Blvd.   (858) 715-6824   Point Loma: 3960 W. Point Loma Blvd. (619) 222-7404
La Mesa: 9158 Fletcher Pkwy.   (619) 462-4232   Rancho Bernardo: 17210 Brndo. Ctr. Dr. (858) 675-3353

LOW-FAT MUFFINS†
Apple Cinnamon Bran, Cranberry Orange Bran, or Fruit Medley Bran
96% fat-free, made from scratch, and served warm from the oven. Analysis for 1 muffin.
✓✓ CALORIES: Excellent Choice (80)   ✓✓ CHOLESTEROL: Excellent Choice (0 mg)
✓✓ FAT: Excellent Choice (½ g)*   ✓ SODIUM: Good Choice (110 mg)
PROTEIN: 2 g, CARBOHYDRATE: 17 g

LOW-FAT SOUPS & CHILIES†
Chicken Tortilla Soup, Classic Chicken Noodle Soup, Santa Fe Black Bean Chili, Tomato Parmesan & Vegetable, Old Fashioned Vegetable, or Vegetable Medley Soup. 1 cup serving contains:
✓ CALORIES: Good Choice (90 to 190)   ✓✓ CHOLESTEROL: Excellent Choice (0 to 30 mg)
✓✓ FAT: Excellent Choice (1 to 3 g)   SODIUM: High (450 to 990 mg)
PROTEIN: 2 to 17 g, CARBOHYDRATE: 5 to 26 g

FAT-FREE PREPARED SALAD†
Aunt Doris' Red Pepper Slaw. ½ cup contains:
✓✓ CALORIES: Excellent Choice (70)   ✓✓ CHOLESTEROL: Excellent Choice (0 mg)
✓✓ FAT: Excellent Choice (0 g)   SODIUM: High (480 mg)
PROTEIN: 18 g, CARBOHYDRATE: 18 g

LOW-FAT PREPARED SALADS†
*Carrot Raisin, Oriental Ginger Slaw with Krab, Baja Bean & Cilantro,
Gemelli Pasta with Chicken in a Citrus Vinaigrette, German Potato, Mandarin Krab,
Mandarin Noodles with Broccoli, Mandarin Shells with Almonds, Moroccan
Marinated Vegetables, Southern Dill Potato, Spicy Southwestern Pasta. ½ cup contains:*
✓ CALORIES: Good Choice (70 to 180)   ✓✓ CHOLESTEROL: Excellent Choice (0 to 5 mg)
✓✓ FAT: Excellent Choice (3 g)*   SODIUM: Carrot Raisin or Oriental Ginger 80 mg;
others 180 to 380 mg
PROTEIN: 1 to 9 g, CARBOHYDRATE: 8 to 29 g

DESSERTS†
*Chocolate, Tapioca, Vanilla or Rice Pudding, Nutty Waldorf Salad,
Vanilla Soft Serve (½ cup), or Small Chocolate Chip Cookie.*
✓ CALORIES: Good Choice (70 to 140)   ✓✓ CHOLESTEROL: Excellent Choice (0 to 20 mg)
✓✓ FAT: Excellent Choice to Low (3 to 4 g)   SODIUM: Rice Pudding, Soft Serve, Waldorf Salad
or Cookie 50 to 90 mg; others 160 to 220 mg
PROTEIN: 1 to 4 g, CARBOHYDRATE: 10 to 24 g

Nutrition information supplied by Souplantation.

† Side dish guidelines are ⅓ of entree guidelines
✓ Good Choice   ✓✓ Excellent Choice

Spices Thai Café provides you with an excellent selection of Thai cuisine. All dishes are individually prepared with natural ingredients and exotic spices. For your health and pleasure, we use vegetable oil for cooking and no MSG. Some dishes are quite spicy but can be made mild upon request. For vegetarian dishes we use vegetarian chicken. We look forward to your visit! $-$$

Spices Thai Café

3810 Valley Centre Dr., Ste. 903, San Diego, CA 92130 (858) 259-0889
16441 Bernardo Center Dr., San Diego, CA 92128 (858) 674-4665

LARB KAI

Minced chicken spiced with lime juice, chili, rice powder and fresh mint.

✓✓ CALORIES: Excellent Choice (305) ✓✓ CHOLESTEROL: Excellent Choice (55 mg)
✓ FAT: Good Choice (17 g)* SODIUM: High (1865 mg)
EXCHANGES: 2¾ Meat (extra lean), ½ Bread, ½ Veg, ¼ Fruit, 2¾ Fat
PROTEIN: 22 g, CARBOHYDRATE: 15 g

TOM YUM KAI

Chicken in hot and sour soup with fresh mushrooms.

✓✓ CALORIES: Excellent Choice (195) ✓✓ CHOLESTEROL: Excellent Choice (55 mg)
✓✓ FAT: Excellent Choice (3 g) SODIUM: High (2760 mg)
EXCHANGES: 2¾ Meat (extra lean), ½ Bread, ¼ Veg, ¼ Fruit
PROTEIN: 24 g, CARBOHYDRATE: 18 g

CHICKEN WITH SWEET BASIL

Chicken breast mixed with sliced green chili, basil, onion and mushrooms.

✓✓ CALORIES: Excellent Choice (290) ✓✓ CHOLESTEROL: Excellent Choice (55 mg)
✓ FAT: Good Choice (16 g)* SODIUM: High (2405 mg)
EXCHANGES: 2¾ Meat (extra lean), ¼ Bread, 1¼ Veg, 2¾ Fat
PROTEIN: 22 g, CARBOHYDRATE: 14 g

SEA BASKET ☘

Steamed assorted fesh seafood and vegetables. Served with three kinds of sauce (not included in analysis).

✓ CALORIES: Good Choice (600) CHOLESTEROL: High (530 mg)
✓ FAT: Good Choice (11 g)* SODIUM: Moderate (780 mg)**
EXCHANGES: 9¼ Meat (extra lean), 8¼ Veg
PROTEIN: 78 g, CARBOHYDRATE: 48 g

PHAD THAI NOODLES – SPECIAL REQUEST ☘

Pan fried rice noodles with tofu, vegetables, egg and bean sprouts.
Request tofu and vegetables instead of pork and request no peanuts.

· ✓ CALORIES: Good Choice (485) CHOLESTEROL: Moderate (210 mg)
FAT: Moderate (24 g)* SODIUM: High (5320 mg)
EXCHANGES: 2 Meat, 2 Bread, 1½ Veg, ¼ Fruit, 3¼ Fat
PROTEIN: 22 g, CARBOHYDRATE: 48 g

---

* Primarily unsaturated fat

** If you request no added salt

☘ at least 2 fruit/vegetable servings

Star of India offers a large selection of vegetarian meals, as well as chicken, lamb and seafood, and fresh homemade breads, desserts and yogurt. Meals are cooked to order and can be requested mild, medium, or hot. Many of our most popular dishes are prepared using the Tandoor, a tall cylindrical clay oven that allows the fat to drip away while retaining the flavor. $

Star of India

La Jolla: 1000 Prospect St., La Jolla 92037   (858) 459-3355
Del Mar: 3860 Valley Ctr. Dr., San Diego 92010   (858) 792-1111
Downtown: 423 F Street, San Diego 92101   (619) 544-9891

CHICKEN TIKKA KABAB

Tandoori-prepared boneless chicken marinated with fresh herbs and spices.

✓ CALORIES: Good Choice (385)   CHOLESTEROL: Moderate (195 mg)
✓✓ FAT: Excellent Choice (8 g)   ✓✓ SODIUM: Excellent Choice (295 mg)**
EXCHANGES: 10 Meat (extra lean)
PROTEIN: 72 g, CARBOHYDRATE: 1 g

TANDOORI PRAWNS

Prawns marinated in yogurt, garlic ginger, vinegar and fresh herbs, and cooked in the Tandoor oven.

✓✓ CALORIES: Excellent Choice (260)   CHOLESTEROL: High (500 mg)
✓✓ FAT: Excellent Choice (3 g)*   SODIUM: Moderate (700 mg)**
EXCHANGES: 7½ Meat (extra lean)
PROTEIN: 54 g, CARBOHYDRATE: 1 g

KARAHI CHICKEN ☗

Boneless chicken sautéed with bell peppers, onion and tomatoes in a delicately spiced curry.

✓ CALORIES: Good Choice (410)   ✓ CHOLESTEROL: Good Choice (105 mg)
✓ FAT: Good Choice (15 g)   SODIUM: Moderate (805 mg)**
EXCHANGES: 4¼ Meat, 4½ Veg, ½ Fat
PROTEIN: 37 g, CARBOHYDRATE: 32 g

PRAWN PEPPER MASALA ☗

Prawns cooked with fresh green peppers, onions and spices.

✓✓ CALORIES: Excellent Choice (300)   CHOLESTEROL: Moderate (250 mg)
✓✓ FAT: Excellent Choice (6 g)*   SODIUM: Moderate (865 mg)**
EXCHANGES: 3¾ Meat (extra lean), 4½ Veg, ½ Fat
PROTEIN: 33 g, CARBOHYDRATE: 32 g

ALOO GOBI ☗

Cauliflower and potatoes cooked with herbs and spices.

✓✓ CALORIES: Excellent Choice (195)   ✓✓ CHOLESTEROL: Excellent Choice (0 mg)
✓✓ FAT: Excellent Choice (4 g)*   ✓✓ SODIUM: Excellent Choice (90 mg)**
EXCHANGES: ¾ Bread, 4¼ Veg, ½ Fat
PROTEIN: 8 g, CARBOHYDRATE: 38 g

BENGAN BHARTHA ☗

Eggplant baked in clay oven with onions, peas and tomatoes.

✓✓ CALORIES: Excellent Choice (325)   ✓✓ CHOLESTEROL: Excellent Choice (0 mg)
✓✓ FAT: Excellent Choice (7 g)*   SODIUM: High (1445 mg)
EXCHANGES: 1 Bread, 8½ Veg, 1 Fat
PROTEIN: 13 g, CARBOHYDRATE: 62 g

☗ at least 2 fruit/vegetable servings
✓ Good Choice   ✓✓ Excellent Choice

Su Casa, serving Authentic Mexican Cuisine and innovative Seafood Specialties, was voted "Best in La Jolla" in the 1999 La Jolla Light Readers' Poll. With numerous awards and distinctions, including 8 California Gold Medals for Food Excellence, Su Casa continues its winning tradition. A cozy atmosphere with fireplaces and a garden patio has made Su Casa a favorite with locals and travelers alike! $-$$

Su Casa 6738 La Jolla Blvd., La Jolla, CA 92037 (858) 454-0369

CARNE ASADA TACOS
Three "Street Style" soft tacos filled with green tomatillo salsa, cilantro, onions & spices. Served with black beans & Mexican rice (not included, see analyses below).
- ✓ CALORIES: Good Choice (500)
- ✓✓ CHOLESTEROL: Excellent Choice (70 mg)
- ✓✓ FAT: Excellent Choice (9 g)
- ✓ SODIUM: Good Choice (420 mg)**

EXCHANGES: 5¼ Meat (extra lean), 3¾ Bread, 1 Veg, ¾ Fat
PROTEIN: 46 g, CARBOHYDRATE: 60 g

CHICKEN AL CHIPOTLE
A tender skinless chicken breast, charbroiled & dipped in a delicious spicy chipotle sauce, choose between medium or hot. Served with Mexican rice & refried beans (not included, see rice analysis below). Analysis includes two flour tortillas, but not sour cream or guacamole.
- ✓ CALORIES: Good Choice (575)
- ✓ CHOLESTEROL: Good Choice (130 mg)
- ✓ FAT: Good Choice (17 g)
- SODIUM: Moderate (720 mg)**

EXCHANGES: 6¾ Meat (extra lean), 2½ Bread, 1½ Veg, 2¼ Fat
PROTEIN: 55 g, CARBOHYDRATE: 48 g

VERDE CRAB ENCHILADAS
Awarded California Gold Medal. Two enchiladas stuffed with snow crabmeat, covered with green tomatillo sauce, served with sour cream, guacamole, rice & beans. Rice, beans & sour cream not included, see rice analysis below.
- ✓ CALORIES: Good Choice (470)
- ✓ CHOLESTEROL: Good Choice (80 mg)
- ✓ FAT: Good Choice (17 g)*
- SODIUM: High (1160 mg)

EXCHANGES: 3¾ Meat (extra lean), 2½ Bread, 1 Veg, 2¾ Fat
PROTEIN: 34 g, CARBOHYDRATE: 46 g

CEVICHE TOSTADAS
Fresh white fish marinated in lime juice & spiced with pico de gallo, olives & onions. Served on top of two tostadas with a side of Mexican rice.
- ✓ CALORIES: Good Choice (555)
- ✓✓ CHOLESTEROL: Excellent Choice (40 mg)
- ✓ FAT: Good Choice (19 g)*
- SODIUM: High (1515 mg)

EXCHANGES: 2½ Meat, 3¾ Bread, 1¾ Veg, 7¼ Fat
PROTEIN: 28 g, CARBOHYDRATE: 69 g

FRESH LOCAL SEABASS ☺
Grilled seabass served with steamed vegetables and a baked potato. Analysis includes a plain potato.
- ✓ CALORIES: Good Choice (520)
- ✓✓ CHOLESTEROL: Excellent Choice (70 mg)
- ✓✓ FAT: Excellent Choice (6 g)*
- ✓✓ SODIUM: Excellent Choice (170 mg)**

EXCHANGES: 5½ Meat (extra lean), 3 Bread, 1¾ Veg
PROTEIN: 56 g, CARBOHYDRATE: 60 g

VEGETABLE ENCHILADA ☺
A large red corn tortilla wrapped around & filled with sauteed vegetables, yellow squash, onions & cilantro. Served with refried beans and Mexican rice (not included, see rice analysis below).
- ✓ CALORIES: Good Choice (365)
- ✓✓ CHOLESTEROL: Excellent Choice (35 mg)
- ✓ FAT: Good Choice (19 g)*
- SODIUM: Moderate (890 mg)**

EXCHANGES: 1 Meat (extra lean), 1½ Bread, 2 Veg, ¼ Fruit, 3 Fat
PROTEIN: 15 g, CARBOHYDRATE: 38 g

MEXICAN RICE CAL: 195, FAT: 13 g, CHOL: 0, SOD: 435 mg; EXCH: 1 Br, ½ Veg, 2½ Fat; PRO: 2 g, CARB: 18 g

BLACK BEANS CAL: 120, FAT: ½ g, CHOL: 0, SOD: 135 mg; EXCH: ½ Meat, 1¼ Br, ¼ Veg, ¼ Fat; PRO: 8 g, CARB: 22 g

* Primarily unsaturated fat

** If you request no added salt

SUBWAY® restaurants are committed to serving fresh, high quality, nutritious foods. We bake Italian white and honey wheat bread fresh throughout each day and use only garden fresh veggies. Each sandwich and salad is made to your exact specifications, right before your eyes.

We've added light mayonnaise as a condiment which provides you with 50% less calories and fat per serving than regular mayonnaise. To further reduce fat and calorie intake, try mustard, vinegar, or our fat-free dressings. Baked Lay's Low-Fat Potato Crisps and Fat-Free Rold Gold Pretzels are also offered. Party Platters and Giant 6' Party Subs are available for your healthy entertaining! $

Over 100 San Diego County **SUBWAY®** locations. For the one nearest you, call (619) 688-9255.

All regular Subway Sandwiches include: Onions, Lettuce, Tomatoes, Pickles, Green Peppers and Olives.
*Available upon request: Cheese, Olive Oil Blend, Mayonnaise, Bacon, Light Mayonnaise, Mustard, Vinegar, Salt, Pepper and Hot Peppers. **Nutritional Information stated below is for 6" regular (not double meat) wheat Subs** and includes bread, meat/poultry, and all veggies. No cheese or condiments are included in values stated below. Addition of ingredients from standard sandwich formula may alter nutrition content.*

ROASTED CHICKEN BREAST FILLET

✓✓ CALORIES: Excellent Choice (350) ✓✓ CHOLESTEROL: Excellent Choice (50 mg)
✓✓ FAT: Excellent Choice (6 g) SODIUM: Moderate (980 mg)
EXCHANGES: 2½ Meat, 2½ Bread, 1 Veg
PROTEIN: 27 g, CARBOHYDRATE: 47 g

ROAST BEEF

✓✓ CALORIES: Excellent Choice (305) ✓✓ CHOLESTEROL: Excellent Choice (20 mg)
✓✓ FAT: Excellent Choice (5 g) SODIUM: Moderate (940 mg)
EXCHANGES: 1½ Meat, 2½ Bread, 1 Veg
PROTEIN: 20 g, CARBOHYDRATE: 45 g

SUBWAY CLUB®

✓✓ CALORIES: Excellent Choice (310) ✓✓ CHOLESTEROL: Excellent Choice (25 mg)
✓✓ FAT: Excellent Choice (5 g) SODIUM: High (1350 mg)
EXCHANGES: 1½ Meat, 2½ Bread, 1 Veg
PROTEIN: 21 g, CARBOHYDRATE: 46 g

TURKEY BREAST & HAM

✓✓ CALORIES: Excellent Choice (295) ✓✓ CHOLESTEROL: Excellent Choice (25 mg)
✓✓ FAT: Excellent Choice (5 g) SODIUM: High (1360 mg)
EXCHANGES: 1 Meat, 2½ Bread, 1 Veg
PROTEIN: 18 g, CARBOHYDRATE: 46 g

TURKEY BREAST

✓✓ CALORIES: Excellent Choice (290) ✓✓ CHOLESTEROL: Excellent Choice (20 mg)
✓✓ FAT: Excellent Choice (4 g) SODIUM: High (1405 mg)
EXCHANGES: 1 Meat, 2½ Bread, 1 Veg
PROTEIN: 18 g, CARBOHYDRATE: 46 g

HAM

✓✓ CALORIES: Excellent Choice (300) ✓✓ CHOLESTEROL: Excellent Choice (30 mg)
✓✓ FAT: Excellent Choice (5 g) SODIUM: High (1320 mg)
EXCHANGES: 1 Meat, 2½ Bread, 1 Veg
PROTEIN: 19 g, CARBOHYDRATE: 45 g

VEGGIE DELITE™

✓✓ CALORIES: Excellent Choice (240) ✓✓ CHOLESTEROL: Excellent Choice (0 mg)
✓✓ FAT: Excellent Choice (3 g)* ✓ SODIUM: Good Choice (595 mg)
EXCHANGES: 2½ Bread, 1 Veg
PROTEIN: 9 g, CARBOHYDRATE: 44 g

Nutrition information supplied by Subway®

† Side dish guidelines are 1/3 of entree guidelines

✓ Good Choice ✓✓ Excellent Choice

Sushi on the Rock, a ten-year institution in downtown La Jolla, boasts a high-energy, exuberant atmosphere where healthy food and good taste converge from the partnership of long-time friends executive chef Andrew Sasloe, sushi chef/owner Paul Johnson and his lovely wife Celeste. The sushi menu is perfectly complemented by exciting Asian-influenced favorites. $$

Sushi On the Rock

7734-A Girard Avenue, La Jolla, CA 92037 (858) 456-1138

ROCKIN' LETTUCE CUPS – SPECIAL REQUEST† ☺

Lettuce leaves served with grilled chicken, fresh vegetables and teriyaki sauce. <u>Request no noodles</u>.

CALORIES: Moderate (360)   CHOLESTEROL: High (130 mg)
✓ FAT: Good Choice (6 g)   SODIUM: High (860 mg)
EXCHANGES: 6¾ Meat (extra lean), ¾ Bread, 1¾ Veg
PROTEIN: 52 g, CARBOHYDRATE: 24 g

RAINBOW WARRIOR ☺

Tofu, vegetable rainbow roll.

✓ CALORIES: Good Choice (450)   ✓✓ CHOLESTEROL: Excellent Choice (0 mg)
✓ FAT: Good Choice (12 g)*   ✓ SODIUM: Good Choice (575 mg)**
EXCHANGES: ¾ Meat, 3½ Bread, 3¼ Veg, 2 Fat
PROTEIN: 13 g, CARBOHYDRATE: 74 g

BARRIO ROLL

Tuna, cilantro and serrano chili reverse roll, served with salsa.

✓ CALORIES: Good Choice (415)   ✓✓ CHOLESTEROL: Excellent Choice (65 mg)
✓✓ FAT: Excellent Choice (4 g)*   SODIUM: Moderate (845 mg)**
EXCHANGES: 4½ Meat (extra lean), 2¾ Bread, 1¼ Veg
PROTEIN: 39 g, CARBOHYDRATE: 54 g

ORANGE CRUSH – SPECIAL REQUEST ☺

Asparagus, cucumber, wasabi tobiko wrapped with salmon and avocado. <u>Request less avocado</u> (1 oz).

✓ CALORIES: Good Choice (565)   CHOLESTEROL: High (320 mg)
✓ FAT: Good Choice (18 g)*   SODIUM: Moderate (625 mg)**
EXCHANGES: 5¼ Meat, 2¾ Bread, 1 Veg, 1 Fat
PROTEIN: 46 g, CARBOHYDRATE: 54 g

CHICKEN (OR SHRIMP) STIR-FRY ☺

Fresh vegetables stir-fried with chicken and teriyaki sauce. Analysis is for chicken; shrimp is similar.

✓ CALORIES: Good Choice (380)   ✓ CHOLESTEROL: Good Choice (85 mg)
✓✓ FAT: Excellent Choice (9 g)   SODIUM: High (1165 mg)
EXCHANGES: 4½ Meat (extra lean), 1 Bread, 4 Veg, 1 Fat
PROTEIN: 38 g, CARBOHYDRATE: 39 g

SESAME CRUSTED TUNA – SPECIAL REQUEST ☺

Ahi tuna encrusted with sesame seeds and served with fresh vegetables. <u>Request no butter</u>.

✓ CALORIES: Good Choice (600)   ✓✓ CHOLESTEROL: Excellent Choice (75 mg)
✓ FAT: Good Choice (16 g)*   SODIUM: High (1455 mg)
EXCHANGES: 5½ Meat (extra lean), 2¾ Bread, 2 Veg, 1½ Fat
PROTEIN: 49 g, CARBOHYDRATE: 61 g

GRILLED SHRIMP SALAD ☺

Grilled shrimp on top of baby lettuce leaves mixed with lemon dressing.

✓✓ CALORIES: Excellent Choice (205)   CHOLESTEROL: Moderate (230 mg)
✓✓ FAT: Excellent Choice (9 g)*   SODIUM: Moderate (860 mg)**
EXCHANGES: 3½ Meat (extra lean), ½ Veg, 1½ Fat
PROTEIN: 26 g, CARBOHYDRATE: 5 g

---

* Primarily unsaturated fat

** If you request no added salt

☺ at least 2 fruit/vegetable servings for entrée, 1 for side dish

Since 1979, Leo Sciuto and his sons have been serving San Diegans a tasty mix of Mexican food & spirits at their 4 popular Tio Leo's locations. Leo's main objective was to serve not only great food, but also generous portions with reasonable prices. Come and taste for yourself! $

Tio Leo's

Del Mar: 3510 Valley Centre Dr.	(858) 350-1468
Mission Gorge: 6333 Mission Gorge Road	(619) 280-9944
Mira Mesa: 10787 Camino Ruiz	(858) 695-1461
Morena/Napa: 5302 Napa Street	(619) 542-1462

POLLO ASADA TACOS

Two grilled chicken tacos, with Tio Leo's special seasoning. Includes two whole wheat tortillas. Served with black beans and Mexican coleslaw (see analyses below).

✓ CALORIES: Good Choice (550)　　　CHOLESTEROL: Moderate (160 mg)
✓ FAT: Good Choice (20 g)　　　SODIUM: Moderate (800 mg)**
EXCHANGES: 7¾ Meat (extra lean), 1½ Bread, ¾ Veg, 1¼ Fat
PROTEIN: 62 g, CARBOHYDRATE: 30 g

GRILLED EGGPLANT TACOS ☙

Two delicious marinated eggplant tacos grilled to perfection. Served with cabbage, pico de gallo and feta cheese in a corn tortilla. Served with black beans and Mexican coleslaw (see analyses below).

✓ CALORIES: Good Choice (395)　　　✓✓ CHOLESTEROL: Excellent Choice (25 mg)
✓ FAT: Good Choice (14 g)　　　✓ SODIUM: Good Choice (540 mg)**
EXCHANGES: ½ Meat, 3¼ Bread, 2½ Veg, 2¼ Fat
PROTEIN: 12 g, CARBOHYDRATE: 61 g

VEGETARIAN BURRITO

Black beans, pinto beans, rice and cheese rolled in a whole wheat or flour tortilla with pico de gallo. Served with Mexican coleslaw (see analysis below).

✓ CALORIES: Good Choice (565)　　　✓✓ CHOLESTEROL: Excellent Choice (15 mg)
✓ FAT: Good Choice (13 g)　　　SODIUM: Moderate (825 mg)**
EXCHANGES: 1¼ Meat, 5¾ Bread, ¾ Veg, 1 Fat
PROTEIN: 25 g, CARBOHYDRATE: 89 g

POLLO ASADA RICE BOWL

Chicken breast with Spanish rice, black beans, pico de gallo & avocado. Tortillas not included in analysis.

CALORIES: Moderate (685)　　　✓ CHOLESTEROL: Good Choice (130 mg)
✓ FAT: Good Choice (17 g)　　　SODIUM: High (1035 mg)
EXCHANGES: 7½ Meat (extra lean), 4 Bread, 1 Veg, ¼ Fruit, 2 Fat
PROTEIN: 63 g, CARBOHYDRATE: 70 g

BLACK BEAN TOSTADA ☙

Black beans with feta cheese, avocado, lettuce and pico de gallo. Analysis does not include shell.

✓ CALORIES: Good Choice (440)　　　✓✓ CHOLESTEROL: Excellent Choice (20 mg)
✓ FAT: Good Choice (16 g)　　　SODIUM: Moderate (875 mg)**
EXCHANGES: 1¼ Meat, 2½ Bread, 2 Veg, ¼ Fruit, 2½ Fat
PROTEIN: 23 g, CARBOHYDRATE: 57 g

BLACK BEANS

CAL: 148, FAT: 1 g*, CHOL: 0, SOD: 269 mg; EXCH: ¾ Meat, 1¾ Bread; PROT: 10 g, CARB: 27 g

MEXICAN COLESLAW ☙

CAL: 131, FAT: 9 g*, CHOL: 0, SOD: 137 mg; EXCH: ¼ Bread, ¾ Veg, 1½ Fat; PROT: 3 g, CARB: 12 g

BLACK BEAN SOUP

CAL: 302, FAT: 8 g, CHOL: 0, SOD: 539 mg; EXCH: 1 Meat, 2½ Bread, ½ Veg, 1 Fat; PROT: 16 g, CARB: 43 g

☙ at least 2 fruit/vegetable servings for entrée, 1 for side dish

　　　✓ Good Choice　✓✓ Excellent Choice

Consistently rated one of the top restaurants in San Diego by the Zagat Guide, Chef Josh Thomsen oversees Trattoria Acqua's Northern Italian cuisine with a Mediterranean influence. Trattoria Acqua offers its diners stunning views of the Pacific Ocean and La Jolla Cove. Other distinctions awarded have been "Best Italian" Restaurant in San Diego for the past four years by the San Diego Restaurant Association and one of San Diego's Top Ten Restaurants by Gourmet Magazine. Visit our website at www.trattoriaacqua.com. $$

Trattoria Acqua
1298 Prospect Street, La Jolla, CA 92037 (858) 454-0709

SPIGOLA ALLA PROVENCALE – SPECIAL REQUEST
Oven roasted striped bass with vine-ripened tomatoes cooked with herbs de Provence, shaved fennel and balsamic syrup. Request no oil drizzled over fish when done.
- ✓ CALORIES: Good Choice (450)
- FAT: Moderate (24 g)*
- ✓ CHOLESTEROL: Good Choice (135 mg)
- ✓✓ SODIUM: Excellent Choice (175 mg)**

EXCHANGES: 4¼ Meat (extra lean), ¼ Bread, 3¾ Veg, 3¾ Fat
PROTEIN: 35 g, CARBOHYDRATE: 28 g

PIZZA AGLI ORTAGGI (½ PIZZA)
Created by syndicated food columnist and cookbook author Jeanne Jones. Mushrooms, bell peppers, zucchini and red onions with tomato sauce and low fat mozzarella cheese. Analysis is for ½ of a pizza.
- ✓ CALORIES: Good Choice (370)
- ✓ FAT: Good Choice (11 g)
- ✓✓ CHOLESTEROL: Excellent Choice (25 mg)
- SODIUM: High (1505 mg)

EXCHANGES: 1½ Meat, 2¾ Bread, 1½ Veg, ¾ Fat
PROTEIN: 21 g, CARBOHYDRATE: 51 g

SALMONE CON FINOCCHI
A 7-oz. portion of Atlantic salmon seasoned, oven roasted and placed on a bed of saffron braised fennel and French green lentils. The sauce is a pomegranate-curry reduction and the plate is garnished with coriander and an Indian rice cracker called a Pompaddom (Pompaddom not included in analysis.)
- ✓ CALORIES: Good Choice (575)
- FAT: Moderate (22 g)*
- ✓ CHOLESTEROL: Good Choice (105 mg)
- ✓✓ SODIUM: Excellent Choice (290 mg)**

EXCHANGES: 6½ Meat, 1½ Bread, 1¼ Veg, ½ Fruit, 1¾ Fat
PROTEIN: 55 g, CARBOHYDRATE: 37 g

ORECCHIETTE CON GAMBERETTI E ASPA
Orecchiette pasta with spicy shrimp, Italian cured ham, broccoli, white beans, white wine and lemon zest.
- ✓ CALORIES: Good Choice (560)
- ✓✓ FAT: Excellent Choice (9 g)
- CHOLESTEROL: Moderate (165 mg)
- ✓ SODIUM: Good Choice (580 mg)**

EXCHANGES: 3¾ Meat (extra lean), 4¾ Bread, ¼ Veg, ¾ Fat
PROTEIN: 41 g, CARBOHYDRATE: 76 g

ANITRA SUL INDIVIE – SPECIAL REQUEST
Roasted and sliced breast of duck served with endive braised in orange and honey. Garnished with toasted almonds, currants and a sauce of passion fruit. Analysis does not include skin. Request steamed vegetables and less oil (1 tsp).
- ✓ CALORIES: Good Choice (545)
- FAT: Moderate (22 g)
- CHOLESTEROL: Moderate (195 mg)
- ✓✓ SODIUM: Excellent Choice (215 mg)**

EXCHANGES: 7 Meat, 2¾ Veg, ½ Fruit, 1¾ Fat
PROTEIN: 59 g, CARBOHYDRATE: 28 g

* Primarily unsaturated fat
** If you request no added salt

Trellises Garden Grille at the Town and Country Resort Hotel has been recognized for its impeccable service and delicious cuisine for over 45 years. Trellises' menu features creative appetizers, healthy light entrees, a variety of pastas and pizzas, fresh fish, shellfish, vegetable entrees and lavish desserts. We invite you to join us at Trellises where celebrations and special events are our specialty. $$

Trellises Garden Grille

Town & Country Hotel 500 Hotel Circle North, San Diego, CA 92108 (619) 291-7131

GULF SHRIMP AND PASTA

Gulf shrimp sautéed in garlic, shallots and mushrooms. Served over pasta.

✓ CALORIES: Good Choice (600) CHOLESTEROL: Moderate (170 mg)
✓ FAT: Good Choice (19 g)* ✓ SODIUM: Good Choice (445 mg)**
EXCHANGES: 2¾ Meat (extra lean), 4¼ Bread, 1½ Veg, 3 Fat
PROTEIN: 34 g, CARBOHYDRATE: 73 g

SWORDFISH CAPONATA

Grilled swordfish served over caponata.

✓ CALORIES: Good Choice (525) ✓ CHOLESTEROL: Good Choice (115 mg)
✓ FAT: Good Choice (14 g)* ✓✓ SODIUM: Excellent Choice (300 mg)**
EXCHANGES: 8¼ Meat (extra lean), 5¾ Veg, ¼ Fat
PROTEIN: 66 g, CARBOHYDRATE: 33 g

ATHENIAN GREENS

Fresh spinach, tomatoes, bell peppers, cucumbers and feta cheese.

✓✓ CALORIES: Excellent Choice (265) ✓✓ CHOLESTEROL: Excellent Choice (25 mg)
✓ FAT: Good Choice (17 g) SODIUM: HModerate (670 mg)
EXCHANGES: ½ Meat, 4 Veg, 3 Fat
PROTEIN: 12 g, CARBOHYDRATE: 23 g

OVEN POACHED SALMON

Poached salmon served with red potatoes and asparagus.

✓ CALORIES: Good Choice (490) ✓ CHOLESTEROL: Good Choice (120 mg)
FAT: Moderate (21 g)* SODIUM: High (4585 mg)
EXCHANGES: 5¾ Meat, 1¼ Bread, ¼ Veg, ¼ Fruit, 1¼ Fat
PROTEIN: 47 g, CARBOHYDRATE: 26 g

TODAY'S OCEAN CATCH

Fresh catch of the day sautéed with spinach, carrots, garlic and shallots.
Analysis is for halibut, other fish is similar.

✓ CALORIES: Good Choice (475) ✓✓ CHOLESTEROL: Excellent Choice (65 mg)
✓ FAT: Good Choice (20 g)* ✓✓ SODIUM: Excellent Choice (235 mg)**
EXCHANGES: 5 Meat (extra lean), 4½ Veg, ¼ Fruit, 2¾ Fat
PROTEIN: 48 g, CARBOHYDRATE: 29 g

 at least 2 fruit/vegetable servings
✓ Good Choice ✓✓ Excellent Choice

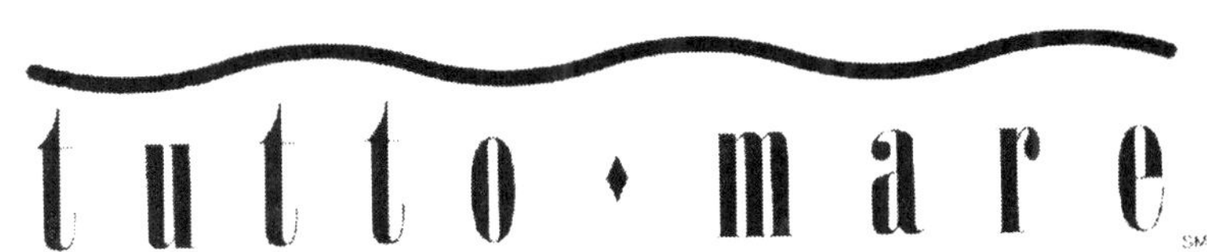

Located in The Plaza at La Jolla Village, Tutto Mare offers a variety of specialties representing the coastal regions of Italy -- whole fish baked in an oak-fire oven, housemade pastas, charcoal-grilled meats, fowl and fresh fish. Hours: Monday 11:30 am to 10:30 pm, Tuesday to Thursday 11:30 am to 11 pm, Friday 11:30 am to 11 pm, Saturday 5 pm to 11 pm, Sunday 5 pm to 10 pm. $$

Tutto Mare   4365 Executive Drive, San Diego, CA 92121   (858) 597-1188

CARPACCIO DI TONNO TIEPIDO AL BALSAMICO

Thinly sliced seared rare ahi tuna, julienne vegetable slaw and balsamic vinegar reduction.
✓✓ CALORIES: Excellent Choice (270)　　✓✓ CHOLESTEROL: Excellent Choice (50 mg)
✓✓ FAT: Excellent Choice (8 g)*　　✓✓ SODIUM: Excellent Choice (270 mg)**
EXCHANGES: 3½ Meat (extra lean), 2¾ Veg, ¼ Fruit, 1¼ Fat
PROTEIN: 29 g, CARBOHYDRATE: 22 g

SAGGIO DI RIVIERA

Mixed organic baby greens, grilled calamari, mixed citrus sections and lemon vinaigrette.
✓✓ CALORIES: Excellent Choice (285)　　CHOLESTEROL: Moderate (265 mg)
✓ FAT: Good Choice (15 g)*　　✓✓ SODIUM: Excellent Choice (55 mg)**
EXCHANGES: 2½ Meat (extra lean), ¼ Veg, ¾ Fruit, 2¾ Fat
PROTEIN: 20 g, CARBOHYDRATE: 18 g

GRIGLIATA MISTA DI PESCE

Mixed seafood grill of calamari, fresh fish and fresh water prawns.
Served with steamed vegetables and roasted potatoes.
✓ CALORIES: Good Choice (510)　　CHOLESTEROL: Moderate (295 mg)
✓ FAT: Good Choice (16 g)*　　✓✓ SODIUM: Excellent Choice (270 mg)**
EXCHANGES: 6 Meat (extra lean), 2 Bread, 1¼ Veg, ¼ Fruit, 2 Fat
PROTEIN: 50 g, CARBOHYDRATE: 44 g

SPAGHETTINI TUTTO MARE

Thin spaghetti, black mussels, clams, langostino and garlic in a spicy tomato sauce.
CALORIES: Moderate (840)　　✓ CHOLESTEROL: Good Choice (125 mg)
✓ FAT: Good Choice (19 g)*　　✓ SODIUM: Good Choice (420 mg)**
EXCHANGES: 6¼ Meat (extra lean), 5¼ Bread, 2 Veg, 3 Fat
PROTEIN: 64 g, CARBOHYDRATE: 98 g

PESCE FRESCO

Fresh fish of the day grilled with fresh herbs and served with
steamed seasonal vegetables. Analysis for halibut.
✓ CALORIES: Good Choice (435)　　✓ CHOLESTEROL: Good Choice (95 mg)
✓ FAT: Good Choice (14 g)*　　✓✓ SODIUM: Excellent Choice (205 mg)**
EXCHANGES: 8¼ Meat (extra lean), 1¾ Veg, ¼ Fruit, 1½ Fat
PROTEIN: 66 g, CARBOHYDRATE: 12 g

* Primarily unsaturated fat
** If you request no added salt

Healthy Dining in San Diego **117**

The Vegetarian Zone is approaching its 25th anniversary. To celebrate our success and to meet customers' requests, we are now offering business catering services as well as on-site private parties and specially prepared treats from our healthy bakery. We do not use refined sugar, white flour, iceberg lettuce or meat in any of our products. In the past few years, The Vegetarian Zone has received numerous awards including "One of Top 50 Vegetarian Restaurants in the United States" (1996) from Natural Living Today, and "...one of the two best [vegetarian restaurants] in the West" (1996) by Vegetarian Times. The Vegetarian Zone was voted in the top 3 for "Best Healthy Restaurants in San Diego County" from 1997-1999 by the San Diego Union-Tribune Poll and was named "Best Health Restaurant" by Metropolitan Magazine (1999). $

The Vegetarian Zone

2949 Fifth Avenue, San Diego, CA 92103 (619) 298-7302

SPLIT PEA SOUP (8 OZ)†

✓✓ CALORIES: Moderate (350)   ✓✓ CHOLESTEROL: Excellent Choice (0 mg)
✓✓ FAT: Excellent Choice (1 g)*   SODIUM: Moderate (205 mg)
EXCHANGES: 1¾ Meat (extra lean), 4 Bread, ¾ Veg
PROTEIN: 24 g, CARBOHYDRATE: 63 g

MUSHROOM APHRODITE (3 MUSHROOMS)†

CALORIES: Moderate (280)   ✓✓ CHOLESTEROL: Excellent Choice (0 mg)
FAT: High (11 g)*   SODIUM: High (510 mg)**
EXCHANGES: 1½ Bread, 1¾ Veg, 2¼ Fat
PROTEIN: 12 g, CARBOHYDRATE: 35 g

CURRIED VEGETABLES ☺

✓✓ CALORIES: Excellent Choice (333)   ✓✓ CHOLESTEROL: Excellent Choice (<1 mg)
✓✓ FAT: Excellent Choice (2 g)*   SODIUM: Moderate (909 mg)**
EXCHANGES: 2 Bread, 5½ Veg, ¼ Fruit, ¼ Fat
PROTEIN: 13 g, CARBOHYDRATE: 69 g

VEGETARIAN CHICKEN WITH VEGETABLES ☺

Served with rice (not included in analysis).

✓✓ CALORIES: Excellent Choice (347)   ✓✓ CHOLESTEROL: Excellent Choice (0 mg)
✓ FAT: Good Choice (12 g)*   ✓ SODIUM: Good Choice (578 mg)**
EXCHANGES: 3¼ Meat (extra lean), 1¾ Bread, 3 Veg, 2¼ Fat
PROTEIN: 32 g, CARBOHYDRATE: 30 g

MAPLE BAKED CUSTARD (DESSERT)†

✓✓ CALORIES: Excellent Choice (74)   ✓✓ CHOLESTEROL: Excellent Choice (39 mg)
✓✓ FAT: Excellent Choice (2 g)   ✓✓ SODIUM: Excellent Choice (120 mg)**
EXCHANGES: ¾ Meat, ¼ Bread, ¼ Milk, ¼ Fat
PROTEIN: 6 g, CARBOHYDRATE: 8 g

---

† Side dish guidelines are 1/3 of entree guidelines

☺ at least 2 fruit/vegetable servings

✓ Good Choice   ✓✓ Excellent Choice

Whole Foods Market

8825 Villa La Jolla Drive, La Jolla, CA 92037 (858) 642-6700

711 University Avenue (Hillcrest), San Diego, CA 92103 (619) 294-2800

ASIAN GINGER SALMON (6 OZ. FILET)

The very intense, Asian inspired sauce makes this dish a consistent favorite.

✓✓ CALORIES: Excellent Choice (280) ✓✓ CHOLESTEROL: Excellent Choice (70 mg)

✓ FAT: Good Choice (18 g)* SODIUM: High (1005 mg)

EXCHANGES: 3¼ Meat, 1¾ Fat

PROTEIN: 28 g, CARBOHYDRATE: 1 g

RAPID DRAGON GREENS (8 OZ. SERVING)

Chard, kale, cabbage and carrots with just a hint of raspberry make this salad stand out above the rest.

✓✓ CALORIES: Excellent Choice (225) ✓✓ CHOLESTEROL: Excellent Choice (0 mg)

✓ FAT: Good Choice (16 g)* SODIUM: Moderate (810 mg)**

EXCHANGES: 1¾ Veg, 3¼ Fat

PROTEIN: 5 g, CARBOHYDRATE: 18 g

POACHED SALMON (6 OZ. FILET)

White wine, lemons and dill complement the salmon perfectly in this dish

✓✓ CALORIES: Excellent Choice (220) ✓ CHOLESTEROL: Good Choice (80 mg)

✓✓ FAT: Excellent Choice (9 g)* ✓✓ SODIUM: Excellent Choice (145 mg)**

EXCHANGES: 3¾ Meat

PROTEIN: 29 g, CARBOHYDRATE: 1 g

IT'S ALIVE (8 OZ. SERVING)

Tons of sprouts and cubes of tofu mingle with a spicy Szechwan sauce to create this very exceptional salad.

✓✓ CALORIES: Excellent Choice (120) ✓✓ CHOLESTEROL: Excellent Choice (0 mg)

✓✓ FAT: Excellent Choice (6 g)* ✓ SODIUM: Good Choice (315 mg)**

EXCHANGES: ½ Meat, 1¼ Veg, ½ Fat

PROTEIN: 10 g, CARBOHYDRATE: 10 g

GRILLED VEGETABLES (16 OZ. SERVING)

We grill a variety of vegetables to choose from daily.

✓✓ CALORIES: Excellent Choice (115) ✓✓ CHOLESTEROL: Excellent Choice (0 mg)

✓✓ FAT: Excellent Choice (2 g)* ✓✓ SODIUM: Excellent Choice (40 mg)**

EXCHANGES: 4 Veg, ¼ Fat

PROTEIN: 5 g, CARBOHYDRATE: 22 g

* Primarily unsaturated fat
** If you request no added salt

Part III

Health Resource Guide

It's probably easier to live a more healthful lifestyle in Southern California than anywhere in the country. The agreeable climate, gentle pace, health-conscious mindset, and accessibility to health-oriented products and services all promote a healthier way of life.

Healthful living includes more than healthy dining. So in the Health Resource Guide that follows, you'll find an array of "tools" to further support your healthful lifestyle. We think you'll find this guide useful, informative and interesting. The *Healthy Dining* team recognizes the Health Resource Guide organizations for their contributions to a healthier community.

Index

AMERICAN CANCER SOCIETY

8880 Rio San Diego Drive, Suite 100
San Diego, CA 92108-1635
(619) 299-4200

It's difficult to keep up with all the emerging research today on diets and nutrients that may either cause or prevent cancer. Fortunately, you don't have to.

While these studies contribute to our knowledge about the health effects of different components of our diets, they also show that no single food or diet is a magic bullet for preventing cancer. Rather, it's the balance of a variety of healthy foods combined with regular physical activity that lowers cancer risk and contributes to overall good health.

Here are the American Cancer Society's recommendations for your best defense against cancer:

Plant Power: No one knows exactly what combination of vitamins and nutrients reduce cancer risk, but we do know that nutritional supplements don't offer the same protection as fruits, vegetables and grains. The best advice is to eat foods from plant sources and plenty of them. These foods are loaded with cancer-fighting nutrients and antioxidants and should be a large part of every meal.

Cut the Fat: High-fat diets are associated with increased cancer risk, so good health relies on fat-conscious eating decisions. The American Cancer Society recommends limiting foods from animal sources, which can be high in fat. When you do eat meat or dairy, choose lean cuts and low-fat dairy options. Also try baking and broiling foods instead of frying.

Step it Up: Moderate activity for at least 30 minutes a day helps keep your body fit and may reduce your risk of cancer, especially colon cancer. If you are heavier than your recommended weight, increase physical activity and reduce caloric intake. Physical activity doesn't have to be strenuous to be beneficial. It can be as simple as walking, jogging, gardening or doing housework -- anything that you enjoy doing that keeps you moving.

Booze Clues: Alcohol offers few nutrients and can increase the risk of cancer, especially of oral, esophageal, liver and breast cancer. The risk of breast cancer can increase with just a few drinks per week; women at high risk for breast cancer might consider not drinking at all. Limit alcohol consumption, if you drink at all to no more than one drink per day for women or two drinks a day for men.

More than just cancer prevention, a healthy diet and regular activity can reduce your risk of heart disease, help prevent obesity, and increase your energy levels. Smart habits can lead to a long lifetime of health and happiness. It is never too early or too late to start.

If you're worried about cancer, remember this. Wherever you are, if you want to talk to us about cancer, call us. We're here to help you. Just call **1-800-ACS-2345 or visit www.cancer.org.**

AMERICAN DIABETES ASSOCIATION

225 Broadway
San Diego, CA 92101
(619) 234-9897

10445 Old Placerville Road
Sacramento, CA 95827
1-800-DIABETES

Western Region
Serving California and Nevada

The American Diabetes Association is the nation's leading nonprofit health organization providing diabetes research, information and advocacy. The mission of the organization is to "prevent and cure diabetes, and to improve the lives of all people affected by diabetes." To fulfill this mission, the American Diabetes Association funds research, publishes scientific findings, and provides information, education programs and other services to people with diabetes, their families, health care professionals, and the public.

The 1-800-DIABETES program is the cornerstone of the Association's information programs. 1-800-DIABETES is a toll-free help line for people who have questions and concerns about diabetes. Through 1-800-DIABETES, people can request information and literature about diabetes-related topics, including exercise, nutrition and self-management.

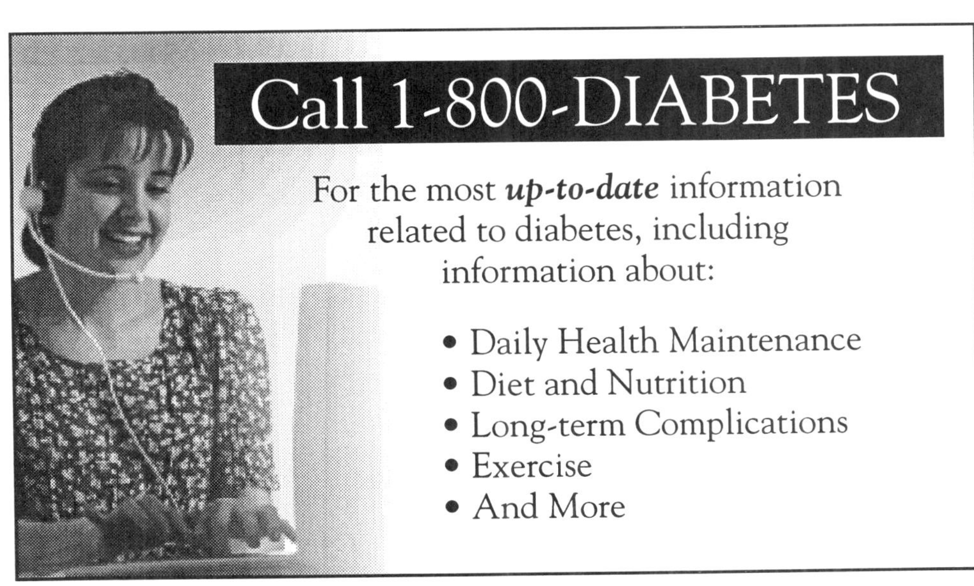

AMERICAN HEART ASSOCIATION

1415 Fifth Avenue
San Diego, CA 92103
(619) 291-7454

Heart disease is the leading cause of death in America, claiming almost one million lives a year. Stroke is the third leading cause of death and the number one cause of disability. The American Heart Association is the nation's oldest and largest voluntary health agency fighting these diseases. Through lifesaving research and preventive education, together we can reduce disability and death from heart disease and stroke.

The soul of the American Heart Association is its people – especially the tireless local volunteers who devote their skills, time and energy for a cause that is "close to their hearts." Donations come from individuals and businesses who understand the need for research and appreciate the value of the work we are doing in the community. For more information, call (619) 291-7454 or reach us online at http:\\www.americanheart.org.

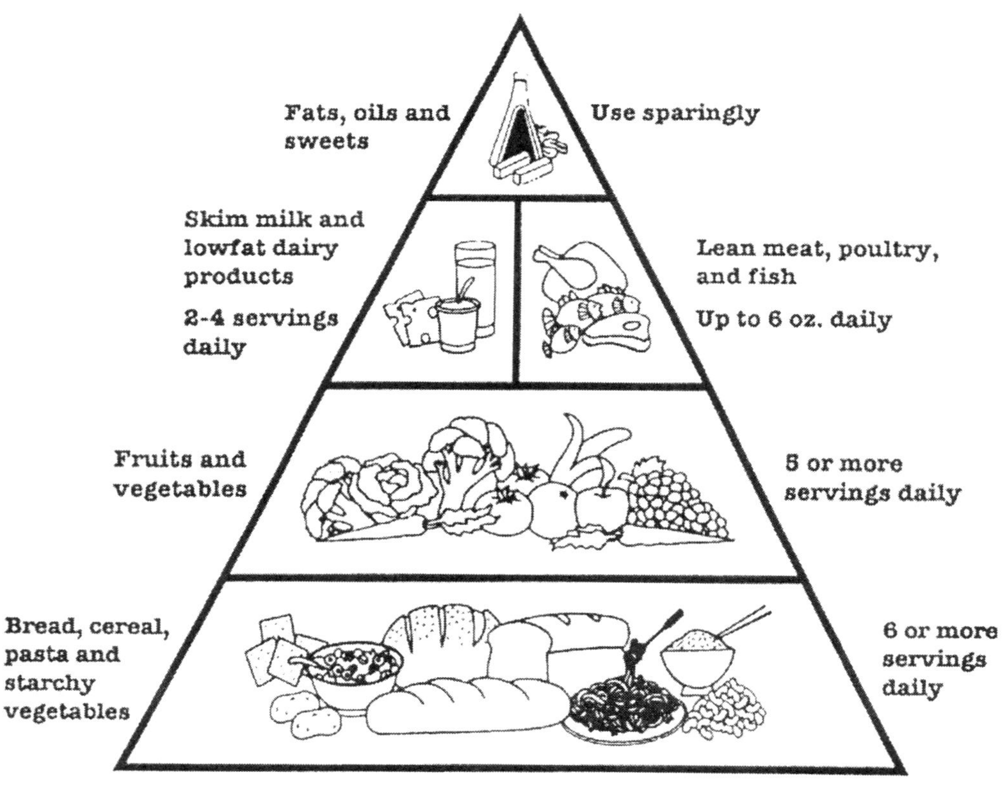

California 5 A Day Campaign

**CANCER PREVENTION and NUTRITION
California Department of Health Services**
**601 N. 7th Street, P.O. Box 942732, MS-662
Sacramento, CA 94234-7320**

Did you know that eating 5 servings of fruits and vegetables every day is one of the most important choices you can make to improve your health? Fruits and vegetables can reduce the risk of cancer, heart disease, high blood pressure and diabetes. They are low in fat and rich in vitamin A, vitamin C, fiber and other nutrients important to good health.

The *California 5 A Day Campaign* encourages Californians to eat 5 or more servings of fruits and vegetables every day as part of a healthy lifestyle to reduce the risk of diet-related diseases, especially cancer and heart disease. The *Campaign* conducts social marketing programs, including the *California Children's 5 A Day – Power Play! Campaign, Latino 5 A Day Campaign, Women's 5 A Day Campaign*, and *Retail 5 A Day Campaign*, all of which offer a variety of materials to help reach the 5 A Day goal.

**Go to the web site for more information
www.ca5aday.com
or call 1-888-EAT-FIVE**

SAN DIEGO COUNTY CERTIFIED FARMERS' MARKETS

Take a bite of San Diego's fresh produce! More than 6,000 farmers work to make agriculture a billion-dollar industry in San Diego County. Many of our county's growers operate small family farms, with 65% harvesting nine acres or less. They have developed a reputation for quality, high-value specialty crops. Visiting one of the Farmers' Markets in San Diego County allows you to experience agriculture. These Farmers' Markets are certified by the State, ensuring that the produce is being sold by the grower, is grown in California and meets all California quality standards. These criteria ensure that you receive the freshest produce for the right price. For more information visit the San Diego Farm Bureau's website at www.sdfarmbureau.org.

CERTIFIED FARMERS' MARKETS SCHEDULE

Tuesday:
Coronado: 2:30 to 6:00 p.m. - Corner of 1st & B Sts. (Ferry Landing & Marketplace)
Escondido: 2:00 to 6:00 p.m - Grand Ave. & Broadway

Wednesday:
Carlsbad: 2:00 to 5:00 p.m. - Roosevelt St. between Grand Ave. & Carlsbad Village Dr.
El Cajon, World Market: 4:00 to7:00 p.m. - Corner of Main & Magnolia, 168 Main St.
Ocean Beach: 4:00 to 7:00 p.m. (Winter), 4:00 to 8:00 p.m. (Summer) - 4900 block of
     Newport Ave.
San Marcos: 8:00 to 11:00 a.m. - San Marcos Restaurant Row

Thursday:
Chula Vista: 3:00 to 6:00 p.m. - 3rd Ave. & Center St.
Julian Farmers Market (Seasonal): 2:30 to 6:30 p.m. - 2907 Washington
Oceanside (downtown): 9:00 a.m. to 12:30 p.m. - Pier View and Hill St.

Friday:
Encinitas (downtown): 2:00 to 5:00 p.m. - 3rd & C (Moonlight Beach parking lot)
La Mesa Village: 3:00 to 6:00 p.m. - Allison St. (East of Spring St.)
Rancho Bernardo Winery: 9:00 a.m. to 12:00 p.m. - Paseo del Verano Norte

Saturday:
Del Mar: 1:00 to 4:00 p.m. - (City Hall Parking Lot) Corner of Camino Del Mar & 10th St.
Pacific Beach: 8:00 a.m. to 12:00 p.m. - (Promenade Mall) Mission Blvd. between Reed &
     Pacific Beach Dr.
Poway: 8:00 to 11:00 a.m. - (Old Poway Park) Corner of Midland & Temple
Temecula: 8:00 a.m. to 12:00 p.m. - 3rd & Front St.
Vista: 8:00 to 11:00 a.m. - Corner of Eucalyptus & Escondido Ave. (City Hall parking lot)

Sunday:
Hillcrest: 9:00 a.m. to 12:00 p.m. - Corner of Normal & Cleveland Sts. (DMV parking lot)
La Jolla: 9:00 a.m. to 1:00 p.m. - La Jolla Elementary School, Girard & Center
Solana Beach: 2:00 to 5:00 p.m. - 124 Lomas Santa Fe Dr. (SB Plaza parking lot)

HENRY'S MARKETPLACE

**15 locations in San Diego and more to come.
Call (619) 258-2900 for the one nearest you.**

Henry's Marketplace was founded in 1941 by Henry Boney. To this day, it is still run by the Boney family and has 15 stores in the San Diego area!

Henry's is known for its farm fresh produce at great prices, but did you know that Henry's also carries bulk bin items like healthy cereals, beans and pastas? How about the finest seafood, hormone-free beef and poultry? We also have one of Southern California's largest selections of natural vitamins and supplements, natural cosmetics, plus much more, like...

- 10% off retail every day on all major brands of vitamins, supplements and herbs.
- 10% off retail every day on all natural cosmetics, body care products and books.
- Save an additional 10% off retail on all major brands of vitamins and supplements, herbs, natural cosmetics, body care products and books when you purchase $100 or more of these items.
- Seniors 55+ receive 10% off retail on all Henry's brand vitamins and supplements with their Henry's Senior Discount Card.
- Henry's has a registered dietitian on staff, available to answer your nutrition questions. See stores for details.

In a nutshell, Henry's is quality products, great prices, friendly and knowledgeable people -- all for you! Call (619) 258-2900 to find the Henry's Marketplace nearest you.

Henry's Marketplace...
"Your stepping stores to better health!"

LA COSTA RESORT AND SPA

WEIGHT MANAGEMENT PROGRAM

Costa del Mar Road
Carlsbad, CA 92009
(760) 438-9111

Mission Statement:

The La Costa Spa Weight Management Program is designed to educate individuals in achieving and maintaining optimal weight and health using the latest research and assistance. Our expert exercise physiologists and registered dietitians provide nutrition education, mind-body exercises, exercise classes and programs.

Eight Week Weight Management Program

Prescreen:
Includes a fitness consultation. Weight, measurements, and fat percentages determined. Discussion of results.

Session One:
Increasing basal metabolism, calculating caloric intake, basics of cardiovascular health, flexibility, and weight training. Eating awareness, behavioral change techniques. Receive nutrition diary.

Session Two:
Introduction to basic nutrition, covering proper amounts of carbohydrates, proteins and fats. Basics of menu planning. Types of fat, essential fatty acids, healthy fats. Introduction of basic weight training for home use. Receive workout diary.

Session Three:
Introduction of basic weight body training for gym use. Food demonstration.

Session Four:
Discussion of supplements and weight loss products. Cardiovascular session. Flexibility session.

Session Five:
Dining out strategies. Cardiovascular session.

Session Six:
Cardio-cross training. Food demonstration.

Postscreen:
Fitness consultation. Weight, measurements, and body fat percentages are taken and compared with those at the outset of the program.

Personal Chefs International

(619) 680-3741

"If you had a Personal Chef, your dinner would be ready!"

- Would you like to enjoy healthy, delicious dinners in your own home, but have someone else do the shopping, cooking and cleanup?

- We will come to your home with our own utensils, shop for your groceries, prepare your meals, then package and refrigerate or freeze them for you to enjoy at your leisure.

- We offer customized menus featuring a variety of dietary alternatives filled with mouthwatering dishes.

- We have chefs that specialize in low-fat, low-salt, vegetarian, diabetic and Ornish diets. We also have chefs that will create menus customized to a diet of your choice such as Kosher, Atkins or Zone.

- While we pride ourselves on our versatility, we also understand the importance of good old-fashioned comfort food.

"Helping you and your family by offering healthy dining alternatives to enjoy in the privacy of your own home."

A Personal Chef is a great gift idea for:

•Working Couples •Busy Singles •Expecting Parents
•Seniors •Families with Newborns

Contact our Personal Chef Referral Line:
(619) 680-3741

Basic Personal Chef Service includes ten entrees for two people. However, programs are available to accommodate singles as well as families. Please ask about our fresh daily programs, as well as small and large dinner party services.

Make your reservation today!
Personal Chefs International
(619) 680-3741

SAN DIEGO DIETETIC ASSOCIATION

The San Diego Dietetic Association (SDDA) is a group of nutrition experts dedicated to promoting healthy lifestyles and food choices and selections throughout the community. To locate a Registered Dietitian in your area, contact the National Center for Nutrition and Dietetics at 1-800-366-1665 or online http://www.eatright.org.
SDDA's website address is http://www.dietitian.org/dietitian/sdda/home.

Good nutrition is important through every stage of life, from conception through the "golden years." A Registered Dietitian can help you improve your overall health.

You may need a Registered Dietitian if ...

... You are eating for 2

... The media  has you confused about nutrition

... You are tired of eating on the  run

... Want to make changes in your life that will lead to a healthier lifestyle

... You have ? ? ? ? ? about food labels

YMCA of San Diego County

Over 13 locations in San Diego County.
Call (858) 292-4034 to find the one nearest you.

Good health lets us all enjoy the goodness of life. That's why you'll find caring instructors at the YMCA. Effective fitness programs make the YMCA a leader in health enhancement that you can count on. Programs include Y's Way to Fitness, Step Aerobics, Aerobics, Water Exercise, Fitness Evaluations, and Strength Training.

The YMCA of San Diego County is an original in our community. It is the oldest and largest youth and family service organization in the county. For over 118 years, the YMCA of San Diego County has been dedicated to improving the quality of human life and to helping all people realize their fullest potential as children of God through development of the spirit, mind and body.

Men, women and children of all ages, races and socio-economic backgrounds participate in a wide variety of programs at over 13 branches in child care, camping, sports and skill development, aquatics, leadership development, social services and health enhancement. For more information, call **(858) 292-4034** for a location near you or visit our home page at http://www.ymca.org.

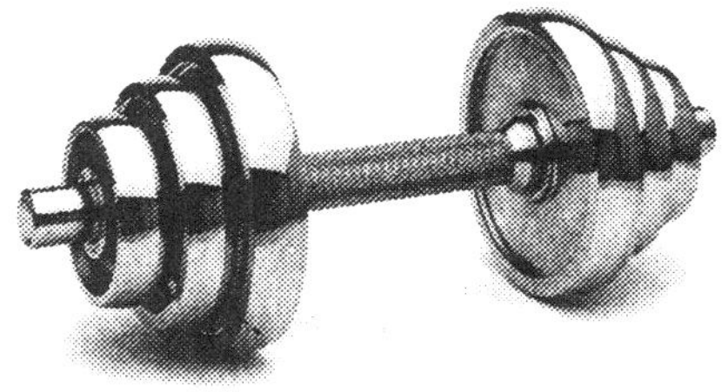

Fitness programs like aerobics and weight training.

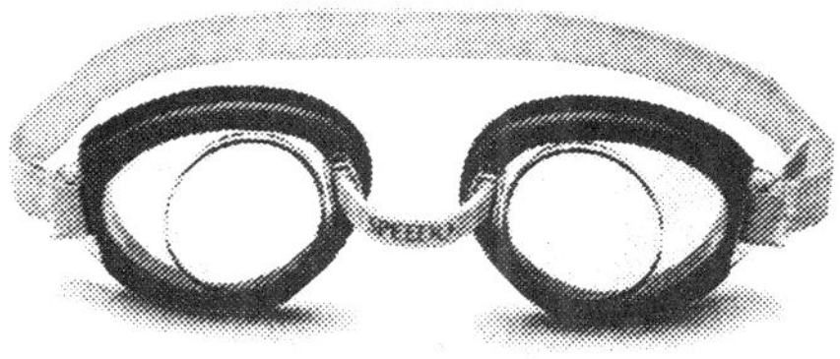

Progressive aquatics program for every age and skill level.

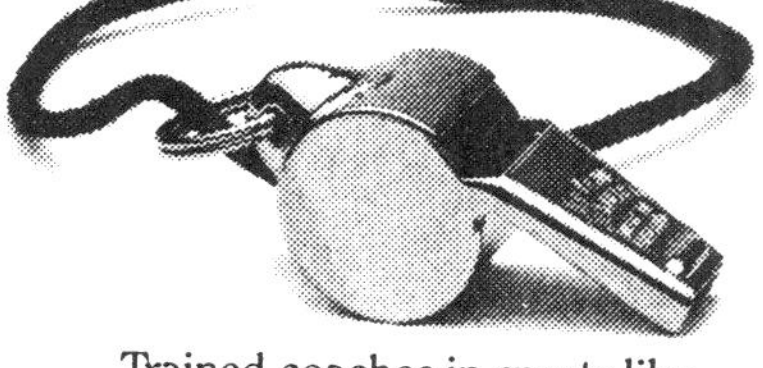

Trained coaches in sports like basketball, soccer, and volleyball.

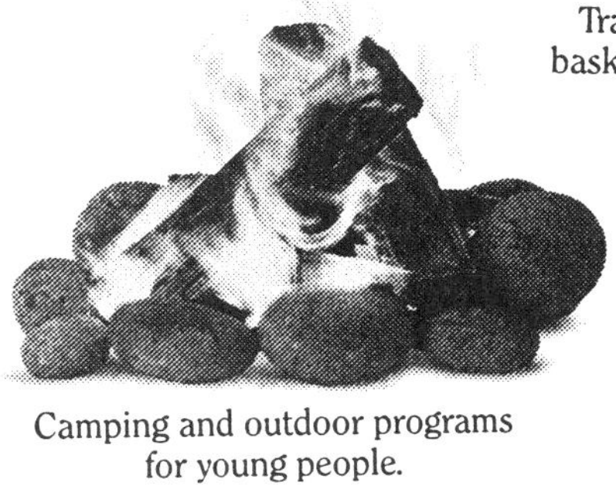

Camping and outdoor programs for young people.

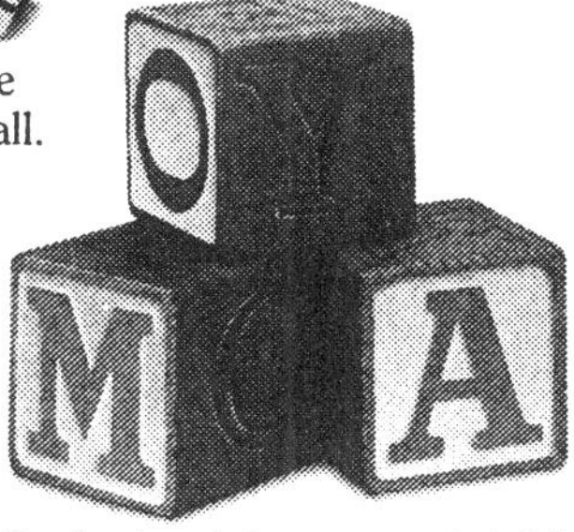

Professional day care and child development services.

Part IV
Chefs' Recipes

Healthy Dining in San Diego is pleased to present a diverse selection of recipes created by chefs of restaurants featured in this book. We are delighted that so many restaurants have elected to participate in this section of *Healthy Dining*, sharing some of their culinary "trade secrets" with *Healthy Dining* readers. The recipes include a wide range of selections --- varying ethnic and regional origins, combinations of flavors, preparation time required, preparation difficulty, and types of dishes (soups, entrees, salads, etc.)

The Recipe Index

On pages 134 through 136 you'll find the Recipe Indexes, first arranged by the type of dish, then by the name of the restaurant that submitted the recipe. Many recipes could easily fall into more than one category within the Recipe Index. For example, a seafood salad could be under either the salads or seafood category. We suggest that you scan the entire Recipe Index to identify dishes that may appeal to you.

Nutritional analysis and modification of the recipes

With few exceptions, the recipes represent dishes that appear on the restaurant's menu page in *Healthy Dining*. We've stated on each recipe page that "This nutritional analysis corresponds to the recipe below. The restaurant version may differ." This notice indicates: (1) The recipe originally submitted to us for nutrition analysis was in bulk quantity and was adjusted to make 4 to 6 servings. In the process, we may have reformulated the recipe slightly so that amounts are expressed in convenient units – for example, ½ cup and not 7 /12 of a cup; (2) We may have substituted more common ingredients; or (3) We may have adjusted the quantities of some ingredients to further improve the nutrition profile.

Unfamiliar ingredients

When an ingredient is included that might be unfamiliar to the "average" cook, we've given some explanation and direction for finding it. If you need further explanation, please call the restaurant, a cooking school, or a specialty market. Or use your creativity and try your own substitutions!

Talk to us!

We wish you enjoyment and satisfaction, challenge and variety in experimenting with the recipes included. We're eager to get your feedback on the recipes included -- please return the questionnaire at the back of your book.

Recipe Index
by Type of Cuisine

Recipe Index
by Restaurant Name

ASIAN CHICKEN SALAD WITH MANGO MUSTARD VINAIGRETTE ☻

Nutrition Information per Serving:

✓ CALORIES: Good Choice (580) ✓ CHOLESTEROL: Good Choice (130 mg)
✓ FAT: Good Choice (17 g) ✓✓ SODIUM: Excellent Choice (170 mg)
EXCHANGES: 6¾ Meat, 1 Veg, 3½ Fruit, 2 Fat
PROTEIN: 50 g, CARBOHYDRATE: 60 g

This nutrition analysis corresponds to the recipe below. The restaurant version may differ.

Ingredients (4 servings):

1½ lb. skinless chicken breasts
pinch ground Chinese peppercorn
pinch ground ginger (optional)
pinch coriander seed†
pinch fennel seed†
pinch cinnamon†
pinch anise†

2 Granny Smith apples,
 julienned
1 cup pea sprouts
1 cup bean sprouts
1½ cups radicchio, julienned
1 cup carrots, julienned

Dressing:

2 cups mango puree††
2 tsp. grained mustard

3 Tbs. rice vinegar
3 Tbs. olive oil

†Five spice powder can be substituted for the above seasonings.
††Can be prepared by pureeing mango pieces.

Directions:

1. Combine spices and sprinkle over chicken. Grill or bake at 350° for 10 to 15 minutes, or until chicken is done. Chill and slice into strips.
2. Combine remaining salad ingredients (apple, sprouts, radicchio and carrots) and toss well.
3. Blend mango, grained mustard and rice vinegar together. Blend in olive oil last.
4. Arrange chicken over salad and drizzle dressing over the top or serve dressing separately.

Recipe supplied by:

Café Japengo
8960 University Center Lane
San Diego, CA 92122
(858) 450-3355

BOK CHOY SALAD ✆

by Patti T. Milligan, MS, RD, Corporate Nutritionist for Henry's Marketplace in San Diego

Nutrition Information per Serving:

✓✓ CALORIES: Excellent Choice (320)   ✓✓ CHOLESTEROL: Excellent Choice (5 mg)
✓ FAT: Good Choice (19 g)*   ✓ SODIUM: Good Choice (390 mg)
EXCHANGES: ½ Bread, 4¼ Veg, 2½ Fat
PROTEIN: 8 g, CARBOHYDRATE: 33 g

This nutrition analysis corresponds to the recipe below. The restaurant version may differ.

*Primarily unsaturated fat

Ingredients (4 servings):

Salad:

2 Tbs. margarine
¼ cup sesame seeds
2 tsp. sugar
3 oz. package ramen noodles, broken in pieces
4 small green onions with tops
1 head of bok choy

Dressing:

2 Tbs. olive oil
2 Tbs. orange juice
⅛ cup red wine vinegar
1 Tbs. low sodium soy sauce

Directions:

Salad:

1. Melt margarine in a small saucepan.
2. Add noodles and cook on medium heat for 5 minutes.
3. Add sugar and cook one minute more. Add sesame seeds and cook 30 seconds more (or until golden).
4. Chop onions and shred bok choy with a knife (a food processor shreds the bok choy too finely); mix in a large bowl.
5. Add noodle mixture, toss, and chill.

Dressing:

1. Mix all ingredients together in a bowl and chill.
2. Toss with salad and serve. (If you wish to reduce the amount of fat in the dish, pour a small amount of dressing on each salad and put the remainder on the table for guests to use at their own discretion).

Recipe supplied by:

Henry's Marketplace
15 San Diego locations
Call (619) 258-2900 for the one nearest you.

   ✆ at least 2 fruit/vegetable servings

MANGO CHUTNEY CHICKEN PASTA SALAD

Nutrition Information per Serving:

- ✓ CALORIES: Good Choice (490)
- ✓ FAT: Good Choice (11 g)
- ✓✓ CHOLESTEROL: Excellent Choice (65 mg)
- SODIUM: Moderate (730 mg)

EXCHANGES: 3¼ Meat (extra lean), 2¼ Bread, 1½ Fruit, 1½ Fat

PROTEIN: 31 g, CARBOHYDRATE: 66 g

This nutrition analysis corresponds to the recipe below. The restaurant version may differ.

Ingredients (6 servings):

Mango Chutney†:

1½ mangos
¼ cup rice vinegar
3 Tbs. sugar
¾ tsp. salt
¼ cup raisins, seedless
½ piece star anise
½ medium cinnamon stick (1½ inches)
½ Tbs. ginger root, peeled & quartered
½ small jalapeno, seeded & deveined
2 garlic cloves
½ tsp. each ground cumin and coriander
¼ tsp. ground turmeric
1 Tbs. canola oil

Pasta Salad:

3 boneless, skinless chicken
  breasts (16 oz.)
½ cup nonfat mayonnaise
½ cup nonfat sour cream
¼ cup mango chutney
½ tsp. salt
8 oz. dry pasta
2 Tbs. cilantro, chopped
1 medium green onion, chopped
1 can (11 oz.) mandarin oranges,
  drained (or 1 fresh)
½ cup coconut
¼ cup sliced almonds

† To save time, you can also purchase prepared mango chutney.

Directions:

Mango Chutney:

1. Peel mangos and dice into ½ inch cubes.
2. In a small bowl, toss mango with vinegar, sugar, salt, raisins, anise and cinnamon.
3. Make a seasoning paste by pureeing ginger, jalapeno, garlic, cumin, coriander, and turmeric in a food processor.
4. Heat paste in a saucepan with oil and stir for 30 seconds over medium-high heat.
5. Add mangos and cook, stirring occasionally until mangos are tender. Cool.
6. Discard cinnamon stick & star anise. Keep covered and chilled and use for up to one month.

Pasta Salad:

1. Grill chicken, cool, and cut into cubes. Set aside.
2. In a large bowl, combine mayonnaise, sour cream, mango chutney and salt.
3. Toss with grilled chicken and let marinate at least 2 hours.
4. Cook pasta and drain. Mix pasta with sauce and chicken. Add cilantro, green onion and mandarin oranges; toss gently.
5. Sprinkle with coconut and sliced almonds before serving.

Recipe supplied by:

Personal Chefs International
(619) 680-3741

ORIENTAL PASTA CHICKEN SALAD 🍎

Nutrition Information per Serving:

✓ CALORIES: Good Choice (525) ✓ CHOLESTEROL: Good Choice (130 mg)
✓ FAT: Good Choice (17 g) ✓ SODIUM: Good Choice (450 mg)
EXCHANGES: 6¾ Meat (extra lean), 1 Bread, 1¾ Veg, ½ Fruit, 2¼ Fat
PROTEIN: 55 g, CARBOHYDRATE: 40 g

This nutrition analysis corresponds to the recipe below. The restaurant version may differ.

Ingredients (4 servings):

Salad:	Dressing:
6 oz. buckwheat soba noodles (dry weight)	**⅓ cup frozen apple juice**
1½ lb. chicken breast	**⅓ cup rice vinegar**
4 cups Napa cabbage	**3 Tbs. sesame oil**
¾ cup green onion	**¾ tsp. Mongolian fire oil†**
½ bell pepper	**1 tsp. ginger root, minced**
¾ cup snow peas	**1 tsp. garlic, minced**
¾ cup dressing	**¼ tsp. salt**
4 green onion stems	**½ tsp. pepper**

† Mongolian fire oil can be found in most supermarkets in the Asian section or in specialty stores.

Directions:

1. Mix all ingredients of dressing well and set aside.
2. Cook soba noodles according to package directions, rinse and cool; set aside.
3. Grill chicken breast until done, and allow to cool. Once cooled, slice chicken.
4. While chicken is grilling, chop the Napa cabbage and green onions, thinly slice bell pepper, and blanch snow peas.
5. In a large bowl, mix soba noodles, Napa cabbage, bell pepper, green onions, ½ cup snow peas and dressing.
6. Top the salad with sliced chicken, remaining snow peas and green onion stems.

Recipe supplied by:

Sushi On the Rock
7734-A Girard
La Jolla, CA 92037
(858) 456-1138

   🍎 at least 2 fruit/vegetable servings

SAGGIO DI RIVIERA ❧

Field greens with grilled calamari, mixed citrus, extra virgin olive oil and lemon.

Nutrition Information per Serving:

✓✓ CALORIES: Excellent Choice (285)   CHOLESTEROL: Moderate (265 mg)
✓ FAT: Good Choice (15 g)*   ✓✓ SODIUM: Excellent Choice (55 mg)
EXCHANGES: 2½ Meat (extra lean), ¼ Veg, ¾ Fruit, 2¾ Fat
PROTEIN: 20 g, CARBOHYDRATE: 18 g

This nutrition analysis corresponds to the recipe below. The restaurant version may differ.
*Primarily unsaturated fat

Ingredients (4 servings):

1 lb. calamari (5-6 pieces/person)	1 orange
¼ cup extra virgin olive oil	1 lemon
¼ cup lemon juice	1 lime
8 cups mixed field greens	1 grapefruit

Directions:

1. Clean calamari. Leave the bodies whole and the tentacles cleaned and separated.
2. Mix olive oil and lemon juice in a bowl.
3. Divide the dressing in two portions, one small portion for basting the calamari, the rest reserved for the dressing.
4. Baste calamari with part of the dressing and place on grill (BBQ is good).
5. Cook on all sides, approximately 3-4 minutes maximum.
6. Toss field greens with remaining dressing. Place on 4 large plates.
7. Peel citrus and separate into sections.
8. Place grilled calamari around plate and garnish with citrus sections.

Recipe supplied by:

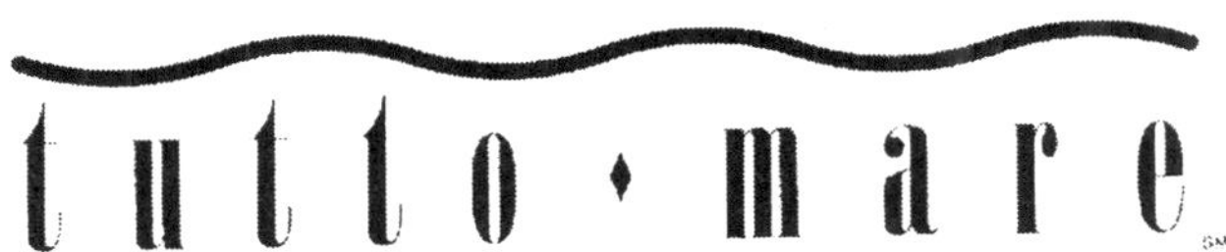

Tutto Mare
4365 Executive Drive
San Diego, CA 92121
(858) 597-1188

SPICES' SHRIMP SALAD

<table>
<tr><td colspan="2">Nutrition Information per Serving:</td></tr>
<tr><td>✓✓ CALORIES: Excellent Choice (150)</td><td>CHOLESTEROL: Moderate (220 mg)</td></tr>
<tr><td>✓✓ FAT: Excellent Choice (4 g)*</td><td>✓ SODIUM: Good Choice (490 mg)</td></tr>
<tr><td colspan="2" align="center">EXCHANGES: 3¼ Meat (extra lean), ¼ Veg, ½ Fat</td></tr>
<tr><td colspan="2" align="center">PROTEIN: 25 g, CARBOHYDRATE: 3 g</td></tr>
<tr><td colspan="2">This nutrition analysis corresponds to the recipe below. The restaurant version may differ.
*Primarily unsaturated fat</td></tr>
</table>

Ingredients (4 servings):

4 cups lettuce, torn	**1 Tbs. fish sauce**
2 tsp. olive oil	**1 Tbs. + 1 tsp. lime juice**
1 lb. medium sized shrimp	**2 green onions, chopped**
2 tsp. lemon grass, minced	**1 tsp. chili powder**
1 Tbs. shallots, minced	**¼ cup mint leaves, chopped**

1. Wash and tear lettuce. Place in a large bowl.
2. Heat olive oil in a skillet over medium-high heat. Add shrimp and sauté for about 2-3 minutes or until shrimp is done.
3. Combine remaining ingredients in a small bowl and wisk together.
4. Toss shrimp, lettuce, and dressing lightly.

Recipe supplied by:

Spices Thai Café
3810 Valley Centre Drive, Suite 903
San Diego, CA 92130
(858) 259-0889
16441 Bernardo Center Drive
San Diego, CA 92128
(858) 674-4665

THREE SEAS SALAD ☆

Nutrition Information per Serving:

✓✓ CALORIES: Excellent Choice (330)   CHOLESTEROL: High (310 mg)
✓✓ FAT: Excellent Choice (9 g)*   SODIUM: Moderate (830 mg)
EXCHANGES: 6½ Meat (extra lean), ¾ Veg, 1¼ Fat
PROTEIN: 52 g, CARBOHYDRATE: 7 g

This nutrition analysis corresponds to the recipe below. The restaurant version may differ.

*Primarily unsaturated fat

Ingredients (4 servings):

Three Seas Salad:
8 cups mixed salad greens
1 tomato
1 hard-boiled egg
12 oz. crab
12 oz. shrimp
tuna salad, prepared

Tuna Salad:
¼ cup celery, chopped
¼ cup onion, chopped
¼ cup low fat mayonnaise
6 oz. can tuna, packed in water
salt and pepper to taste
(not included in analysis)

Directions:

1. Combine ingredients for tuna salad in a small bowl.
2. Wash salad greens and toss in a separate large bowl.
3. Clean and cook crab and shrimp and add to the salad greens.
4. Slice tomato and hard-boiled egg and add to green salad.
5. Top the green salad with spoonfuls of tuna salad.
6. Serve with a low fat or fat free dressing of your choice (not included in analysis).

Recipe supplied by:

SandCrab Cafe
2229 Micro Place
Escondido, CA 92029
(760) 480-CRAB (2722)

TOFU EGG-FREE SALAD

Nutrition Information per Serving:

✓✓ CALORIES: Excellent Choice (105) ✓✓ CHOLESTEROL: Excellent Choice (0 mg)
✓✓ FAT: Excellent Choice (7 g)* SODIUM: Moderate (660 mg)
EXCHANGES: 1 Meat, ¼ Veg, ¾ Fat
PROTEIN: 8 g, CARBOHYDRATE: 4 g

This nutrition analysis corresponds to the recipe below. The restaurant version may differ.

*Primarily unsaturated fat

Ingredients (4 servings):

1 lb. tofu, firm	1 tsp. lemon juice
1½ Tbs. Veganaise†	½ tsp. turmeric
1 tsp. mustard	⅛ tsp. curry powder
2 Tbs. green onions	1 tsp. salt
2 Tbs. parsley	

†Mayonnaise substitute found in the refrigerator case of natural food stores.

Directions:

1. Crumble tofu into a bowl.
2. In a separate bowl, combine Veganaise and all other ingredients.
3. Mix with tofu and blend well.

Recipe supplied by:

Jimbo's...Naturally!
Escondido: 1633 S. Centre City Parkway
Escondido, CA 92025
(760) 489-7755

Del Mar: 12853 El Camino Real
San Diego, CA 92130
(858) 793-7755

ANTHONY'S SPECIAL GRILLED SHRIMP ❦

Skewers of shrimp and vegetables served with vegetables and rice.

Nutrition Information per Serving:

✓ CALORIES: Good Choice (555)   CHOLESTEROL: Moderate (275)

✓✓ FAT: Excellent Choice (3 g)*   ✓ SODIUM: Good Choice (540 g)

EXCHANGES: 4¼ Meat (extra lean), 4¾ Bread, 3½ Veg, ¼ Fat

PROTEIN: 41 g, CARBOHYDRATE: 91 g

This nutrition analysis corresponds to the recipe below. The restaurant version may differ.

*Primarily unsaturated fat

Ingredients (4 servings):

48 medium shrimp (approx. 1¼ lb.)
shelled, cleaned & deveined

2 onions, cut into 16 wedges

2 green peppers, cut into 16 wedges

3 Tbs. Lawry's Honey Mustard Sauce

8 skewers

6 cups vegetable medley (broccoli, carrots, zucchini, cauliflower)

Sprinkle of garlic parsley spice

6 cups cooked rice

Directions:

1. Thread each skewer with the following: onion, 2 shrimp, bell pepper, 2 shrimp, bell pepper, 2 shrimp, onion.
2. Mesquite grill or barbecue shrimp skewers, basting with honey mustard glaze.
3. Cook for 3 minutes on each side over hot flame, or just until shrimp turn pink. Do not overcook.
4. Steam veggies; sprinkle with garlic parsley spice and toss to coat.
5. Put rice on center of the plate, top with the shrimp skewers. Evenly distribute veggies around the rice in a circle.

Recipe supplied by:

Anthony's Fish Grotto

San Diego Bay: Harbor Dr. at Ash St.
(619) 232-5103
Chula Vista: Hwy. 5 at "E" St.
(619) 425-4200
La Mesa: Highway 8 at Severin Dr.
(619) 463-0368
Rancho Bernardo: Bernardo Center Dr. to Avena Pl.
(858) 451-2070

CAMERONES RANCHEROS ☙

Mouth watering shrimp, bell pepper, onions and tomatoes sautéed in a delicious ranchera salsa.
Serving suggestion: Serve with Mexican rice, black beans and/or tortillas.

Nutrition Information per Serving:

✓✓ CALORIES: Excellent Choice (240)   CHOLESTEROL: High (335 mg)
✓✓ FAT: Excellent Choice (3 g)*   SODIUM: Moderate (885 mg)
EXCHANGES: 5 Meat (extra lean), 2 Veg
PROTEIN: 38 g, CARBOHYDRATE: 14 g

This nutrition analysis corresponds to the recipe below. The restaurant version may differ.

*Primarily unsaturated fat

Ingredients (4 servings):

Ranchera Salsa:

½ lb. onion
1 lb. tomatoes
2 bell pepper
½ Tbs. California chilies
½ Tbs. cilantro

1¼ tsp. garlic powder
1¼ tsp. white pepper
½ tsp. salt
1 tsp. chicken base

Camerones:

½ tsp. soybean oil
1½ lb. large shrimp

Directions:

Ranchera Salsa:

1. Cut onions, tomatoes and bell pepper into 1" pieces.
2. Place in a large pot and add just enough water to cover bottom of pan.
3. Add chopped chilies and cilantro, garlic powder, white pepper, salt and chicken base.
4. Simmer over low heat for 45-60 minutes. Stir occasionally but carefully so as not to blend ingredients but just to keep vegetables from sticking to the bottom.

Camerones:

1. Heat oil slightly in a sauté pan.
2. Add shrimp and sauté until just pink.
3. Add the shrimp to the ranchera salsa and simmer a few more minutes.

Recipe supplied by:

Eva's Cocina & Cantina
6690 Mission Gorge Rd.
San Diego, CA 92120
(619) 284-5874

CORIANDER SEARED AHI ☘

Ahi seared with coriander, served with a cucumber and roma tomato salad.

Nutrition Information per Serving:

✓ CALORIES: Good Choice (375)　　✓✓ CHOLESTEROL: Excellent Choice (50 mg)
✓ FAT: Good Choice (16 g)*　　　　　SODIUM: Moderate (680 mg)
EXCHANGES: 3½ Meat (extra lean), 3½ Veg, 2 Fat
PROTEIN: 37 g, CARBOHYDRATE: 27 g

This nutrition analysis corresponds to the recipe below. The restaurant version may differ.
*Primarily unsaturated fat

Ingredients (4 servings):

2 Tbs. pine nuts
4 cucumbers
4 roma tomatoes
¼ cup fresh basil
¼ cup cilantro
¼ cup light soy sauce

1 Tbs. + 1 tsp. peanut oil
16 oz. ahi tuna
½ cup coriander seeds
2 basil tops
2 Tbs. sesame seeds
low-fat or non-fat citrus vinaigrette
(not included in analysis)

Directions:

1. Toast pine nuts.
2. Thinly slice cucumbers.
3. Chop tomatoes, basil and cilantro.
4. Mix cucumbers, tomatoes, basil, cilantro, toasted pine nuts, and soy sauce.
5. Heat peanut oil in a sauté pan over high heat.
6. Lightly dust ahi with coriander seeds and sear in the hot sauté pan.
7. Toss salad with dressing of choice (not included in analysis) and place on a plate with ahi.
8. Garnish with basil and sesame seeds.

Recipe supplied by:

Pacific Coast Grill
437 South Highway 101
Solana Beach, CA 92075
(858) 794-4632

IMPERIAL SHRIMP 🍎

Nutrition Information per Serving:

✓✓ CALORIES: Excellent Choice (245)   CHOLESTEROL: Moderate (280 mg)
✓✓ FAT: Excellent Choice (9 g)*   SODIUM: Moderate (695 mg)
EXCHANGES: 4¼ Meat (extra lean), 1¼ Veg, 1¼ Fat
PROTEIN: 33 g, CARBOHYDRATE: 8 g

This nutrition analysis corresponds to the recipe below. The restaurant version may differ.

*Primarily unsaturated fat

Ingredients (4 servings):

1 Tbs. cooking oil	½ tsp. salt
1¼ lb. shrimp, deveined and butterflied	¼ tsp. sugar
2 cups broccoli, chopped	1 Tbs. rice cooking wine
1½ cup mushrooms, sliced	¼ tsp. white pepper
¾ cup snow peas	¼ cup chicken broth, no salt added
½ tsp. garlic, fresh, minced	2 tsp. corn starch
½ tsp. ginger, fresh, minced	1 Tbs. sesame oil

Directions:

1. Heat oil in a skillet over medium-high heat.
2. Add shrimp and quickly sauté until it just starts to turn pink. Do not cook through. Remove from skillet.
3. In a separate pot, parboil vegetables. Do not overcook.
4. Combine remaining ingredients except cornstarch and sesame oil in skillet and stir.
5. Add shrimp and vegetables. Stir-fry until shrimp is done.
6. Add sesame oil and then cornstarch to thicken sauce.

Recipe supplied by:

Chin's Szechwan Cuisine

Carlsbad: 2958 Madison St.	(760) 434-7115
Encinitas: 1506 Encinitas Blvd.	(760) 753-3903
Escondido: 445 N. Escondido Blvd.	(760) 480-4115
Oceanside: 4140 Oceanside Blvd.	(760) 631-4808
Oceanside: 2241 El Camino Real	(760) 439-3600
Rancho Bernardo: 15721A Bernardo Hts. Pky.	(858) 676-0166
San Marcos: 631 S. Rancho Santa Fe Rd.	(760) 591-9648
Scripps Ranch: 9978 Scripps Ranch Blvd.	(858) 566-0031
Vista: 600 E. Vista Way	(760) 732-3880

     🍎 at least 2 fruit/vegetable servings

PACIFIC COAST BOUILLABAISE

Traditional seafood soup.

Nutrition Information per Serving:

✓ CALORIES: Good Choice (400) CHOLESTEROL: Moderate (215 mg)
✓ FAT: Good Choice (16 g)* ✓ SODIUM: Good Choice (455 mg)
EXCHANGES: 4½ Meat (extra lean), 1¼ Bread, ¾ Veg, 1½ Fat
PROTEIN: 46 g, CARBOHYDRATE: 28 g

This nutrition analysis corresponds to the recipe below. The restaurant version may differ.

*Primarily unsaturated fat

Ingredients (4 servings):

3 Tbs. olive oil	2 pinches saffron threads
1 fennel bulb, sliced	¼ tsp. black pepper
4 shallots, diced	salt to taste
4 garlic cloves, diced	(not included in analysis)
8 cups fish or vegetable stock	4 oz. sea bass
2 Tbs. pernod (anise flavored liquor, optional)	4 oz. salmon
8 plum tomatoes, quartered	6 shrimp
6 small red potatoes, cubed	6 mussels
2 bunches fresh thyme, chopped	6 clams
2 Tbs. fresh Italian parsley, chopped	4 oz. calamari

Directions:

1. Warm olive oil in nonstick saucepan over medium heat.
2. Add fennel and cook for 3 minutes, lowering heat if necessary to keep fennel from browning.
3. Stir in garlic and shallots and cook for 2 minutes.
4. Add stock, pernod, tomatoes, potatoes, thyme, parsley and saffron. Season with salt and pepper if desired (not included in analysis).
5. Cover and simmer for 20 minutes, or until the vegetables are cooked but still firm.
6. Add the fish, shrimp, mussels, clams and calamari.
7. Cover and simmer until the fish and shrimp are opaque.

Recipe supplied by:

French Market Grille
15717 Bernardo Heights Parkway
San Diego, CA 92128
(858) 485-8055

PESCADO ENVUELTO ☙

Fish wrapped in banana leaf and served with tomato slices, green pepper slices and salsa.

Nutrition Information per Serving:

✓ CALORIES: Good Choice (375) ✓✓ CHOLESTEROL: Excellent Choice (60 mg)
✓ FAT: Good Choice (16 g)* SODIUM: Moderate (975 mg)
EXCHANGES: 3¾ Meat (extra lean), 2¾ Veg, 2¾ Fat
PROTEIN: 28 g, CARBOHYDRATE: 27 g

This nutrition analysis corresponds to the recipe below. The restaurant version may differ.

*Primarily unsaturated fat

Ingredients (4 servings):

1 lb. white fish (cod) without skin	**Salsa Espanola Tropical:**
4 banana leaves approx. 10" by 6"†	¼ cup diced onion
8 slices ripe tomato	¼ cup diced bell pepper
8 strips (¼-inch) roasted green pepper or chilies	¼ cup diced tomato
4 Tbs. olive oil	2 Tbs. tomato sauce
4 cups vegetables (onion, carrots, green and yellow zucchini)	½ tsp. each cumin & white pepper
2 Tbs. orange juice	1 tsp. each minced garlic and salt
2 Tbs. achiote paste††	⅓ cup water
	½ cup pureed mango
	¼ cup white wine

†Foil can be substituted for banana leaves.

††Achiote paste can be found at Whole Foods Market or other specialty stores.

Directions:

1. Mix Salsa Espanola Tropical and let flavors mix for at least one hour.
2. Roast green peppers or chili strips and set aside.
3. Clean and fillet fish into pieces about ¼ inch thick.
4. Evenly divide the fish, tomato slices, salsa and roasted peppers or chilies and place on the four bananas leaves. Drizzle with 2 Tbs. of the olive oil.
5. If using banana leaves, fold them tamale style. Fasten with shoestring-size banana leaves. If using foil, wrap ingredients, making a packet with the foil.
6. Steam in a double boiler, or, bake, grill or BBQ them. Cook until fish flakes easily with a fork.
7. Grill or sauté the vegetables with the remaining olive oil. Mix orange juice and achiote paste together and drizzle over vegetables.
8. Serving suggestion: Add diced red peppers and onion to black beans and serve on the side (not included in analysis).

Recipe supplied by:

Casa de Pico
Bazaar del Mundo
Old Town San Diego State Historic Park
2754 Calhoun St., San Diego, CA 92110
(619) 296-3267

POACHED SALMON

Nutrition Information per Serving:

✓✓ CALORIES: Excellent Choice (340)   ✓ CHOLESTEROL: Good Choice (120 mg)
  ✓ FAT: Good Choice (14 g)*   ✓✓ SODIUM: Excellent Choice (245 mg)
EXCHANGES: 5¾ Meat, ¼ Fat
PROTEIN: 44 g, CARBOHYDRATE: 1 g

This nutrition analysis corresponds to the recipe below. The restaurant version may differ.
*Primarily unsaturated fat

Ingredients (4 servings):

½ cup white wine   2 lbs. salmon fillets
½ tsp. garlic, dried   1 Tbs. dill weed, dried
¼ tsp. white pepper   2 Tbs. lemon juice
¼ tsp. salt

1. Mix first four ingredients (wine through salt) together and pour into 9" x 13" baking dish.
2. Cut the salmon fillets into 2½" pieces.
3. Place into the baking dish.
4. Sprinkle the salmon pieces with dill and pour on the lemon juice.
5. Cover the dish with foil and bake at 400° for 25 minutes, or until the salmon flakes easily with a fork.

Recipe supplied by:

Whole Foods
8825 Villa La Jolla Drive
La Jolla, CA 92037
(858) 642-6700

711 University Avenue (Hillcrest)
San Diego, CA 92103
(619) 294-2800

POLYNESIAN DUNGENESS CRAB STACK ⚘

Mango, pea shoots, cucumber, tomato, avocado and peanuts served with spicy ginger lime dressing.

Nutrition Information per Serving:

✓✓ CALORIES: Excellent Choice (280) ✓✓ CHOLESTEROL: Excellent Choice (45 mg)
✓✓ FAT: Excellent Choice (10 g)* SODIUM: Moderate (780 mg)
EXCHANGES: 2 Meat (extra lean), 1 Bread, ¾ Veg, ¼ Fruit, 1¾ Fat
PROTEIN: 18 g, CARBOHYDRATE: 33 g

This nutrition analysis corresponds to the recipe below. The restaurant version may differ.
*Primarily unsaturated fat

Ingredients (4 servings)†:

Crab Stack:

1 cup pea shoots, cut in 2" pieces
1 cup mango, diced in ½" pieces
1 cup cucumber, seeded & sliced
1 cup red onion, thinly sliced
1 cup roma tomatoes, seeded & sliced
½ avocado, diced in ½" pieces
8 oz. Dungeness crab meat, squeeze dry
¼ cup peanuts, ground & toasted
1½ Tbs. cilantro leaves
ginger lime dressing

Ginger Lime Dressing:

½ tsp. garlic, minced
1 Tbs. chile paste
2 Tbs. ginger root, minced
3 Tbs. fish sauce
3 Tbs. lime juice
¼ cup + 1 Tbs. water
¼ cup + 1 Tbs. sugar

† For the most effective presentation, the restaurant suggests using a tubular mold that is open at both ends (1 per person) for preparation.

Directions:

1. Combine ingredients of ginger lime dressing in a medium-sized bowl and set aside.
2. Place the four tubular molds on the serving plates. Beginning with pea shoots and ending with crabmeat, place each ingredient in turn into the four tubular molds. Pack firmly. If you're not using molds, stack ingredients on the plates.
3. Garnish with peanuts and cilantro leaves, and drizzle with dressing.
4. Take off the mold by pressing down on the stack and lifting the tube at the same time.

Recipe supplied by:

Roppongi Restaurant, Bar & Cafe
875 Prospect Street
La Jolla, CA 92037
(858) 551-5252

⚘ at least 2 fruit/vegetable servings

RANCHOS SIETE MARE

Hot, fresh seafood soup served with two corn tortillas.

Nutrition Information per Serving:

✓✓ CALORIES: Excellent Choice (335)　　CHOLESTEROL: Moderate (175 mg)
✓✓ FAT: Excellent Choice (7 g)*　　SODIUM: Moderate (615 mg)
EXCHANGES: 4¼ Meat (extra lean), 1½ Bread, 1 Veg, ¼ Fat
PROTEIN: 49 g, CARBOHYDRATE: 38 g

This nutrition analysis corresponds to the recipe below. The restaurant version may differ.

*Primarily unsaturated fat

Ingredients (4 servings):

8 cups water
1 cup (8 oz.) ranchero sauce†
1 cup (8 oz.) pico de gallo
4 oz. lobster
4 oz. white fish
4 oz. scallops

2 oz. calamari
4 oz. salmon
4 oz. shrimp
4 mussels
8 corn tortillas

†Found in the Mexican food section of most supermarkets. It may have the name *salsa ranchero*.

Directions:

1. Clean all fish.
2. In large pot, add water and heat (but not to boiling).
3. Add ranchero sauce and pico de gallo.
4. Add lobster, white fish, scallops and calamari.
5. When fish is ½ done, add salmon, shrimp and mussels.
6. Cover and bring to a boil.
7. Cook until all fish is cooked thoroughly.
8. Serve with two warm corn tortillas.

Recipe supplied by:

Ranchos Cocina
1830 Sunset Cliffs Blvd., #H
Ocean Beach (619) 226-7619
4705 Point Loma Ave.
Ocean Beach (619) 224-9815

SALMON CON FINOCCHI ⭐

A 7-oz. portion of Atlantic salmon seasoned, oven roasted and placed on a bed of saffron braised fennel and French green lentils. The sauce is a pomegranate-curry reduction and the plate is garnished with coriander. This dish was created by Chef Josh Thomsen for your enjoyment!

Nutrition Information per Serving:

CALORIES: Moderate (625)   ✓ CHOLESTEROL: Good Choice (105 mg)
✓ FAT: Good Choice (20 g)*   ✓✓ SODIUM: Excellent Choice (120 mg)
EXCHANGES: 6 Meat, 2 Bread, 1 Veg, 1¼ Fruit, 1¼ Fat
PROTEIN: 54 g, CARBOHYDRATE: 58 g

This nutrition analysis corresponds to the recipe below. The restaurant version may differ.

*Primarily unsaturated fat

Ingredients (4 servings):

Lentils:
1 cup white onion, diced
1 cup carrots, diced
1 Tbs. vegetable oil
12 cups chicken broth,
   fat & sodium free
1 cup dry lentils

Fennel:
8 pcs. fennel bulb,
   quartered
1 Tbs. saffron†

Pomegranate Syrup:
12 oz. pomegranate juice†
¼ cup + 2 Tbs. orange juice
½ mango, diced
⅛ tsp. curry powder

Fish:
4 7-oz. cuts Atlantic
   salmon steaks
kosher salt to taste
   (not included in analysis)
white pepper to taste
1 Tbs. vegetable oil

Garnish:
4 Tbs. cilantro leaves

†Saffron and pomegranate juice can be found in Indian specialty stores.

Directions:

1. Heat 1 Tbs. vegetable oil in a pot until warm. Add carrots and onion; sauté until onions are translucent. Add lentils and broth and cook until lentils are soft, about 15 minutes. Drain, reserving remaining broth. Reserve lentils warm.
2. Boil fennel in remaining chicken broth and saffron until tender.
3. Combine fennel with lentils. Reserve warm.
4. Combine ingredients of pomegranate syrup in a sauté pan. Reduce to a syrup. Pour into a food processor and puree. Strain through a fine mesh strainer.
5. Season salmon with salt and pepper on both sides. Place in a hot sauté pan with 1 Tbs. vegetable oil. Sauté until golden, about 2 minutes on medium heat on each side. Place in the oven for 3 minutes at 350°.
6. In the center of a large dinner plate, place lentil/fennel mixture, top with salmon, cilantro, and pour the syrup around the plate.

Recipe supplied by:

Trattoria Acqua
1298 Prospect Street
La Jolla, CA 92037
(858) 454-0709

    ⭐ at least 2 fruit/vegetable servings

SEAFOOD ENCHILADAS

Lobster, shrimp, scallops with leeks, roasted bell peppers and tomatoes, topped with traditional salsa.

Nutrition Information per Serving:

✓✓ CALORIES: Excellent Choice (315)   ✓ CHOLESTEROL: Good Choice (130 mg)
✓✓ FAT: Excellent Choice (6 g)*   SODIUM: High (1450 mg)
EXCHANGES: 3¼ Meat (extra lean), 2 Bread, ¾ Veg, 1 Fat
PROTEIN: 29 g, CARBOHYDRATE: 35 g

This nutrition analysis corresponds to the recipe below. The restaurant version may differ.
*Primarily unsaturated fat

Ingredients (4 servings, 2 tacos each):

6 oz. lobster   4 garlic cloves, minced
6 oz. shrimp   3 Tbs. tomato, diced
6 oz. scallops   ½ cup roasted bell pepper, chopped
1 Tbs. olive oil   8 corn tortillas
½ cup leeks, diced   2 cups traditional salsa

Directions:

1. Sauté lobster, shrimp and scallops in oil for 5 minutes over medium - high heat.
2. Add leeks and garlic and sauté for an additional 2 minutes.
3. Add tomato and roasted bell pepper and sauté another minute.
4. Warm corn tortillas.
5. Fill tortillas with seafood mixture, roll, and place seam side down in serving dish.
6. Top with salsa.
7. Serve with your choice of sides.

Recipe supplied by:

Los Cabos
1255 El Camino Real, Ste. G-7
San Diego, CA 92130
(858) 792-2226

SHRIMP SCAMPI

Nutrition Information per Serving:

✓✓ CALORIES: Excellent Choice (300)   CHOLESTEROL: Moderate (275 mg)
✓ FAT: Good Choice (15 g)*   ✓ SODIUM: Good Choice (325 mg)
EXCHANGES: 4¼ Meat (extra lean), ¾ Veg, 3 Fat
PROTEIN: 31 g, CARBOHYDRATE: 6 g

This nutrition analysis corresponds to the recipe below. The restaurant version may differ.
*Primarily unsaturated fat

Ingredients (4 servings):

¼ cup oil
8 mushrooms, sliced
1 Tbs. + 1 tsp. garlic, minced
1¼ lb. shrimp, peeled and deveined

¾ cup white wine
1 large tomato, diced
2 tsp. chives
2 lemons, juiced

Directions:

1. Pre-heat oil in skillet on medium - high heat.
2. Add sliced mushrooms and sauté 1-2 minutes.
3. Add minced garlic and sauté until golden brown.
4. Add shrimp and sauté approximately 3-4 minutes, turning often.
5. Add wine, tomatoes, chives and lemon juice. Simmer approximately 3-4 minutes.
6. Serve immediately.

Recipe supplied by:

Bully's East
2401 Camino Del Rio S., San Diego, CA 92108
(619) 291-2665

Bully's La Jolla
5755 La Jolla Blvd., La Jolla, CA 92037
(858) 459-2768

Bully's Del Mar
1404 Camino Del Mar, Del Mar, CA 92014
(858) 755-1660

TRENETTE VERDE MARE

Spinach pasta, prawns, sea scallops, mussels, olive oil and garlic.

Nutrition Information per Serving:

✓ CALORIES: Good Choice (545)   CHOLESTEROL: High (320 mg)
✓ FAT: Good Choice (11 g)*   ✓ SODIUM: Good Choice (530 mg)
EXCHANGES: 4¾ Meat (extra lean), 3 Bread, ½ Veg, 1¾ Fat
PROTEIN: 52 g, CARBOHYDRATE: 56 g

This nutrition analysis corresponds to the recipe below. The restaurant version may differ.

*Primarily unsaturated fat

Ingredients (4 servings):

12 oz. fresh pasta
1 Tbs. + 1 tsp. olive oil
¼ cup garlic
2 roma tomatoes
1 cup fresh basil, chopped
12 mussels

12 oz. sea scallops
1 cup white wine
12 oz. prawns
salt and pepper to taste
   (not included in analysis)

Directions:

1. Cook pasta according to package directions.
2. In medium size sauté pan, add olive oil, garlic, tomatoes, basil, mussels, sea scallops and ½ cup wine.
3. Sauté over medium heat until the mussels begin to open.
4. Add remaining wine, prawns, salt and pepper (salt and pepper not included in analysis).
5. Cook for two minutes; prawns should be bright orange.
6. Toss with cooked pasta and garnish with fresh Italian parsley sprigs or basil.

Recipe supplied by:

Prego Ristorante
1370 Frazee Road
San Diego, CA 92108
(619) 294-4700

CHEF'S WHITE OMELETTE

Omelette with artichoke hearts, grilled chicken, dill, green onion and Swiss cheese.

Nutrition Information per Serving:

✓ CALORIES: Good Choice (405) ✓ CHOLESTEROL: Good Choice (95 mg)
✓ FAT: Good Choice (17 g) SODIUM: Moderate (630 mg)
EXCHANGES: 6¾ Meat (extra lean), ¾ Veg, 1¾ Fat
PROTEIN: 51 g, CARBOHYDRATE: 9 g

This nutrition analysis corresponds to the recipe below. The restaurant version may differ.

Ingredients (4 servings):

8 oz. boneless, skinless chicken breast
Non-stick vegetable spray
1 cup canned artichoke hearts

2 tsp. dried dill
3 cups egg whites, whisked
1 cup Swiss cheese, grated

Directions:

1. Chop chicken into bite sized pieces.
2. Lightly spray a large non-stick pan and heat over medium - high heat.
3. Add artichoke hearts, chicken and dill; cook until chicken is done, remove from pan and keep warm.
4. Cook ½ of the amount of egg whites in pan.
5. Cook gently, pulling the cooked whites to the center of the pan while tipping liquid eggs to cooking surface.
6. When set to desired consistency, sprinkle ½ of the chicken mixture and ½ cup Swiss cheese over the left side of the eggs. Fold the right side of the eggs over the left and lightly press down on the omelette to seal.
7. Repeat the same procedure for the next omelette.
8. Divide each omelette in half and enjoy!

Recipe supplied by:

Sbicca
215 15th Street
Del Mar, CA 92014
(858) 481-1101

Enchiladas Verdes de Pollo ☺

Seasoned chicken wrapped in corn tortillas, topped with tomatillo sauce & Parmesan cheese.

Nutrition Information per Serving:

✓ CALORIES: Good Choice (440)
✓ FAT: Good Choice (14 g)

✓✓ CHOLESTEROL: Excellent Choice (35 mg)
SODIUM: Moderate (790 mg)

EXCHANGES: 1¾ Meat, 2¾ Bread, 1¾ Veg, 1¾ Fat
PROTEIN: 26 g, CARBOHYDRATE: 54 g

This nutrition analysis corresponds to the recipe below. The restaurant version may differ.

Ingredients (6 servings, 2 enchiladas each):

1 dozen corn tortillas
4 lbs. whole chicken or chicken parts
4 cloves garlic, peeled
2 yellow onions
2 tsp. salt
1 Tbs. black peppercorns
2 Tbs. vegetable oil
1 each green **and** red bell pepper
1 large tomato
4 oz. (½ cup) tomato sauce
1 tsp. garlic powder

Verde Sauce:
4 lbs. fresh tomatillos
4 yellow chilies
1 medium yellow onion
1 small bunch cilantro
1 tsp. salt
½ tsp. sugar
6 cloves garlic
1 quart water

Directions:

Verde Sauce:
1. Wash vegetables. Peel off outer skin of tomatillos, onion & garlic.
2. Put all ingredients in a 2 quart sauce pan, cover with water and boil for 15 to 20 minutes or until tomatillos are tender. Allow to cool slightly.
3. Puree all ingredients (in portions to prevent overspill) in blender for 30 seconds.

Enchiladas:
1. Place chicken in a 6-quart pot. Cover with water. Add garlic cloves, 1 onion (quartered), 1 tsp. salt, and pepper. Bring to a boil and cook for 45 minutes.
2. Cool. Remove chicken from pot. Remove and discard skin and shred chicken.
3. Chop bell peppers, tomato, and remaining onion. In a large skillet, heat oil and sauté onion, peppers and tomato. Add ¼ cup water, tomato sauce and remaining seasonings. Simmer about 20 minutes until water is reduced.
4. To make enchiladas, dip the tortillas in a little bit of the Verde sauce to soften. Divide the chicken evenly between the 12 tortillas and roll. Arrange in a glass baking dish so that the loose edge of the roll is at the bottom of the dish.
5. Top the enchiladas with Verde Sauce and bake in a 350° oven for 15 - 20 min.
6. Sprinkle with Parmesan cheese and serve.

Recipe supplied by:

Rancho el Nopal
Bazaar del Mundo
Old Town San Diego State Historic Park
2754 Calhoun St., San Diego, CA 92110
(619) 295-0584

POLLO AL LIMONE E ROSMARINO

Chicken sautéed with garlic, fresh rosemary, lemon juice and white wine.

Nutrition Information per Serving:

✓✓ CALORIES: Excellent Choice (250)   ✓ CHOLESTEROL: Good Choice (90 mg)
✓✓ FAT: Excellent Choice (7 g)   ✓✓ SODIUM: Excellent Choice (80 mg)
EXCHANGES: 4¾ Meat (extra lean), 1 Fat
PROTEIN: 34 g, CARBOHYDRATE: 3 g

This nutrition analysis corresponds to the recipe below. The restaurant version may differ.

Ingredients (4 servings):

1 lb. chicken breast, boneless, skinless
1 Tbs. olive oil
1 Tbs. fresh garlic, minced
1 to 1½ Tbs. fresh rosemary, chopped
¼ cup lemon juice
1½ cups white wine

Directions:

1. Heat olive oil over medium-high heat in a skillet.
2. Place chicken in skillet and cook until golden brown on one side.
3. Turn chicken and add garlic, rosemary, lemon juice and wine.
4. Cook until chicken is done. Place on a serving platter.
5. Pour sauce remaining in pan over chicken.
6. We recommend serving with steamed vegetables and potatoes (not included in analysis).

Recipe supplied by:

Andiamo! Italian Restaurant
5950 Santo Road
San Diego, CA 92124
(858) 277-3501

Santa Fe Chicken

Ingredients (5 servings):

⅓ green bell pepper
olive oil spray
¼ cup onions, chopped
1 tsp. garlic, minced
¼ cup flour

5 skinless chicken breasts (5 oz. each)
4 oz. baked tortilla chips
16 oz. enchilada sauce
2 oz. low-fat mozzarella, grated

Directions:

1. Roast green bell peppers in broiler. Dice when cool and set aside.
2. Spray skillet with olive oil. Sauté onion and garlic.
3. Dust chicken with flour and place in skillet. Brown and remove.
4. Spray 13" x 9" pan with olive oil. Place chips on bottom of pan.
5. Place chicken and onion on top of chips.
6. Pour enchilada sauce over all.
7. Sprinkle mozzarella cheese on top of each piece of chicken, and then top with roasted pepper.
8. Cover and bake 30-40 minutes at 425°.

Recipe supplied by:

Daily's Restaurant
8915 Towne Centre Drive
San Diego, CA 92122
Phone (858) 453-1112
Fax (858) 453-1393

TERIYAKI CHICKEN SANDWICH

with a delicious teriyaki sauce that adds that special touch to
lots of dishes -- chicken, rice, stir-fries, -- even sandwiches!

Nutrition Information per Serving:

✓ CALORIES: Good Choice (570) ✓ CHOLESTEROL: Good Choice (130 mg)
✓✓ FAT: Excellent Choice (9 g) SODIUM: High (1120 mg)
EXCHANGES: 6¾ Meat (extra lean), 4 Bread, ¼ Fruit, ½ Fat
PROTEIN: 60 g, CARBOHYDRATE: 65 g

This nutrition analysis corresponds to the recipe below. The restaurant version may differ.

Ingredients (4 servings):

Teriyaki Sauce (makes 2 cups):
1 cup soy sauce
¼ cup burgundy wine
½ cup water
3 oz. pineapple juice
1 Tbs. fresh ginger root, chopped
⅓ cup brown sugar
Corn starch to thicken (1 to 2 tsp.)

Chicken Sandwich:
4 chicken breasts, skinless (6 oz. each)
4 Tbs. teriyaki sauce (recipe at left)
4 whole wheat buns (4 oz. each)
4 slices tomato
4 leaves of lettuce
4 pineapple slices, fresh (½ oz. each)

Directions:

Teriyaki Sauce:
1. Chop fresh ginger root and puree in a blender with the water.
2. In a large pot, bring soy sauce, wine and pineapple juice to a boil. Set aside.
3. Add pureed ginger liquid to pot and reheat.
4. Add brown sugar when mixture reaches boiling point.
5. Reduce heat. Thicken mixture with corn starch, cooking for an additional 2 to 4 minutes, stirring frequently.
6. Save some of this teriyaki sauce for other delicious meals.

Chicken Sandwich:
1. Broil chicken breasts.
2. Glaze each chicken breast with 1 Tbs. teriyaki sauce.
3. Crown with pineapple rings and place on toasted wheat buns with lettuce and tomato.

Recipe supplied by:

St. Germain's
C A F E

St. Germain's Cafe
1010 S. Hwy. 101
Encinitas, CA 92024
(760) 753-5411

SHISH KABOB 🍎

Juicy marinated chunks of filet mignon, skewered and charbroiled to perfection with charbroiled vegetables.

Nutrition Information per Serving:

✓ CALORIES: Good Choice (425)   ✓ CHOLESTEROL: Good Choice (130 mg)
✓ FAT: Good Choice (17 g)   ✓✓ SODIUM: Excellent Choice (270 mg)
EXCHANGES: 6 Meat, 3½ Veg, ½ Fat
PROTEIN: 47 g, CARBOHYDRATE: 22 g

This nutrition analysis corresponds to the recipe below. The restaurant version may differ.

Ingredients (4 servings):

Shish Kabob:	Marinade:
1½ lb. filet mignon	1¼ cup chopped onion
3 large tomatoes	1½ tsp. salt
2 large onions	¾ tsp. pepper
3 bell peppers	¼ cup vegetable oil

Directions:

1. Cut filet mignon, tomato, onion and bell pepper into chunks.
2. Combine ingredients for marinade.
3. Marinate meat and vegetables at least 12 hours in refrigerator.
4. Skewer meat and vegetables and charbroil until meat is completely done.
5. We recommend serving with basmati rice.

Recipe supplied by:

Bandar
825 4th Avenue
San Diego, CA 92101
(619) 238-0101

HONEY THYME PORK LOIN

Roasted pork loin glazed with honey and seasoned with garlic, dijon, and thyme.

Nutrition Information per Serving:

✓✓ CALORIES: Excellent Choice (270)   ✓✓ CHOLESTEROL: Excellent Choice (55 mg)

✓✓ FAT: Excellent Choice (5 g)   ✓✓ SODIUM: Excellent Choice (220 mg)

PROTEIN: 21 g, CARBOHYDRATE: 51 g

Nutrition information supplied by Healthy Gourmet.

Ingredients (9 servings):

2 lb. pork loin	1 tsp. thyme leaves
1 Tbs. canola oil	1 tsp. cracked black peppercorns
1 Tbs. shallots, chopped	1⅔ cup beef broth, no salt added
2 cloves garlic, minced	3 Tbs. cornstarch
2 Tbs. tomato paste	½ tsp. salt
1 Tbs. dijon mustard	⅓ cup water
5 Tbs. red wine vinegar	½ cup chicken broth, no salt added
1 cup honey	

Directions:

1. Heat oil and brown pork tenderloin in a medium size pan.
2. Remove pork and pour off excess oil.
3. Add chopped shallots, minced garlic, tomato paste, and mustard. Sauté for 1-2 minutes. Add the red wine vinegar and deglaze (cook until the mixture thickens as the vinegar evaporates).
4. Add honey, thyme, and cracked peppercorns.
5. Generously spoon glaze on the pork; put in a roasting pan. Set remaining glaze aside for later use.
6. Roast at medium heat (300°) until pork reaches an internal temperature of 160° (about 1 hour). Don't overcook the pork or it will be dry.
7. Add beef broth to remaining glaze in sauté pan and simmer for one minute. Stir in mixture of cornstarch, salt, water, and chicken broth. Let mixture cook until sauce thickens.

Recipe supplied by:

Healthy Gourmet
1-888-EZ-MEALS (396-3257)
Conveniently located pick-up around San Diego County

ANGEL HAIR PASTA WITH SMOKED TOMATOES ✿

Pasta smothered with smoked roma tomatoes, onions, basil, roasted garlic and Asiago cheese.

Nutrition Information per Serving:

✓ CALORIES: Good Choice (495) ✓✓ CHOLESTEROL: Excellent Choice (5 mg)
✓✓ FAT: Excellent Choice (8 g)* ✓✓ SODIUM: Excellent Choice (285 mg)
EXCHANGES: ¼ Meat, 5¼ Bread, 1¼ Veg, 1 Fat
PROTEIN: 17 g, CARBOHYDRATE: 89 g

This nutrition analysis corresponds to the recipe below. The restaurant version may differ.
*Primarily unsaturated fat

Ingredients (4 servings):

Main Dish:
Salsa Cruda (see recipe)
16 oz. angel hair pasta, dry weight
4 Tbs. asiago cheese

Salsa Cruda:
2 lb. tomatoes, cored, halved
1 onion, julienned
4 Tbs. fresh basil, julienned
2 tsp. fresh garlic, minced
¼ tsp. black pepper
½ tsp. salt
2 Tbs. canola oil

Directions:

Salsa Cruda:
1. For optimal flavor, grill the tomatoes, cut side down on a BBQ using hickory chips or if you prefer, roast the tomatoes in the oven (you will not achieve the "smoked" flavor with the oven method). Once cooked, dice tomatoes and place into a large bowl.
2. Combine all remaining ingredients in the bowl and set aside.

Pasta:
1. Cook the pasta according to package directions.
2. Add the salsa cruda to a saucepan and bring to a simmer.
3. Place cooked pasta in a serving bowl and pour the hot salsa over the top of the pasta.
4. Sprinkle with asiago cheese.

Recipe supplied by:

Rock Bottom
8980 Villa La Jolla Dr.
La Jolla, CA 92037
(858) 450-9277

619 G St. (in the Gaslamp)
San Diego, CA 92101
(619) 231-7000

ANGEL HAIR PASTA WITH TOMATOES, BASIL & GARLIC

Nutrition Information per Serving:

✓ CALORIES: Good Choice (520)   ✓ CHOLESTEROL: Good Choice (130 mg)
✓ FAT: Good Choice (19 g)*   ✓✓ SODIUM: Excellent Choice (65 mg)
EXCHANGES: 4 Bread, 1 Veg, 3¾ Fat
PROTEIN: 17 g, CARBOHYDRATE: 70 g

This nutrition analysis corresponds to the recipe below. The restaurant version may differ.
*Primarily unsaturated fat

Ingredients (4 servings):

16 oz. fresh angel hair pasta, uncooked
¼ cup olive oil
2½ Tbs. garlic, minced
4 tomatoes, chopped

¾ cup white wine
½ cup vegetable stock
¼ cup basil, chopped

Directions:

1. Cook pasta according to package directions and set aside.
2. Heat olive oil in a pan over medium-high heat.
3. Add garlic and sauté until golden brown.
4. Add tomatoes and cook for 1 minute on medium heat to allow juices to release.
5. Deglaze pan with white wine; cook until the wine is reduced by ½.
6. Add vegetable stock and cook until the stock is reduced by ½.
7. Finish the sauce by adding the basil and remove from heat.
8. Toss the pasta with the sauce.

Recipe supplied by:

Bernard'O Restaurant
12457 Rancho Bernardo Road
San Diego, CA 92128
(858) 487-7171

CAPELLINI DI POMODORO AL FRESCO ☙

Nutrition Information per Serving:

✓ CALORIES: Good Choice (510)   ✓✓ CHOLESTEROL: Excellent Choice (10 mg)
✓✓ FAT: Excellent Choice (7 g)*   ✓✓ SODIUM: Excellent Choice (60 mg)
EXCHANGES: 5¼ Bread, 3 Veg, 1 Fat
PROTEIN: 21 g, CARBOHYDRATE: 98 g

This nutrition analysis corresponds to the recipe below. The restaurant version may differ.
*Primarily unsaturated fat

Ingredients (4 servings):

16 oz. pasta, dry weight	4 tsp. sugar
1 Tbs. olive oil	1 cup white wine
4 tsp. garlic, minced	1 cup chicken broth, no salt added
4 tsp. oregano, dry	8 cups tomatoes, chopped
½ tsp. pepper	2 cups basil, fresh, chopped

Directions:

1. Cook pasta according to package directions.
2. Heat oil in a large sauté pan over medium - high heat.
3. Sauté garlic in olive oil until golden brown.
4. Add oregano, pepper, sugar, white wine and chicken stock.
5. Toss in fresh tomatoes and cook until hot.
6. Reduce heat slightly and toss in pasta.
7. Sprinkle chopped basil over pasta.
8. Serve immediately.

Recipe supplied by:

Nicolosi's
5351 Adobe Falls Road
San Diego, CA 92120
(619) 287-5757

Serving San Diego since 1952

☙ at least 2 fruit/vegetable servings

SPICY SOUTHWESTERN PENNE PASTA ☙

Pasta with sweet peppers, onions, capers and tomatoes.

Nutrition Information per Serving:

✓ CALORIES: Good Choice (395) ✓✓ CHOLESTEROL: Excellent Choice (10 mg)
✓✓ FAT: Excellent Choice (10 g)* ✓ SODIUM: Good Choice (310 mg)
EXCHANGES: ¼ Meat, 3½ Bread, 1¾ Veg, 1½ Fat
PROTEIN: 13 g, CARBOHYDRATE: 64 g

This nutrition analysis corresponds to the recipe below. The restaurant version may differ.

*Primarily unsaturated fat

Ingredients (6 servings):

1 lb. ziti, penne or fusili pasta
2 Tbs. olive oil
2½ cups onion, sliced
4 cloves garlic, diced
1 yellow bell pepper,
  cut into thin strips
1 lb. tomatoes, cubed
salt & pepper to taste
  (not included in analysis)

½ cup olives, sliced
3 Tbs. capers
½ tsp. dried oregano
2 tsp. red pepper flakes
¼ cup fresh basil, chopped
¼ cup fresh cilantro, chopped
½ cup Monterey Jack or parmesan
  cheese, grated

Directions:

1. Prepare pasta according to package directions, drain and place into a large bowl.
2. In a large skillet, heat oil over high heat.
3. Add onions, garlic and bell pepper; cook stirring until tender, but not brown, about 3 minutes.
4. Add tomatoes, salt and pepper (salt and pepper not included in analysis).
5. Cook over high heat until some of the liquid from the tomatoes has evaporated, approximately 5 minutes.
6. Stir in olives, capers, oregano, red pepper flakes, basil and cilantro.
7. Remove from heat.
8. Add tomato mixture to pasta, toss and sprinkle with cheese.

Recipe supplied by:

Trellises Garden Grille
Town & Country Hotel
500 Hotel Circle North
San Diego, CA 92108
(619) 291-7131

        ☙ at least 2 fruit/vegetable servings

BENGAN BHARTHA 🍎

Eggplant baked in hot oven with onions, peas and tomatoes.

Nutrition Information per Serving:

✓✓ CALORIES: Excellent Choice (240) ✓✓ CHOLESTEROL: Excellent Choice (0 mg)
✓✓ FAT: Excellent Choice (6 g)*   SODIUM: High (1215 mg)
EXCHANGES: 2¼ Bread, 1½ Veg, 1 Fat
PROTEIN: 7 g, CARBOHYDRATE: 44 g

This nutrition analysis corresponds to the recipe below. The restaurant version may differ.

* Primarily unsaturated fat

Ingredients (4 servings):

4 eggplants (about 1½ lb. each)   2 tsp. salt
2 large onions, chopped   ½ tsp. red chili powder
2 large tomatoes, chopped   ½ tsp. garam masala†
4 tsp. vegetable oil   ¼ cup cilantro
¼ lb. green peas

† An Indian spice available at Indian and specialty stores and Henry's Marketplace.

Directions:

1. Roast eggplant in a 300° oven until the skin becomes black and starts separating from the eggplant (about 20 minutes).
2. Remove from oven to cool.
3. When cold, remove skin from the eggplant and mash well in a bowl.
4. In a pan, add oil and heat.
5. Add chopped onions and stir-fry about 5 minutes.
6. Add tomatoes, peas, salt and red chili, and stir-fry again for 5 minutes.
7. Add mashed eggplant and simmer on medium for 10 minutes.
8. Add garam masala and cilantro.

Recipe supplied by:

Star of India

La Jolla: 1000 Prospect Street (858) 459-3355
Del Mar: 3860 Valley Center Drive (858) 792-1111
Downtown: 423 F Street (619) 544-9891

BUDDAH'S DELIGHT 🍎

A delightful combination of nine fresh vegetables lightly stir-fried in a light white sauce.

Nutrition Information per Serving:

✓✓ CALORIES: Excellent Choice (250)   ✓✓ CHOLESTEROL: Excellent Choice (0 mg)

✓✓ FAT: Excellent Choice (4 g)*   SODIUM: High (1545 mg)

EXCHANGES: 1¼ Bread, 5¾ Veg, ¾ Fat

PROTEIN: 9 g, CARBOHYDRATE: 51 g

This nutrition analysis corresponds to the recipe below. The restaurant version may differ.

*Primarily unsaturated fat

Ingredients (2 large servings):

Buddah's Delight:

1 stalk broccoli, chopped

½ small green cabbage, shredded

2 stalks celery, chopped

1½ cups mushrooms, sliced

3 oz. water chestnuts

2 Tbs. cornstarch + 2 Tbs. water, mixed well

3 oz. bamboo shoots

4 oz. baby corn

1 tsp. vegetable oil

1 tsp. garlic, minced

2 tsp. cooking wine

1 cup carrots, chopped

White sauce:

1¾ cups water

1 tsp. salt

2 tsp. chicken powder

pinch pepper

Directions:

1. Mix ingredients of white sauce in a bowl and set aside.
2. Blanch all vegetables in boiling water for 30 seconds. Drain and set aside.
3. Add vegetable oil into a wok or sauté pan, and heat over medium-high heat for 20 seconds.
4. Place garlic into the wok or pan and stir-fry for 5 to 10 seconds, but do not allow to brown.
5. Add cooking wine and white sauce. Then slowly stir in cornstarch/water mixture.
6. Stir until the sauce boils and/or is set to desired consistency.
7. Add all vegetables into the wok or pan and mix well and cook until desired texture.

Recipe supplied by:

Fortune Cookie
16425 Bernardo Ctr. Dr.
San Diego, CA 92128
(858) 451-8958

Bistro Yang
4705 G Clairemont Dr.
San Diego, CA 92117
(858) 483-6893

🍎 at least 2 fruit/vegetable servings

EGGPLANT PARMESAN ♠

<table>
<tr><td colspan="2">Nutrition Information per Serving:</td></tr>
<tr><td>✓✓ Calories: Excellent Choice (300)</td><td>✓✓ Cholesterol: Excellent Choice (35 mg)</td></tr>
<tr><td>✓✓ Fat: Excellent Choice (7 g)*</td><td>✓ Sodium: Good Choice (410 mg)</td></tr>
</table>

Exchanges: 2½ Meat (extra lean), 1 Bread, 4¼ Veg, ¾ Fat

Protein: 24 g, Carbohydrate: 38 g

This nutrition analysis corresponds to the recipe below. The restaurant version may differ.

*Primarily unsaturated fat

Ingredients (8 servings):

Sauce:

1 Tbs. olive oil
1 medium onion, diced
1 large bell pepper, diced
2 garlic cloves, minced
1 lb. tomatoes, diced
½ lb. tomato sauce, no salt added
6 oz. tomato paste, no salt added
½ lb. mushrooms, sliced
1 Tbs. oregano
2 tsp. basil
2 bay leaves
2 Tbs. parsley
2 tsp. sugar
¼ cup dry red wine

Eggplant:

salt (for use on eggplant, see below)
2 large eggplants, 24 slices
¾ cup matzo meal
½ tsp. paprika
½ tsp. oregano
1 egg
¼ cup water
non-stick fat free cooking spray
12 oz. fat free ricotta cheese
6 oz. tofu, crumbled
6 oz. low fat mozzarella cheese, grated
¾ cup parmesan cheese, grated

Directions:

Sauce:
1. Sauté onions & peppers in oil until softened.
2. Add garlic & sauté 1 minute more.
3. Add tomatoes, tomato sauce & tomato paste; simmer 30 minutes.
4. Add mushrooms, oregano, basil, bay leaves, parsley, sugar & wine; simmer 30 minutes more. Remove bay leaves when done.

Eggplant:
1. Sprinkle salt on eggplant slices; let stand for 40 minutes & then drain. Wipe clean.
2. Mix dry ingredients in a shallow bowl. Beat together egg & water in a separate bowl.
3. Dip eggplant slices in liquid, then coat with matzo meal mixture.
4. Place slices on cookie sheet sprayed with non-stick fat free cooking spray; bake in oven at 425° approximately 20 minutes, turning every 5 minutes, until crisp on the outside & tender on the inside.
5. Alternate layers of sauce, eggplant, cheese & tofu in a 10" x 13" baking dish ending with sauce & a sprinkling of parmesan. (Make 8 stacks, 3 layers each).
6. Bake at 350° for 30 minutes. Cool & transfer to serving dishes, 1 stack per serving.

Recipe supplied by:

Personal Chefs International
(619) 680-3741

FILO WITH ARTICHOKE HEARTS, WILD MUSHROOMS AND SUNDRIED TOMATOES ❦

Filo dough stuffed with artichoke hearts, wild mushrooms and sundried tomatoes.

Nutrition Information per Serving:

✓✓ CALORIES: Excellent Choice (300)   ✓✓ CHOLESTEROL: Excellent Choice (75 mg)

✓✓ FAT: Excellent Choice (3 g)*   SODIUM: High (1355 mg)

EXCHANGES: 1¼ Meat (extra lean), 2¼ Bread, 2½ Veg, ¼ Fat

PROTEIN: 20 g, CARBOHYDRATE: 44 g

This nutrition analysis corresponds to the recipe below. The restaurant version may differ.

*Primarily unsaturated fat

Ingredients (6 servings):

Nonstick vegetable spray
2 Tbs. garlic, chopped
1 red onion, thinly sliced
18 artichoke hearts, drained
½ cup sundried tomatoes, thinly sliced
1½ cups wild mushrooms, thinly sliced
2 Tbs. low sodium soy sauce
½ tsp. white pepper
2 eggs
2 cups non-fat cottage cheese

¼ cup parmesan cheese
1 Tbs. oregano, fresh, chopped
1 Tbs. basil, fresh, chopped
1 Tbs. dill, fresh, chopped
salt & pepper to taste
  (not included in analysis)
12 sheets filo dough
½ cup chayote squash, sliced
½ cup baby bok choy, sliced
½ cup yellow squash, sliced
½ cup carrots, sliced

Directions:

1. Preheat oven to 300°.
2. Spray sauté pan with nonstick vegetable spray. Sauté garlic and onions until soft.
3. Add artichoke hearts, sundried tomatoes, wild mushrooms, soy sauce and white pepper. Sauté until mushrooms are soft.
4. Drain cottage cheese completely.
5. Mix eggs with cottage cheese, parmesan cheese, fresh herbs and salt & pepper to taste.
6. Mix the artichoke hearts mixture with the cheese mixture.
7. Take two sheets of filo dough and fold each in half. Spray the edges with vegetable spray and place ¾ cup of the mixture in the middle of the dough. Gather in all corners to the center and push together to close. Repeat the above procedure for the remaining dough.
8. Place the stuffed filo on a cookie sheet sprayed with non-stick cooking spray and bake for 12-15 minutes.
9. Steam remaining vegetables and serve on the side.

Recipe supplied by:

La Costa Resort and Spa

Costa del Mar Road, Carlsbad, CA 92009

(760) 438-9111

❦ at least 2 fruit/vegetable servings

PAHT THAI NOODLES

*A generous portion of chantaboon noodles surrounded by tofu,
ground peanuts, chili powder and bean sprouts.*

Nutrition Information per Serving:

✓ CALORIES: Good Choice (555)　　✓✓ CHOLESTEROL: Excellent Choice (0 mg)
✓✓ FAT: Excellent Choice (10 g)*　　✓ SODIUM: Good Choice (565 mg)
EXCHANGES: ½ Meat, 6¼ Bread, ½ Veg, 1¾ Fat
PROTEIN: 12 g, CARBOHYDRATE: 106 g

This nutrition analysis corresponds to the recipe below. The restaurant version may differ.
*Primarily unsaturated fat

Ingredients (4 servings):

8 oz. chantaboon noodles†
　(rice sticks), dry weight
2 Tbs. oil
1 tsp. garlic, minced
½ cup baked bean curd (tofu)†, diced
3 Tbs. fish sauce
2 Tbs. sugar
¼ cup vinegar

3 Tbs. lime juice
pinch chili powder
2 tsp. paprika
1 cup bean sprouts
1 Tbs. cilantro
1 Tbs. green onion, chopped
1 Tbs. ground unsalted peanuts

†Chantaboon noodles (rice sticks) and baked bean curd (tofu) are available in Asian markets.

Directions:

1. Soak chantaboon noodles (rice sticks) in cold water for 1 to 2 hours or until soft.
2. Heat oil in pan. Add garlic and sauté until light brown.
3. Add bean curd and cook an additional minute.
4. Add noodles. Stir a few seconds.
5. In a separate bowl, mix fish sauce, sugar, vinegar, lime juice, chili powder and paprika. Add to bean curd mix.
6. Stir-fry until noodles are soft.
7. Toss in bean sprouts and serve immediately.
8. Garnish with cilantro, chopped green onion and ground peanuts.

Recipe supplied by:

Royal Thai Cuisine
467 Fifth Avenue
San Diego, CA (619) 230-THAI
737 Pearl Street
La Jolla, CA (858) 551-THAI

ROASTED TOFU

Roasted tofu can be served with vegetables, rice, soup or anything!

Nutrition Information per Serving:

✓✓ CALORIES: Excellent Choice (155)   ✓✓ CHOLESTEROL: Excellent Choice (0 mg)
✓✓ FAT: Excellent Choice (7 g)*   SODIUM: Moderate (770 mg)
EXCHANGES: 2¼ Meat, ¼ Bread
PROTEIN: 17 g, CARBOHYDRATE: 8 g

This nutrition analysis corresponds to the recipe below. The restaurant version may differ.
*Primarily unsaturated fat

Ingredients (4 servings):

**2 lb. firm tofu
¼ cup teriyaki sauce
½ tsp. olive oil**

Directions:

1. Drain tofu well and cut into ¼ inch cubes.
2. Soak tofu for 10 minutes in teriyaki sauce.
3. Brush the olive oil on a cookie sheet.
4. Bake at 325° for 30 - 40 minutes or until golden brown.
5. Serve with vegetables, rice, soup, tortillas, or anything you like.
6. Keep unused portion covered in the refrigerator.

Recipe supplied by:

Ki's
2591 South Highway 101
Cardiff, CA 92007
(760) 436-5236

TOFU JALFARAZI ☙

Tofu sautéed with onion, bell pepper and vegetables.

Nutrition Information per Serving:

✓✓ CALORIES: Excellent Choice (310)   ✓✓ CHOLESTEROL: Excellent Choice (0 mg)
✓ FAT: Good Choice (18 g)*   ✓✓ SODIUM: Excellent Choice (265 mg)
EXCHANGES: 2¾ Meat, 2¼ Veg, 1¾ Fat
PROTEIN: 23 g, CARBOHYDRATE: 19 g

This nutrition analysis corresponds to the recipe below. The restaurant version may differ.
*Primarily unsaturated fat

Ingredients (2 servings):

1 cup firm tofu	½ cup broccoli
½ cup onion	1 Tbs. fresh ginger
4 garlic cloves	2 Tbs. fresh cilantro
2 fresh green chilies	1 Tbs. olive oil
½ cup bell pepper	½ lemon (juice)
½ cup cauliflower	½ tsp. salt (optional, not included in analysis)

1. Drain and cube tofu.
2. Chop onion, garlic cloves, and green chilies.
3. Chop remaining vegetables, ginger and cilantro and set aside.
4. Heat oil in a sauté pan over medium - high heat.
5. Add onion, garlic and green chilies. Sauté for 2-3 minutes.
6. Add tofu and remaining ingredients to sauté pan with lemon juice and salt
7. Cover and cook for approximately five more minutes.

Recipe supplied by:

Café India
3760-5 Sports Arena Blvd.
San Diego, CA 92109
(619) 224-7500

VEGETABLE ENCHILADAS ✑

Corn tortillas filled with vegetables, onions and cilantro.

Nutrition Information per Serving:

✓✓ CALORIES: Excellent Choice (310)   ✓✓ CHOLESTEROL: Excellent Choice (20 mg)
 ✓ FAT: Good Choice (13 g)*   ✓ SODIUM: Good Choice (570 mg)
EXCHANGES: ¾ Meat (extra lean), 1½ Bread, 2 Veg, ¼ Milk, 2 Fat
PROTEIN: 12 g, CARBOHYDRATE: 38 g

This nutrition analysis corresponds to the recipe below. The restaurant version may differ.

*Primarily unsaturated fat

Ingredients (6 servings):

Vegetable Mix:
1½ Tbs. butter
1 cup carrots
1 cup zucchini
¾ cup cauliflower
¾ cup broccoli
1 cup yellow squash
¼ cup onion
¼ cup tomato
¼ cup cilantro
2 Tbs. jalapenos
½ cup chipotle sauce (or salsa)
½ cup nonfat sour cream
¾ cup mozzarella (skim milk), shredded

Enchiladas:
12 6" corn tortillas
vegetable mix
2 cups salsa verde†
¼ cup mozzarella cheese
   (skim milk), shredded
1 cup guacamole

†Salsa verde can be found in the Mexican food section of most grocery stores.

Directions:

Vegetable Mix:
1. Preheat oven to 350°.
2. Cut carrots, zucchini, cauliflower, broccoli, yellow squash, onion and tomato into bite size chunks. Dice cilantro and jalapeno.
3. Add all ingredients except sour cream and cheese to a heavy saucepan.
4. Simmer for 20 minutes (vegetables should be cooked, but still a bit crispy).
5. Add sour cream and cheese and cook for 5 more minutes.

Enchiladas:
1. Fill tortillas with vegetable mix, roll & top with verde sauce, cheese & guacamole.
2. Bake in oven for 10 minutes or until heated through.

Recipe supplied by:

Su Casa
6738 La Jolla Boulevard
La Jolla, CA 92037
(858) 454-0369

   ✑ at least 2 fruit/vegetable servings

VEGETARIAN COMBO 🍎

Ingredients (4 servings):

3 baking potatoes	¼ cup onion, chopped
3 oz. winter squash	1 tomato, chopped
2 Tbs. olive oil (divided)	½ tsp. cumin
2 cups steamed rice (¾ cup dry)	¼ tsp. salt
3 oz. spinach	4 oz. green beans
¼ cup green onion, chopped	1 bell pepper, chopped
1 Tbs. cilantro, chopped	4 Tbs. low-fat yogurt, plain
6 oz. eggplant, cubed	

Directions:

1. Peel potato and winter squash, cube and brush with olive oil.
2. Bake at 400° for 1 hour, turning occasionally.
3. Steam rice and set aside.
4. Wilt spinach with green onion and cilantro in ½ Tbs. olive oil.
5. Sauté eggplant with onion, tomato, cumin and salt in 1 tsp. olive oil.
6. Sauté green beans and bell pepper until soft in ½ Tbs. olive oil.
7. Combine rice with vegetables; heat through before serving.
8. Top with 1 Tbs. yogurt per serving.

Recipe supplied by:

KABUL WEST

Kabul West
9450 Scranton Road, #114G
San Diego, CA 92121
(858) 622-9500

VEGETARIAN TACO

Soft mini tortilla prepared "Baja Style" with chopped onions, cilantro and salsa.
Rich in vitamins and fiber, very tasty, very low in fat, and very healthy!

Nutrition Information per Serving:

✓✓ CALORIES: Excellent Choice (210)   ✓✓ CHOLESTEROL: Excellent Choice (0 mg)
✓✓ FAT: Excellent Choice (1 g)*   ✓✓ SODIUM: Excellent Choice (200 mg)
EXCHANGES: ¼ Meat, 2½ Bread, ¾ Veg, ¼ Fat
PROTEIN: 8 g, CARBOHYDRATE: 44 g

This nutrition analysis corresponds to the recipe below. The restaurant version may differ.

* Primarily unsaturated fat

Ingredients (4 servings):

½ cup rice	1 cup black or pinto beans, cooked
½ cup tomato juice	½ tsp. garlic (granulated)
½ cup water	¼ tsp. oregano
4 corn tortillas (or 8 mini tortillas)	¾ tsp. Italian seasoning
⅓ cup onion, julienne cut	¼ tsp. black pepper
½ cup bell pepper, julienne cut	¾ tsp. red pepper
½ cup zucchini, julienne cut	2 oz. (¼ cup) salsa of your choice
	cilantro (optional)

Directions:

1. Cook rice according to package instructions, except adjust liquid to be ½ cup water and ½ cup tomato juice.
2. "Sauté" the vegetables in a non-stick skillet with 1 Tbs. water (i.e., steam vegetables), stirring constantly.
3. Season with garlic, Italian seasoning, oregano, black and red pepper, and cook 10 minutes, adding more water if necessary.
4. Warm tortillas (i.e., microwave or steam).
5. Place some vegetables, beans, rice, and salsa on each tortilla, roll, and serve.

Recipe supplied by:

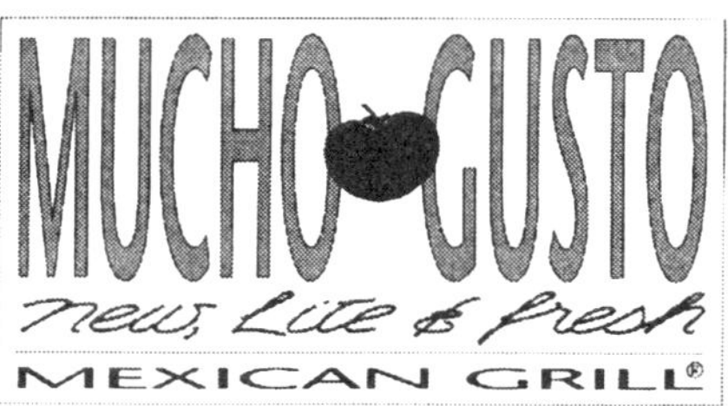

Mucho Gusto
2668 Del Mar Heights Rd., Suite B
Del Mar, CA 92014
(858) 259-6855

5660 Balboa Avenue
San Diego, CA 92117
(858) 505-4111

ZUCCHINI EGGPLANT PIZZA

✓ CALORIES: Good Choice (425)   ✓✓ CHOLESTEROL: Excellent Choice (50 mg)
✓ FAT: Good Choice (15 g)   SODIUM: Moderate (1040 mg)
EXCHANGES: 2¾ Meat, 2½ Bread, ¾ Veg, 1 Fat
PROTEIN: 28 g, CARBOHYDRATE: 45 g

This nutrition analysis corresponds to the recipe below. The restaurant version may differ.

Ingredients (Two 9" pizzas = 6 servings):

Topping:	Pizza Dough:
6 oz. (¾ cup) pizza sauce	2 cups warm water
1 cup eggplant, cut in bite size pieces	1 package dry yeast
½ cup zucchini, grilled	pinch sugar
2 cups grated mozarella cheese, skim milk	5 cups all purpose flour
4 Tbs. grated Romano cheese	2 tsp. salt
	1 tsp. olive oil

Directions:

Dough:

1. Pour 1 cup warm water into a large mixing bowl. Dissolve yeast & sugar in the water. Slowly add 2 cups flour to the yeast/water mixture, stirring with a wooden spoon until completely mixed. Cover bowl with towel and allow mixture to rise in a warm place for 20 minutes.
2. Add remaining water, salt, and an additional 2 cups of flour and mix to combine. Place dough in bowl of a food processor or electric mixer with special dough blade. Add the remaining cup of flour. Mix until dough forms a ball and pulls away from the sides of the bowl. Add more flour if the dough is too sticky.
3. Place on floured counter or board and knead until soft -- 5 to 10 minutes. Roll dough around in a bowl that has been coated with olive oil, making sure the entire surface has a coating of oil. Cover and allow dough to rise for 1 hour in a warm place.
4. Remove from bowl to a counter or board and divide into 2 equal pieces. To make crust, press dough into a flat circle and build up the outside edges.

Topping:

1. Cut eggplant and zucchini in bite sized pieces. Grill zucchini under broiler.
2. Divide ingredients in half.
3. Spread pizza sauce evenly over pizza dough.
4. Sprinkle mozarella cheese evenly over the sauce.
5. Sprinkle eggplant; top with zucchini spaced around the base of the dough.
6. Finish with Romano cheese.
7. Bake at 500° for 10-15 minutes or until crust is golden brown.

Recipe supplied by:

Sammy's
Woodfired Pizza
Carlsbad, Costa Verde, Del Mar, Downtown,
La Jolla, Mission Valley, & Scripps Ranch

Asian Slaw 🍎

Nutrition Information per Serving†:

✓✓ CALORIES: Excellent Choice (105)   ✓✓ CHOLESTEROL: Excellent Choice (0 mg)
✓ FAT: Good Choice (5 g)*   SODIUM: High (1240 mg)
EXCHANGES: ¾ Veg, ¾ Fat
PROTEIN: 4 g, CARBOHYDRATE: 13 g

This nutrition analysis corresponds to the recipe below. The restaurant version may differ.
*Primarily unsaturated fat
† Side dish guidelines are 1/3 of entree guidelines

Ingredients (6 servings):

3 cups red cabbage
3 cups green cabbage
3 cups romaine lettuce
1½ tsp. ginger root
1 clove garlic
1 shallot
¼ cup red wine vinegar

¾ cup low sodium soy sauce
1 Tbs. sweet chili sauce
2 Tbs. honey
½ tsp. crushed chili
⅛ cup sesame oil
¼ bunch cilantro

Directions:

1. Finely shred the red and green cabbage and chop lettuce.
2. Puree the ginger, garlic and shallot in a blender with the vinegar.
3. Blend together the remaining ingredients.
4. Toss cabbage, lettuce and dressing.

Recipe supplied by:

French Gourmet
960 Turquoise Street
San Diego, CA 92109
(858) 488-1725

ORANGE BLOSSOM SMOOTHIE ☺

Nutrition Information per 24 oz. Serving:

✓ CALORIES: Good Choice (460)   ✓✓ CHOLESTEROL: Excellent Choice (0 mg)
✓✓ FAT: Excellent Choice (1 g)   ✓✓ SODIUM: Excellent Choice (115 mg)
PROTEIN: 10 g, CARBOHYDRATE: 104 g

This nutrition analysis corresponds to the recipe below. The restaurant version may differ.

Ingredients (24 oz. serving):

12 oz. orange juice
⅔ cup nonfat vanilla frozen yogurt
½ cup strawberries

½ cup peaches
½ cup bananas
½ cup ice

Directions:

1. In a blender cup, mix in order: orange juice, frozen yogurt, strawberries, peaches, bananas and ice.
2. Blend until smooth.

Recipe supplied by:

Jamba Juice

with 11 area locations in: Carmel Mountain, Del Mar, Hillcrest, Horton Plaza, La Jolla, La Mesa, Mira Mesa, Mission Valley, Pacific Beach, Point Loma, and UCSD La Jolla campus
Call 1-888-JAMBA12 for your nearest location.

☺ at least 2 fruit/vegetable servings

TOMATILLO/CHIPOTLE SALSA

<table>
<tr><td colspan="2">Nutrition Information per 2 Tbs. Serving†:</td></tr>
<tr><td>✓✓ CALORIES: Excellent Choice (10)</td><td>✓✓ CHOLESTEROL: Excellent Choice (0 mg)</td></tr>
<tr><td>✓✓ FAT: Excellent Choice (0 g)</td><td>✓✓ SODIUM: Excellent Choice (75 mg)</td></tr>
</table>

EXCHANGES: ¼ Veg
PROTEIN: ¼ g, CARBOHYDRATE: 2 g

This nutrition analysis corresponds to the recipe below. The restaurant version may differ.

† Side dish guidelines are ⅓ of entrée guidelines

Ingredients for approx. 1 pint (16 servings):

½ lb. tomatillos	½ tsp. salt
1 med. tomato (4 oz.)	½ tsp. sugar
1 dried chipotle chile	1 tsp. rice wine vinegar
½ cup chopped onion (2 oz.)	1 Tbs. lime juice
1 clove garlic, minced	¼ cup cilantro

Directions:

1. Place tomatillos on foil-lined baking sheet. Put in broiler and roast until skin is blackened (approx. 15 minutes), stirring occasionally.
2. Place tomatoes on foil-lined baking sheet. Put in broiler and roast until black, turning after 15 minutes. Roast 30 minutes total.
3. Toast chipotle chile on clean hot griddle until fragrant and aroma is released (approx. 5 seconds). Place in pot with very hot water and soak for approx. 15 minutes until soft. Remove seeds.
4. Place tomatillos, tomatoes and seeded chile in blender with other ingredients. Puree with quick on/off pulses for 20 seconds total.

Recipe supplied by:

La Salsa Fresh Mexican Grill

Locations in Coronado, Downtown, Hillcrest, La Jolla, La Mesa, Mira Mesa, and Pacific Beach.

Part V

Other Editions in the *Healthy Dining* Book Series,

Response Forms,

and

Restaurant Discount Coupons

Healthy Dining in <u>Los Angeles</u>

Participating Restaurants:

A Votre Sante
Acapulco
Allegria
Amazon Bar and Grill
Auberge at Barnabey's Hotel
Bagel Nosh
Barefoot Café and Bar
BeauRivage
Bombay Cafe
Border Grill
Bristol's Café and Bristol Farms' Deli
Ca'Brea
Ca' del Sole
Café El Cholo
Café Pinot
Café Santorini
California Pizza Kitchen
California Wok
California Wok - Los Alamitos
Carrows
Chang's
Chasen's
Chicken Madras
Chin Chin
Ciao
City Wok
Club Sushi
Coco's
Crocodile Café
Crustacean
Curry House
Daily Grill
El Torito
555 East
Four Seasons Hotel – Gardens Restaurant
Fromin's Delicatessen
Gardens on Glendon
Gaylord
Glide'er Inn
The Greek Bistro
Healthy Gourmet
il Moro
Jack Sprat's Grille
Jamba Juice
Jerry's Famous Deli
Joss
Kate Mantilini
Khoury's
King's Pine Avenue Fish House

Koo Koo Roo
La Frite Cafe
La Salsa
Le Colonial
Louise's Trattoria
Maria's Cucina
Marix Tex Mex Cafe
McCormick & Schmick's
Mi Piace
Michael's
Museum of Latin American Art Restaurant
Natalee Thai Cuisine
Nicola's Kitchen
Ocean Avenue Seafood
One Pico at Shutters on the Beach
Pane e Vino
Papa Jon's
Paradise
Parkway Grill
Pasta al Dente
Patina
Pinot Bistro
Pinot at the Chronicle
Pinot Hollywood
Pizzeria Uno
Prego Ristorante
Red
Red Lobster
Reed's
Round Table Pizza
Ruby's
Runaway Bay Restaurant
Sangria
Santa Monica Seafood
Shenadoah Cafe
Sisley Italian Kitchen
Sonora Cafe
Souplantation
Spaghettini
Tacone Wraps
Taix
Tesoro Trattoria
Tower Restaurant
12th Street Grill
Villa Piacere
Whole Foods Market
Woo Lae Oak
Yangtze
Your Place

Healthy Dining in <u>Orange County</u>

Participating Restaurants:

A La Carte
Acapulco Mexican Restaurant
Antonello Ristorante
Au Lac Vegetarian Restaurant
Back Bay Rowing & Running Club
Bagels & Brew
The Beach House
Birraporetti's
Blueberry Hill
Bluewater Grill
Café Hidalgo
Caffé il Farro
California Pizza Kitchen
California Wok
Capistrano's Restaurant
Carrows
China West
Chin Chin
Chin's Chinese Kitchen
Ciao
The Cottage
Culinary Wraps
Disney's PCH Grill
Dolce Ristorante Italiano
El Torito Restaurants
El Torito Grill
Ferdussi Taste of Persia
Great Harvest Bread Co.
Haute Links
The Health Emporium
Healthy Gourmet
Ho Sum Bistro
Hyatt Newporter, Cantori
Hyatt Newporter, Jamboree Cafe
Inca Amazon Grill
Jamba Juice
Java City
JT Schmid's
JW's Calif. Grill, Newport Beach Marriott
Koo Koo Roo
La Fayette
La Salsa
Lotus Cafe
Luigi's D'Italia
Maggiano's Little Italy

McCormick & Schmick's
Mezzanine at the Towers
Mother's Market and Kitchen
The Old Spaghetti Factory
Peppino's Italian Family Restaurant
Pick Up Stix
Pinot Provence
The Quiet Woman
Red Lobster
Redberry Kaffe
Ristorante Rumari
Romeo Cucina
Round Table Pizza
Royal Thai
Ruby's Diner
Rutabegorz
Sagami Japanese Restaurant
Santa Monica Seafood
Sapori Ristorante, Sapori Trattoria
Scott's Seafood Grill & Bar
Sizzler
Souplantation
Spaghettini Italian Grill
Split Rock Tavern
Stix
Subway
SunFlour Natural Bakery
The Taco Company
Thai Spice
Todai Restaurant
Tustin Ranch Golf Club Restaurant
Tutto Mare
230 Forest Avenue
Vie de France
Villa Roma Ristorante Italiano
Villa Romana Trattoria
The Village Farmer
Wahoo's Fish Taco
Walt's Wharf
Waters Lakehouse
Wendy's
Whole Foods Market
Wild Oats Community Market
Your Personal Chef
Z Pizza

To order any of the *Healthy Dining* editions, see page 188 or call 1-800-DINE (3463)

Say "Thank You" to Restaurant Management

Restaurants that honor your special requests and take active steps to serve healthier meals need to hear from you, the consumer. Write a note of thanks on the restaurant's customer comment card. Or…you can photocopy and clip out this sample Thank You note and give it to management. Use your *Healthy Dining* book to select which restaurants to visit, order menu items featured in the book, and tell management whenever possible that you appreciate the restaurant's participation in *Healthy Dining,* that you use the book and recommend it to your friends and family.

You can also give these notes to restaurants that are not in the *Healthy Dining* book. Tell management about the program and encourage them to get involved. Call the *Healthy Dining* office with any names of potential restaurants for future publications.

Restaurants listen to you, the "Healthy Diner." <u>Together</u>, we can lead the way to a healthier community.

<table>
<tr><td>

Dear Restaurant Owner/Manager:

THANK YOU…for serving such satisfying food that is lower in calories, fat, cholesterol, and sodium – and dishes that include fruits and vegetables. The top killers of Americans – heart disease, cancer, stroke and diabetes – are closely linked with diet. Your "healthy" leadership is helping improve – even save – lives in Southern California!

 To learn more about *Healthy Dining*, call 1-800-953-DINE

</td><td>

Dear Restaurant Owner/Manager:

THANK YOU…for serving such satisfying food that is lower in calories, fat, cholesterol, and sodium – and dishes that include fruits and vegetables. The top killers of Americans – heart disease, cancer, stroke and diabetes – are closely linked with diet. Your "healthy" leadership is helping improve – even save – lives in Southern California!

 To learn more about *Healthy Dining*, call 1-800-953-DINE

</td></tr>
<tr><td>

Dear Restaurant Owner/Manager:

THANK YOU…for serving such satisfying food that is lower in calories, fat, cholesterol, and sodium – and dishes that include fruits and vegetables. The top killers of Americans – heart disease, cancer, stroke and diabetes – are closely linked with diet. Your "healthy" leadership is helping improve – even save – lives in Southern California!

 To learn more about *Healthy Dining*, call 1-800-953-DINE

</td><td>

Dear Restaurant Owner/Manager:

THANK YOU…for serving such satisfying food that is lower in calories, fat, cholesterol, and sodium – and dishes that include fruits and vegetables. The top killers of Americans – heart disease, cancer, stroke and diabetes – are closely linked with diet. Your "healthy" leadership is helping improve – even save – lives in Southern California!

 To learn more about *Healthy Dining*, call 1-800-953-DINE

</td></tr>
</table>

Thank You notes are also available at www.healthy-dining.com

$3.00 OFF
your next purchase of *Healthy Dining*

We want to know more about you and your thoughts about *Healthy Dining*. So we'll give you $3.00 off your next copy of *Healthy Dining* if you'll return this questionnaire (information is confidential). To thank you, we will contact you when new editions are published and offer $3.00 off the retail price. You may also order now at the discount price (see reverse side).

1. How did you learn about *Healthy Dining in San Diego*?

    ____ Newspaper   ____ Family or friend   ____ Dietitian
    ____ Radio   ____ Restaurant   ____ Personal Trainer/Fitness Ctr.
    ____ Television   ____ Health Organization   ____ Special Event _________
    ____ Store _________   ____ Physician   ____ TrEAT Yourself Well Campaign
    ____ Workplace   ____ Internet   ____ Other ______________

2. Are you on any of these special diets?

    ____ Weight loss   ____ Low-cholesterol   ____ Diabetic   ____ General health-conscious
    ____ Low-fat   ____ Low-sodium   ____ Vegetarian   ____ Other _____________

3. Please rate the following features of the book:

	Very helpful	Moderately helpful	Not needed
Chapters on general nutrition	____	____	____
List of restaurants offering healthier items	____	____	____
Specific menu items available at these restaurants	____	____	____
Numerical values of fat, calories, cholesterol, etc.	____	____	____
"Excellent Choice" (✓✓) and "Good Choice" (✓) categories	____	____	____
Restaurant coupons	____	____	____
Chefs' recipes section	____	____	____

4. Please list your favorite restaurants from this book:

5. What other restaurants would you like to see in the next edition?

6. Please list your favorite recipes from the Chefs' Recipes section:

7. On average, how many times <u>per month</u> do you dine out? ______ Do you use the coupons? ______

8. Is this book primarily used by: ___ female ___ male ___ both ____ how many?

9. What is the age of the primary user of this book?
    ____ Under 30   ____ 30 to 45   ____ 45 to 60   ____ over 60

10. What other food or health-related publications do you read? (Health Magazine, Berkeley Wellness, Nutrition Action Healthletter, Eating Well, Cooking Light, etc.)

11. Would you or any of your personal contacts like more information about: ____ fund-raising ______ seminars or community events ______ wholesale prices for *Healthy Dining* books?

    Other Comments?

Please complete name and address on reverse side, fold and mail. Photocopy acceptable. SD5

Fold on lines with address on outside.

Name: ________________________

Address: ________________________

____

Stamp

Healthy Dining
8305 Vickers Street, Suite 106
San Diego, CA 92111

Special **$3.00 OFF** any *Healthy Dining* books.

Order as many as you want at the special discount! It's our thank-you for answering our questionnaire. You will also receive the $3.00 discount on future editions. Orders normally processed within 1 week.

Quantity		Price
______ *Healthy Dining in San Diego*	$19.95 - $3.00 discount = $16.95	__________
______ *Healthy Dining in Orange County*	$19.95 - $3.00 discount = $16.95	__________

for information about *Healthy Dining in Los Angeles* call (858) 541-2049

	Subtotal	__________
	Tax (7¾% in San Diego)	__________
	Postage ($1.75 for 1st book + 50¢ each for additional books)	__________

____ Check enclosed   Phone (   ) _______________   Total __________

____ VISA/Mastercard # ____________________________ exp.______ Signature________________

Please fill out questionnaire on reverse and your name & address above. If sending check, make to *Healthy Dining* and fasten your check securely to this sheet or use a separate envelope. Thanks.

Coupons

$3.00 OFF
your next purchase of *Healthy Dining*
See page 188 for details.

Healthy Dining in San Diego

Healthy Dining Entrée for $1.99!

Acapulco

Buy one Healthy Dining entrée at regular price and receive another Healthy Dining entrée of equal or lesser value for $1.99!

Valid at all San Diego Acapulco locations.

Not valid with any other advertised special, banquet or for carry out. Exp. 12/02

Healthy Dining in San Diego

Free Entrée

Andiamo!
Italian Restaurant

Andiamo!

With purchase of one entrée of equal or greater value. Maximum $8.00
Not valid with any other offer or on major holidays.

5950 Santo Road
San Diego, CA 92124
(858) 277-3501

Healthy Dining in San Diego

Healthy Dining in San Diego

Coupon   *Healthy Dining in San Diego*   Coupon

$3.00 OFF

Bernard'O

Any meal $8.00 or More
For up to 4 members in party.
Not valid with any other offer.

12457 Rancho Bernardo Rd.
San Diego, CA 92128
(858) 487-7171

Coupon   *Healthy Dining in San Diego*   Coupon

Free Masala Chai (Ginger Tea)

Café India

With purchase of an entrée.
Not valid with any other offer.

3760-5 Sports Arena Blvd.
San Diego, CA 92109
(619) 224- 7500

Coupon   *Healthy Dining in San Diego*   Coupon

Free Entrée

when a 2nd LUNCH
or DINNER ENTRÉE of equal
or greater value is purchased.
Holidays excluded. Tipping should be
15 to 20% of check before discount.
Not valid with any other offer.

CASA DE BANDINI
MEXICAN RESTAURANT

Casa de Bandini

Bazaar del Mundo, Old Town
San Diego State Historic Park
2754 Calhoun St., San Diego (619) 297-8211

Coupon   *Healthy Dining in San Diego*   Coupon

Free Entrée

when a 2nd LUNCH
or DINNER ENTRÉE of equal
or greater value is purchased.
Holidays excluded. Tipping should be
15 to 20% of check before discount.
Not valid with any other offer.

CASA DE PICO
MEXICAN RESTAURANT

Casa de Pico

Bazaar del Mundo, Old Town
San Diego State Historic Park
2754 Calhoun St., San Diego, (619) 299-7124

Coupon   *Healthy Dining in San Diego*   Coupon

Free Entrée

when a 2nd LUNCH
or DINNER ENTRÉE of equal
or greater value is purchased.
Holidays excluded. Tipping should be
15 to 20% of check before discount.
Not valid with any other offer.

Casa Guadalajara

Bazaar del Mundo, Old Town
San Diego State Historic Park
4105 Taylor St., San Diego, (619) 295-5111

Healthy Dining in San Diego

Healthy Dining in San Diego

Healthy Dining in San Diego

Healthy Dining in San Diego

Healthy Dining in San Diego

Healthy Dining in San Diego

Healthy Dining in San Diego

Healthy Dining in San Diego

Healthy Dining in San Diego

Healthy Dining in San Diego

Healthy Dining in San Diego

Healthy Dining in San Diego

Healthy Dining in San Diego

Healthy Dining in San Diego

Healthy Dining in San Diego

Healthy Dining in San Diego

Healthy Dining in San Diego

Healthy Dining in San Diego

Healthy Dining in San Diego

Healthy Dining in San Diego

Healthy Dining in San Diego

Healthy Dining in San Diego

Healthy Dining in San Diego

Healthy Dining in San Diego

Healthy Dining in San Diego

Coupon

Dinner for Two only $11.99

Not valid with any other offer.

Pizza Nova

Hillcrest: 3955 Fifth Ave.
Point Loma: 5120 N. Harbor Dr.
Solana Beach: 945 Lomas Santa Fe Dr.

Healthy Dining in San Diego

Coupon · Coupon

Free Entrée

With purchase of one entrée of equal or greater value.
Not valid with any other offer.

Ranchos Cocina

1830 Sunset Cliffs Blvd., #H
4705 Point Loma Ave.

Healthy Dining in San Diego

Coupon · Coupon

Free Entrée

when a 2nd LUNCH
or DINNER ENTRÉE of equal
or greater value is purchased.
Holidays excluded. Tipping should be
15 to 20% of check before discount.
Not valid with any other offer.

Rancho El Nopal

Bazaar del Mundo, Old Town
San Diego State Historic Park
2754 Calhoun St., San Diego, (619) 295-0584

Healthy Dining in San Diego

Coupon · Coupon

$3.00 OFF

Any Large Pizza.

Not valid with any other discount
or offer. Good at participating
San Diego locations.

Round Table Pizza locations:

Casa de Oro, Chula Vista, Clairemont,
Encinitas, Escondido, La Jolla, La Mesa,
Oceanside, Pacific Beach, Poway,
Rancho Bernardo, Rancho Penasquitos,
Rancho San Diego, Tierrasanta, Santee,
Solana Beach, University City, Vista.

Healthy Dining in San Diego

Coupon · Coupon

20% OFF
Entire Meal

Alcoholic beverages excluded
Up to 4 in party.
Not valid with any other offer.

Royal Thai Cuisine

467 Fifth Avenue
San Diego, CA 92101 (619) 230-THAI
737 Pearl Avenue
La Jolla, CA 92037 (858) 551-THAI

Healthy Dining in San Diego

Healthy Dining in San Diego

Healthy Dining in San Diego

Healthy Dining in San Diego

Healthy Dining in San Diego

Healthy Dining in San Diego

Healthy Dining in San Diego

Healthy Dining in San Diego

Healthy Dining in San Diego

Healthy Dining in San Diego

50% OFF

**Second entrée with purchase
of one entrée of equal
or greater value.**

Not valid with any other offer.

Star of India

1000 Prospect St., La Jolla (858) 459-3355
3860 Valley Ctr. Dr., San Diego (858) 481-2767
423 F St., San Diego (619) 544-98910

Free 6" Sub

**Buy any regular (not double meat)
6" Sub at regular price, and get another
regular 6" Sub of equal or lesser price FREE!**
Not valid with any other offer.

Over 100
SUBWAY®
locations in San Diego County.
For the one nearest you,
call (619) 688-9255.

Free Meal

**With purchase of one meal
of equal or greater value.**
Solo diners enjoy 50% off one meal.
Not valid with take out orders.
Not valid with any other offer.

Su Casa

6738 La Jolla Blvd.
La Jolla, CA 92037
(858) 454-0369

Complimentary Serving of Flan

With purchase of any entrée.
Valid for up to 4 people,
one coupon per table.
Not valid with any other offer.

Tio Leo's

5302 Napa St. (619) 542-1462
10787 Camino Ruiz (858) 695-1461
3510 Valley Centre Dr. (858) 350-1468
6333 Mission Gorge Rd. (619) 280-9944

10% OFF

**Any item in our full-service
deli department.**

Limit 2 pounds. One coupon per customer.
Not valid with any other special offer.

Whole Foods Market

8825 Villa La Jolla Dr., La Jolla (858) 642-6700
711 University Ave. (Hillcrest) (619) 294-2800

 *Healthy Dining in San Diego*

 *Healthy Dining in San Diego*

 *Healthy Dining in San Diego*

 *Healthy Dining in San Diego*

 *Healthy Dining in San Diego*

Part VI

Indexes

Restaurant Menu Indexes

Other Indexes

Index by Cuisine

Index by Cuisine, continued

Index by Location

Index by Location, continued

Index by Location, continued

Index by Location, continued

Alphabetical Index